Interperspectival Content

Interperspectival Content

Peter Ludlow

OXFORD
UNIVERSITY PRESS

OXFORD
UNIVERSITY PRESS

Great Clarendon Street, Oxford, OX2 6DP,
United Kingdom

Oxford University Press is a department of the University of Oxford.
It furthers the University's objective of excellence in research, scholarship,
and education by publishing worldwide. Oxford is a registered trade mark of
Oxford University Press in the UK and in certain other countries

© Peter Ludlow 2019

The moral rights of the author have been asserted

First Edition published in 2019
First published in paperback 2021

Published in the United States of America by Oxford University Press
198 Madison Avenue, New York, NY 10016, United States of America

British Library Cataloguing in Publication Data
Data available

Library of Congress Cataloging in Publication Data
Data available

ISBN 978–0–19–882379–7 (Hbk.)
ISBN 978–0–19–289758–9 (Pbk.)

Contents

Preface

After I completed my book *Semantics Tense and Time*, I thought I was putting away issues in the philosophy of time (and all things related) for a long time—most likely (I thought) forever. The main idea behind that book was not to stake out a position in the philosophy of time in any case, but rather to illustrate a particular method of doing metaphysics—one in which one tackles issues in the semantics of natural language and metaphysics simultaneously. Given externalist assumptions about the semantics of natural language one could hardly do semantics without doing metaphysics, but it also turned out that sound semantic theory exposed otherwise hidden metaphysical commitments. Metaphysicians thought I was trying to extract metaphysics from semantics, and semanticists thought I was letting pure metaphysical concerns drive the semantic theory. The goal of the book was to illustrate an approach in which you privilege neither.

But, like I say, the discussion of the semantics of tense and the metaphysics of time was actually supposed to be illustrative of a more general methodology, and I really didn't have much at stake in the area or in the positions. However, since that book has appeared, enough philosophers have called me a "crazy tenser" and less often a "crazy presentist" so that I actually started to wonder if it was true, and despite my best efforts to *not* think about the arguments they threw at me, I began to think about them anyway. I also began to think about mistakes I had made in the book and things that I could have and should have done differently. I began to make mental notes on these mistakes, and their possible resolution. These mental notes began to occupy vast amounts of processing time and memory. I began to write things down.

As friends engaged with me on these issues I also began to realize the work on tense was really just one aspect of a bigger phenomenon—one that is commonly called indexicality, but which in this book I will characterize in terms of perspectival position and which I will cash out using *interperspectival contents—or perspectival contents*, for short. So I began to generalize my work to that broader class of contents. And then came the invitations to talk about tense and perspectival content and to write about it, and coupled with my inability to set priorities I accepted these invitations; lecture notes began to appear, and then papers began to appear, and then those papers began to look a lot like book chapters, and before you knew it a book had appeared—this one!

This work has enjoyed the help of a number of people over the years. The general outline of this book took form in a graduate course I taught at the University of Michigan in the Winter Term of 2003. Bits and pieces of the material were also presented at The University of Texas at Austin (at their most excellent Graduate Student Philosophy Conference), the University of Istanbul (the 5th meeting of the Vienna-Istanbul Philosophy Circle), Princeton University, Geneva University, and twice at Rutgers University—once for a semantics workshop organized by Ernie Lepore and once for a "metaphysical mayhem" workshop organized by Dean Zimmerman (with people like Frank Artzenius, Delia Fara, John Hawthorne, Tim Maudlin, Ted Sider, and gazillions of smart graduate students from everywhere providing comments). I've also talked about these matters several times at the Arché research center at St. Andrews University, at the Festival of Science in Rome, Italy in 2012, and in 2018 at the University of Campinas in Brazil, at the invitation of Marco Ruffino.

As usual, I also owe much to informal discussion of these matters with friends and colleagues, including Emiliano Boccardi, Brit Brogaard, Herman Cappelen, Josh Dever, Stacie Friend, Patrick Grim, John Hawthorne, James Higginbotham, Thomas Hofweber, Richard Larson, Ernie Lepore, John Perry, Chiara Repetti-Ludlow, Marco Ruffino, and Jason Stanley, and to many conversations with Larry Sklar over delicacies such as pig entrails and beef tendon with turnips. Yum. Comments on an earlier draft from Kasia Jaszczolt led me to tear apart the manuscript and refocus my thesis, yielding, I believe, a much improved work.

Special thanks are due to Peter Momtchiloff for finding three very excellent anonymous readers for the antepenultimate draft of the manuscript. As I told Peter, I knew that philosophy had people that were that smart, but I didn't know they were also diligent enough to provide comments of that level, care, and substance. They, being anonymous, don't get thanked by name for their efforts, but this work is substantially stronger thanks to those efforts. Finally, I am grateful to Ulyana Savchenko, who miraculously appeared on the mean streets of Playa del Carmen one day and offered to provide comments and corrections on my penultimate draft.

Portions of this book were previously published elsewhere. Parts of Chapter 2 and 3 draw from my paper "Understanding Temporal Indexicals," which appeared in M. O'Rourke and C. Washington (eds.), *Situating Semantics: Essays on the Philosophy of John Perry*, Cambridge: MIT Press, 2006. Other parts of the book drew from a paper called "Tense" which appeared in E. Lepore and B. Smith (eds.), *Blackwell's Handbook of the Philosophy of Language*, Oxford: Blackwell Publishers, 2006. Appendix section A1 is based on my paper "Presentism, Triviality, and the Varieties of Tensism," in D. Zimmerman (ed.), *Oxford Studies in Metaphysics, Vol. II.*, Oxford: Oxford University Press, 2004. Section 6.5 draws on my paper "Tense, the Dynamic Lexicon, and the Flow of Time," which appeared in *Topoi* 34, 2015. Portions of Section 8.1 drew from my (2016) paper "Tense, Perspectival Properties, and Special Relativity," *Manuscrito* 39, 49–74.

Introduction

Suppose, following an example from Perry (1979), that I am sitting in my office one day, painfully aware that I have an important meeting with my boss at three o'clock. I might even utter (1) under my breath as I shuffle papers and take care of administrative minutiae.

(1)   I have a meeting with the boss at three o'clock.

As I dither about in my office, I realize that the clock on my wall hasn't moved off of 2:30 in a while. Puzzled, I check the clock on my computer. It says that it is 3:00. I double-check the time online. I conclude that it is in fact three o'clock and I utter (2).

(2)   Oh no, I have a meeting with the boss *now*!

I immediately get up and run to the boss's office.

My utterance of (2) reflects a piece of knowledge that my utterance of (1) does not and this additional piece of knowledge played a role in my actions. The thought that I expressed with my utterance of (1) was not enough to get me up out of my chair. It was only by coming to have the thought that I expressed with my utterance of (2) that I formed the intention to immediately run over to the boss's office. The question is, what is that extra thing? What is the secret ingredient X?

In this book I will be arguing that the secret ingredient is a special kind of content, which I will call an *interperspectival* content—or *perspectival* content for short. I will be arguing that these perspectival contents are ubiquitous and ineliminable. I will also be arguing that perspectival contents are richer than basic referential contents; they are philosophically exotic. As we will see, they are also critical to the explanation of human actions and emotions.

A case of explaining human action is given above—explaining why I initially did not go to the meeting but later did. A case of explaining human emotions was given by A.N. Prior (1959) in a paper entitled "Thank Goodness That's Over": If my root canal dental surgery is on May 1, on May 2 I will be relieved that it is over with. But my relief can't really be characterized as my being relieved that the root canal is earlier than May 2. Why should that matter unless I know it's *now* May 2 and the root canal is over with; it is in *my* perspectival past?

A similar story holds for anticipatory emotions. On April 30, I may be very nervous and concerned about the operation, but it is hard to make sense of that concern unless I know that *tomorrow* is the root canal. It is in *my* near future. If I lose track of the date, and don't realize it is already April 30, even if I know that the root canal is May 1 I may be much less concerned (here assuming that concern increases as the date approaches).

The examples I just gave involve temporal perspectival contents. They are a function of how things stand, from my perspectival position, in time. Other perspectival contents are locational. They are a function of how things stand, from my perspectival position in space.

For example, if I know the meeting is in my office and know I am in my office, I won't get up and go anywhere because I am already where I need to be. Notice, in this case it isn't enough for me to know the meeting is at a particular spatial location—I need to know I am *there*! If I am confused and think I am in a colleague's office in another part of town I might get up and unknowingly leave the location of the meeting.

Finally, some perspectival contents are *personal*. That is, there can be first person, second person, and third person perspectival contents. We can illustrate the idea of a first person perspectival content with the help of another story from John Perry (1979)—this one autobiographical.

One day John Perry was in the supermarket, pushing his cart, when he noticed a trail of spilt sugar. Perry then muttered to himself, "s/he is making a mess," and then began to follow the trail of sugar to inform the person making a mess. After a couple of left turns, Perry noticed that the trail of sugar was starting to get thicker. He then muttered to himself, "Oh, *I* am making the mess." Perry then bent down and repaired his leaky bag of sugar. Again, the thought that Perry expressed with the words 'I am making a mess' led to his taking action and repairing the bag. The thought that he expressed with 's/he is making a mess' gave rise to a different action (following the trail of sugar). So there was something more, or at least different in the two cases—a secret ingredient X, the perspectival content.

Most analytic philosophers today describe these cases as being indexical constructions and talk about them having "indexical contents." I believe that this way of talking about things has been misleading, for it suggests that what is doing the heavy lifting are the so-called indexical pronouns—'I', 'you', 'now', etc. Contrarily, I believe that the heavy lifting is being done by the predicates—'is making a mess' vs. 'am making a mess'.

This idea about the contents being expressed by predicates (rather than indexical pronouns, as commonly supposed) can also be illustrated with the help of a story once related by the physicist Ernst Mach (1959: 4, n. 1):

Not long ago, after a trying railway journey by night, when I was very tired, I got into an omnibus, just as another man appeared at the other end. 'What a shabby pedagogue that is, that has just entered,' thought I. It was myself; opposite me hung a large mirror. The physiognomy of my class, accordingly, was better known to me than my own.

Philosophers have offered a number of accounts of Mach's plight, but on my view, 'is a shabby pedagogue' and 'am a shabby pedagogue' express different contents when used in the same perspectival position. An utterance of the first predicate is an expression of another's shabbiness. The second predicate ('am a shabby pedagogue') in one's mouth is an expression of one's own shabbiness. In English we signal the deployment of the first person perspectival content by stressing the first person pronoun: "Oh no, *I* am the shabby pedagogue." Other languages will have other ways of doing this—for example by stressing the verb. My point is that the heavy lifting is not being done by the indexical pronoun, but rather by the predicate—or rather, by the content expressed by the predicate.

G.E.M. Anscombe (1975) made a related claim about first person contents, only on her view the first person pronoun does no semantic work at all. If she is right, then we have a perspectival content (or more accurately, an unmediated concept of, in this case, being a shabby pedagogue), and the pronoun is a mere grace note, in the way that the pleonastic pronoun 'it' functions in sentences like 'it is raining'. I won't be following Anscombe down this path; contemporary linguistics has made a strong case for the presence of (sometimes unvoiced) pronominal elements in these constructions.[1] I do believe, however, that Anscombe did us a great service by focusing our attention on the predicates and away from the pronouns. Most philosophers are not apt to think of perspectival contents as being expressed by predicates. But perhaps I can animate the idea with an example from the verbal system of an inflectional language.

When Anglophones like me learn an inflected language—a Romance language like French or Spanish, for example—we are routinely taught to think of some aspects of verbal conjugation as being a morphological feature without much semantic consequence. We thus think of the verbal inflection for person as much ado about nothing—a cruel trick played upon us native English speakers in our attempt to learn a Romance language. Consider, for example, the present indicative conjugation for the Spanish verb 'comer' (to eat).

Yo como (I eat)
Tu comes (you [familiar] eat)
El/Ella/Usted come (he/she/you [formal] eat)
Nosotros comemos (we eat)
Vosotros coméis[2] (you [plural] eat)
Ellos/Ellas/Ustedes comen (they [masc.]/they
      [fem.]/you [plural, formal] eat)

We are also taught that the pronouns can be dispensed with. In the *parlance* of the linguist, Spanish is a "pro-drop language," meaning you can, and frankly probably should, not bother voicing the pronoun. But as the Anglophone student is prone to think: all that work to just say 'eat'! Why bother?

But what if those different verbal forms were actually expressing different contents? That is, what if, on a particular occasion of use, the first person form was expressing a different perspectival content than the other verbal forms did? I believe that this is exactly what these different verb forms are enlisted to do.

In this book my goal is to defend a group of interlocking doctrines related to what philosophers have called "indexical contents," but which,

---

[1] There are also issues such as if someone utters, 'I am a shabby pedagogue' and I reply, 'no you aren't', we are disagreeing. It is hard to see how to make sense of that if you are merely trading expressions of contents.

[2] This form is not used in Latin American Spanish—'*ustedes*' carries the load in the Western hemisphere.

as I noted, I will call *interperspectival contents* (or *perspectival contents* for short). The unifying idea is that language is used to express perspectival contents, which in turn are ineliminable features of reality (and not merely features of language and mind). I'll argue that perspectival contents are not only ineliminable, but also ubiquitous. I'll also argue that with respect to tense, this view does not commit us to presentism, and that it opens the door to a form of A-series/B-series compatibilism (that is, that our theory of time can consistently allow both tensed and untensed accounts of temporal order).

Specifically, there are four different claims that I will be defending (the fourth being methodological):

1) **perspectivalism**—the view that tense and so-called "indexicals," in addition to having referential contents, express interperspectival contents (or perspectival contents for short)—contents that are expressed in different ways from different perspectival positions. These perspectival contents are critical to the explanation of human action and emotion (and many other phenomena) and are irreducible and ineliminable

2) **tensism**—the view that tense, being a kind of perspectival content, is an irreducible and ineliminable perspectival feature of the world (not merely a feature of language and mind). Far from being a projection of linguistic tense, the idea is that metaphysical tense, or temporal perspectival content, is fundamental and that different human languages devise different strategies for expressing those temporal perspectival contents

3) **A-series/B-series compatibility**—the view that one can combine a tenseless ordering of events with tense and other perspectival contents—you can, as it were, paint the perspectival contents over the B-series positions without creating philosophical problems. Furthermore, both the B-series and A-series are critical to a proper understanding of time and temporal phenomena, including the flow of time

4) **semantic accountability**—the methodological claim that semantics lays bare our ontological commitments and we cannot duck those commitments by claiming that only special parts of our language are ontologically committing. Specifically, we are ontologically committed by the language we use for the conduct of

scientific inquiry, ranging from the context of experimentation and discovery to the application of scientific theories, by the use of language in the context of explaining human action and emotion, as well as in our discourse about consciousness, perception, and normative action.

Let's look at each doctrine in more detail.

0.1 Perspectivalism

'Perspectivalism', as I use the term, incorporates three ideas: perspectival position, interperspectival content, and the ineliminability of interperspectival content.

Your *perspectival position* can be understood as the perspective that you yourself have when embedded in a place or time. Whether something is in your future or past depends on your embedded perspective in the scheme of things. Some events happen before others and we can even imagine a timeline in which the sequence of events is arranged by some before/after relation.[3] That timeline contains quite a bit of information, but it does not tell me what is in *my* future and what is in *my* past because to know that I would have to know where *I* currently am on that timeline. Past and future (at least for me) depend on where I am now embedded in that timeline.

So, for example, if I am embedded in a timeline certain events will be future *for me*, and certain events will be past *for me*. Likewise, events do not merely have spatial locations (and not merely locations with respect to me), but some events are spatially *before* me. In Chapter 2, I will illustrate this idea using the metaphor of first person shooter video games, in which objects (e.g. enemy monsters) are not merely spatially located, but are oriented as before you. As we will see, this is not a point about phenomenology. Sometimes people talk about *egocentric space*, and it is related to perspectival position but is not the same thing. Perspectival positions are egocentric spaces anchored in external positions.

---

[3] As we will see, this is not an entirely innocent account of time. More on this in Section 8.2.

I therefore am not using 'perspectival' in the way that Recanati (2007) and Noë (2012) do. As I understand them, they think of perspectival contents as being phenomenological. My idea is that our perspectival positions drastically underdetermine how we experience those positions. As we will see in Chapter 2, different perspectival positions may yield the same phenomenal experience, and a single perspectival position is consistent with any number of phenomenal experiences.

Interperspectival contents are contents that we deploy to attribute attitudes and contents to agents across perspectival positions. We will go into this in some detail in Chapter 3, but the core idea is that the same interperspectival content is expressed differently in different perspectival positions. So, for example, in one perspectival position a thought might be expressed as "Today is a fine day," and in another perspectival position the very same content (interperspectival content) might be expressed as "Yesterday was a fine day." The interperspectival content is stable across these perspectival positions. To save some ink and electrons I will usually refer to this simply as *perspectival content.*

By *contents*, I mean features of the world that are expressed by our language. Sometimes, we use a semantic theory to make explicit what those contents are, and to illuminate how our language expresses contents in a systematic way. On some theories, contents are not features of the world, but something else—psychological objects, for example. I will be arguing that true contents are features of the world.

Sometimes I will talk about these features of the world as being perspectival and sometimes I will talk about them being tensed. When I say that the world is tensed or features of the world are tensed I mean that there are temporal perspectival contents.

In Section 2.2 I will offer some rough guidelines for the various approaches that might be developed, but I want to be clear that my view here is neutral with respect to the various ways of cashing out the metaphysics. To have a neutral way of talking about these options, I talk about "features" of the world and sometimes "aspects" of the world. I use both terms informally, in their pre-theoretical sense, and if they have been deployed as technical terms elsewhere, it is not my intention to deploy those technical meanings.

I believe that my view is neutral with respect to a broad range of positions. One might argue that there are interperspectival *properties* (tensed properties if you prefer) or interperspectival *facts* (tensed facts if you prefer) or alternatively one might argue that properties and facts are not tensed but that propositions or events are. For example: "it was true that there is an event that is boring" and "it will be true that there is an event that is fun."

However we work out the details, we will see that the range of perspectival contents that we might encounter is impressive. Philosophers have observed a multitude of other ways in which we lean on perspectival contents. We rely on them not merely to account for our actions, but also consciousness, ethical agency, and perceptual thought. Cappelen and Dever (2013), who reject the importance of perspectival content (we will come to their objections in Chapter 1), have gathered together a number of different ways in which this point has been expressed. Here are some of them.

Colin McGinn argues that first person perspectival contents are critical to perception and consciousness.

But there is also the kind of thought we operate with when actively engaged in the world, when the world is directly presented to our consciousness; and this seems shot through with indexicality .... It thus seems that what the phenomenologists would call 'being-in-the-world' presupposes indexical thought. (1983: 91)

I believe this is also the point that Susanna Siegel (2016) is driving home in the following passage.

Many contentful experiences seem to have contents that must be specified by the use of *indexical* expressions, such as 'over there', 'to the left', 'here', 'in front of/ behind me', 'just a second ago', 'since a few second ago', and so on. For instance, some auditory experiences seem to present sounds as coming from a direction relative to the ears; some proprioceptive experiences seem to present pressure sensations as located in specific parts of the body; visual experiences seem to present things in locations relative to the eyes and the rest of the body. More generally, contentful experiences present the world from the subject's perspective both in space and in time. If one tried to characterize the perspective aspect of contents in language, it would be natural to use indexical expressions for spatial properties, for the subject herself, and for times.

Here is another way to think about this idea: We don't just perceive perspective-free patches of color like pixels on a two-dimensional screen. We experience things as located relative to our (anchored) egocentric positions. The flattened-patch-of-color description of our experience is the product of analysis. Our core experiences are located relative to our perspectival positions. Without that perspectival element and corresponding perspectival content, there are arguably no experiences—at least not the sorts of experiences we are familiar with.

In the temporal case we could think about the phenomenology of listening to a concert. We don't hear the concert all at once. We are, throughout the concert, experiencing part of it as behind us, and we may be anticipating some portion in front of us. Sometimes, what we anticipate is not what transpires. However we experience it, the temporal aspects are critical. To even perceive a tone, we need to hear part of it as having happened and we need to anticipate that it will continue or perhaps end soon.

David Velleman has observed that first person perspectival content is critical to ethical agency as well.

Kant's framing his maxim in the first person is no accident. He could not have restated it, for example, as "Immanuel Kant will make lying promises when he is in need." Such a third-personal thought would not be a maxim of action, since it could not be acted upon by the thinker until he reformulated it reflexively, in the first person. Insofar as the target of universalization is a practical thought, it is essentially first-personal.   (2006: 121)

Velleman's point is that in the case of Kantian ethics, perspectival thoughts are critical. *I* am supposed to act only on that maxim which *I* could will to be a universal law. To put it another way, I must understand that the ethical principle applies to *me*, and that *I* am to act on it. If *I* make a promise, *I* am to keep it. Thus the moral law speaks to me. It is a law *for* me.

Here again, the temporal element is critical. When I make a promise, that promise has a temporal element to it. I am not to fulfill the promise immediately; I will do so sometime in my future. If I fail to deliver on my promise then I shall perhaps feel remorse at having failed to do so, or perhaps I shall be judged for having failed to do so. If I am being judged it is because I *have failed* to deliver.

I believe perspectival content applies to all norms, even unconscious individual grammatical rules. In my (2011) book *The Philosophy of Generative Linguistics* I proposed an account of grammatical competence in which each of us has individual grammatical rules that are normatively guiding. This is how I put it (2011: 50), using the linguistic rule of subjacency as an example:

Saying we have a rule like subjacency is also thicker than merely saying we cognize it (or at least it can be made thicker). Saying *I* have such a rule invites the interpretation that it is a rule *for me*—that *I* am normatively guided by it.
[emphasis added]

To explain, I have a rule that a WH word like 'who' cannot move out of a complex noun phrase (out of a sentential clause embedded in a noun phrase). Thus this rule tells me that I ought not to say things like 'Who did you hear the story that Thor smote' even though it is clear what it would mean (Who is such that you heard the story that Thor smote them). This rule constitutes part of my linguistic competence, and it may guide my linguistic performance. Describing that rule in an aperspectival way could explain my linguistic *performance*, but it cannot explain my linguistic *competence* (because *I* may or may not act in accord with the rule).

The temporal reflex of this would be the anticipatory nature of my rule following. Consider the following passage from John Lawler's lecture notes,[4] involving the anticipation and repair of a Subjacency violation (he calls it a violation of the Complex Noun Phrase Constraint and also a violation of a Ross Constraint, after the Linguist, John "Haj" Ross, who discovered these facts).

Violations of Ross Constraints are very ungrammatical. Most people never encounter them. We appear to formulate our discourse to avoid them. Occasionally, we get in a bind and see one looming at the end of the clause, and have to do something quick. What we do is often illuminating about the relative importance of syntactic rules.

For instance, consider the following:

?That's the book_i [that Bill married the woman_j [who_j illustrated it_i]].
*That's the book_i [that Bill married the woman_j [who_j illustrated ___i]].

Neither sentence is terrifically grammatical, but the first seems more appropriate (and common as a type) than the second, though the last word in the first sentence still feels strange. The ordinary rule of relative clause formation operating on the last clause should result in its deletion at the end of the clause (and thus the sentence). However, it appears inside another relative, an island, and is thus safe from such "movement" by the Complex NP Constraint.

Sentences like the first one are generated when, at the last minute, the speaker realizes what is going to result, and cancels the deletion, substituting an alternative relative-formation rule (called a **Resumptive Pronoun** in the trade), which merely pronominalizes the coreferential NP, instead of deleting it in the object position.

This is not the way English forms its relative clauses (though other languages use it frequently, e.g, Hebrew), and the sentence is thus ungrammatical. But this

---

[4] http://www-personal.umich.edu/~jlawler/aue/ross.html. Last accessed Jan. 10, 2018.

turns out to be a venial syntactic sin by comparison with a violation of a Ross constraint, which typically produces extreme ungrammaticality.

In other words, when I see an *imminent* violation of a rule on the horizon, I understand that *I* ought to repair it before the violation occurs.

Finally, the writers canvassed by Cappelen and Dever seem to agree that perspectival content (here described as "indexical" content) is not reducible to aperspectival content.

François Recanati:

[N]o transformation from indexical to non-indexical is possible without affecting the cognitive significance of the utterance and therefore changing the thought it expresses.... The irreducibility and indispensability of indexicals is widely acknowledged.   (2007: 243)

Colin McGinn:

The present suggestion, then, is that indexical concepts are ineliminable because without them agency would be impossible: when I imagine myself divested of indexical thoughts, employing only centreless mental representations, I *eo ipso* imagine myself deprived of the power to act.   (1983: 104)

Héctor-Neri Castañeda:

When I act intentionally on an object, I care neither about the Russellian (Kaplanian) propositions beyond as such nor about their Fregean (Kaplanian) first referents. These are not crucial. What I need is to bring those doxastic referents somehow into my experience through my thinking indexical (that is, experiential) references... the singular proposition that mobilizes my powers of deliberation and action is the indexical truth within my grasp.   (1989: 126)

Indexical reference is personal, ephemeral, confrontational, and executive. Hence, it is not reducible to nonindexical reference to what is not confronted.
(1989: 170)

So perspectival contents are important and ineliminable, but what are they and how do they work?

Now clearly, it is not *prima facie* obvious how the same perspectival content can be expressed in different ways from different perspectival positions, nor for that matter, what perspectival positions and interperspectival contents *are.* Explaining this will take some care, and we will get into the details of how this works in Chapters 2 and 3.

0.2 Tensism

'Tensism', as I use the term, refers to the idea that tense is not merely a feature of language and thought, but that it reflects some further, irreducible, perspectival feature of the world. For the purposes of this book, let's call someone who endorses this kind of metaphysical position a *tenser*. Let's call someone who rejects this claim and thinks that reality is fundamentally aperspectival a *detenser*.[5]

According to the *detenser*, so-called tense operators in natural language should be analyzed in terms of a series of events related by tenseless Spacetime positions—for example, they might be related by the earlier-than/later-than relation.[6] We can think of these events being lined up on a timeline (or perhaps the timeline is nothing more than the ordering of these events). All of the events on the timeline are equally real, from the birth of Queen Elizabeth II to the event of your reading this book to the birth of the first child in the year 2500. Following McTaggart (1908, 1927), we can call this series of events *the B-series*.

To take a very simple case of a detensing semantics, consider the utterance u, of a sentence having the form 'PAST(E)', where 'E' refers to a particular event and 'PAST' is the past tense morpheme. In this case the semantics might look as follows: 'Past(E)' is true iff (the time of) E is earlier than (the time of) u. The analysis is aperspectival because E is earlier than u from every perspectival position (although this needs to be qualified for relativistic effects—see Section 8.1). E is earlier than u on the "view from nowhere."

The analysis of tense sketched above is a *regimentation* in the sense of Burgess (1984); although tense expressions appear in the object language (here as the morpheme 'PAST'), such expressions do not appear in the metalanguage—they are analyzed away in favor of the earlier-than/later-than relation.

The detenser frequently argues that tense is merely a feature of languages (linguistic tense) or the mind (psychological tense) and that we mistakenly project this feature of natural language (or mind) into our metaphysics. In my view, on the other hand, that picture has things

---

[5] This usage is not universal. Some would define 'tenser' to include those who think tense is psychological. My definition, for the purposes of this book, is not so generous.

[6] This is an oversimplification, as we will see.

upside down. Most languages of the world have nothing resembling standard Indo-European tense morphology. Other languages rely upon elements like aspect, evidentials,[7] and modals to talk about temporal features of the world. Even in English we don't have a genuine future tense (clearly 'will' is a modal in 'I will eat'), and for that matter our past tense morpheme '-ed' looks a lot like an aspectual marker (presumably indicating perfect aspect).

Now of course we are good at identifying the ways in which different languages express past, future, etc., but there is no common feature of the *syntax* and *morphology* of these languages that we are picking up on (since they express temporal notions in radically different ways). In the face of these facts, one begins to suspect that there are temporal features of the world and that different languages of the world devise different strategies for talking about those features. If this is right, then linguistic tense may only enter into the picture when we think about how language hooks up with perspectival features of the world. There is no linguistic phenomenon that we mistakenly project onto the world; it is more plausible to think that perspectival aspects of the world are metaphysically prior, and that different languages find different strategies for talking about these aspects of the world.

0.3 A-Series/B-Series Compatibility

In 1908 James McTaggart Ellis McTaggart[8] published a paper that has led to a great philosophical divide in how subsequent philosophers have thought about time. At the heart of the paper was a distinction between the tensed (perspectival) and detensed (aperspectival) conceptions of time—conceptions that McTaggart referred to as the A-theory and the B-theory respectively. McTaggart argued that the conjunction of these two views led to paradox, and subsequent philosophers have largely

---

[7] Evidentials are grammatical elements that encode the source of the information. So for example imagine that English had a suffix '-foo' which when appended to a verb indicated that the event in question was seen with one's own eyes (as opposed to via testimony or inference). Then if I say 'John walkfoo', I am saying that I saw John walk with my own eyes. The past tense is presumably inferred from the nature of perceptual reports. Many languages use elements like this in complementary distribution with past tense morphology.

[8] The repetition of 'McTaggart' is correct. It's a long story involving a wealthy relative/benefactor with the name McTaggart.

chosen to be either A-theorists or B-theorists, but rarely have they chosen to be both at the same time.[9]

I am not prepared to say that the A-*theory* and B-*theory* are compatible, since sometimes those theories come loaded with a lot of philosophical baggage—for example, the supposition that the A-theory is incoherent or that the B-theory rejects the possibility of metaphysical tense (perspectival contents). So my claim here is a more narrow claim about the compatibility of the A-*series* and B-*series*.

When I talk about the *B-series*, I will mean a series of events that are tenselessly related to each other (for example by the earlier-than/later-than relation). In that usage I will take the B-series to be tense free (aperspectival). When I talk about the *A-series* I am talking about an ordered collection of tensed contents (interperspectival contents).

I do not agree with the standard view that the A-series and the B-series are incompatible. To the contrary, not only do I believe that both tensed (perspectival) and detensed (aperspectival) contents exist and that neither is more fundamental, but I believe they are both critical in our temporal reasoning. I will even argue that both are needed for any interesting theory of the flow of time.

What then of the paradox that allegedly comes from the conjunction of A-theoretic and B-theoretic approaches to time? McTaggart's alleged paradox has stood as the great continental divide in the past hundred-plus years of work in the philosophy of time. Some philosophers have become resolute detensers. Others have become fanatical tensers. I'm going to make the case that a hundred years on, enough is enough. It is time for reconciliation.

Historically, tensism has been tied up with the doctrine of presentism. Presentism is the thesis that only present things exist. Future things and events don't exist (at least not yet) and likewise past things and events don't exist (at least not anymore). Another way to put it is that anytime we utter a sentence (or if you prefer, express a proposition) in which we existentially quantify over individuals or events, what we say can only be true if the things we quantify over currently exist or if our existential quantification takes place in the scope of a past or future tense. So, it is fine to say that it *was* the case that there was an x such that x was a

---

[9] Important exceptions include Smith (1993), passage theories like those discussed in Brogaard (2012), and "growing block" theories such as Broad (1923: ch. 2).

dinosaur and x does not presently exist, but we are saying something false if we say that there *is* an x such that it was the case that x was a dinosaur and x does not presently exist.

There are lots of interesting questions to be asked about presentism, but one of the *most* interesting questions has to do with its relation to tensism. Must tensers be presentists? A.N. Prior thought so. I used to think so too. But this issue turns out to be complicated. I will be making the case in this book that tensism does not entail presentism. One can be a tenser and believe in future and past objects and events.

Not to give away too much in advance, the idea will be that a single term like 'now' can express (be used to express) different contents at different times. I don't merely mean that 'now' is used to refer to different times— that much is obvious. What I mean is that the perspectival content (sense content, if you prefer) expressed by 'now' is also different at different times. This is not to say that there is a "moving now." There are, however, different perspectival contents being expressed at different times.

The considerations regarding 'now' apply to past and future tensed verbs (and any tensed expression). In different contexts these verbs will express different perspectival contents. As I will argue, such is to be expected from the theory of the dynamic lexicon that I independently argued for in Ludlow (2014).

What if one doesn't go down this route? That is, what if one wants to endorse tensism *and* presentism? Well, then we head down the path to all kinds of puzzles, not least of which is the question of how a presentist handles complex tenses like the past perfect and phenomena like temporal anaphora—cases where we at least appear to be referring to past and future times and/or events. Such a discussion is very interesting, but not directly related to my core concern here, which is the narrower project of defending perspectival contents. Accordingly, I have moved discussion of such issues to the Appendix, where I explore options for the presentist, and conclude that there are potential solution paths if one wishes to be a presentist.

0.4 Semantic Accountability

Throughout this book I will be drawing on a doctrine that I call *Semantic Accountability*. The basic idea is that meaningful use of language has ontological commitments.

To be clear, I am *not* supposing that the semantics of natural language is extruded from linguistic forms or from the semantics of natural language in isolation. The semantics of natural language is a theory about language–world relations and how we organize and deploy our talk about the world. Accordingly, semantics and metaphysics have to take place hand in hand.

Nevertheless, there is a misperception about this approach to ontology, which is that it is a way to extrude metaphysical conclusions out of syntax or some internalist properties of language. For an example of this misperception, consider the following passage, from Ted Sider.

[F]our-dimensionalism is a metaphysical thesis about the nature of persisting objects. It is not a thesis about language, nor about the analysis of predicates of constituents, nor about the conceptual epistemic priority of predicates of states and predicates of constituents...

The difference between thing-talk and process-talk in no way undermines four-dimensionalism. It is consistent with things and events being in the same ontological category that natural language contains different ways of speaking of things and events. Natural language contains different vocabulary for speaking of persons and inanimate physical objects, but this is no argument against materialism. Nor is the oddness of saying that my thought is spatially located in my brain a compelling argument against the mind-brain identity theory. The objection might have bite if four-dimensionalism were a thesis of ordinary language philosophy, but it seems ineffective against the metaphysical thesis that I uphold.   (Sider 2001: 211–12)

I believe the core of the misunderstanding here is the assumption that the semantic approach to metaphysics aims to read metaphysics or anything else off linguistic *forms*. When we are engaged in the semantics of natural language we are already engaged in language–world relations. Semantics would simply be impossible if we did not have some grasp on the furnishings of the world. Nothing extrudes from the analysis of predicates themselves. Predicates are just bits of syntax.[10]

For example, when I drew on the romance inflectional system to illustrate how different verbal inflections express different perspectival contents, I was not arguing from the existence of the inflectional system

---

[10] Even this may be too strong. Elsewhere (Ludlow 2011) I have argued that even linguistic forms may be contingent in some ways on our environmental embedding conditions. It may be that nothing is "just syntax" but we can concede the formalism about syntax and hold that the semantics is very much about language–world relations.

to this conclusion. That would be a difficult case to make given that not all languages use verbal inflection to represent tense (Chinese is a case in point). And if you were being a stickler about extruding metaphysical tense from each verbal tense, you might conclude that we ought to have more than three metaphysical tenses.

Any case to be made for the reality of perspectival contents has to be made independently. And, as I said, it is my view that different languages have different strategies for expressing these perspectival contents. The illustration from the romance inflectional system is just that—an illustration—offered with the intent of making vivid the kinds of perspectival contents that furnish our world. Whether the encoding of these contents in the inflectional system of some languages is serendipitous, or perhaps reflects some deep connection, need not concern us here.

It should also be emphasized that the ontological commitments of the semantics of our language are not easily recognized. Sometimes the surface form of language can be deceptive. For example, are definite descriptions names, as Frege thought, and thus ontologically committing, or are they definite descriptions in disguise, as Russell thought? Or, to use another example, when we say 'the average family has 2.3 children' are we saying there is such thing as an average family or is 'average' working as a kind of adverb here ('on average a family has 2.3 children')? When I say 'there is a flaw in the argument' am I committed to there being flaws or is 'flaw' modifying something—'the argument is flawed'?[11]

Commitment to Semantic Accountability does not require you to take things at face value, but it does require you to explain exactly why you are not ontologically committed to something when it appears that you are. David and Stephanie Lewis thus respected Semantic Accountability in their (1970) paper on holes. They did not like the idea of being ontologically committed to holes, but understood that there is a lot of hole talk that needs to be accounted for. For example, we seem to quantify over holes (e.g. I can say 'there are seven holes in my cheese') and we even compare these quantities ('there are more holes in my cheese than in yours'). This quantificational language must be accounted for (the Lewises concluded that we were quantifying over hole *linings*). Whether that works or not can be disputed (see Casati and Varzi (1995) for

---

[11] I discussed some of these questions in Ludlow (2011: ch. 6).

discussion) but my point here is that running in the background of their paper is the doctrine of Semantic Accountability.

So it is with tense and perspectival contents. If one is determined to deny the existence of perspectival contents, that is fine, but Semantic Accountability dictates that you owe some analysis of perspectival language in terms of aperspectival contents. It is my view that this cannot be done. This is not to say that all language must be perspectival nor is it to say that we can't create languages that are aperspectival.

In a famous passage in "Concept and Object," Gottlob Frege (1892) took issue with the alleged inability of natural language to allow him to express what he wanted to say about the distinction between concepts and objects.

I have got hold of a distinction of the highest importance. I admit that there is a quite peculiar obstacle in the way of an understanding with my reader. By a kind of necessity of language, my expressions, taken literally, sometimes miss my thought, in that [indem] I mention an object, when what I intend is a concept. I fully realize that in such cases I was relying upon a reader who would be ready to meet me half-way who does not begrudge a pinch of salt.   (1892: 193)

I believe that what Frege is saying is that in his formal language concepts could not be referred to using names (or definite descriptions, but for Frege this came to the same thing). Concepts could only be *used*. I don't really begrudge Frege his "pinch of salt" here. Natural language is very generous about nominalizing predicates. If 'is a horse' expresses a concept, we naturally want to say "it expresses the concept of a horse." I see no problem with creating languages in which this is not allowed.[12]

---

[12] There is room here to say that Frege was talking about the surface grammar of natural language and that logical form, which is to say a level of linguistic representation (what linguists call LF) that is visible to the semantics, might have the properties that Frege was looking for. In many cases I think this is right. There might be (actually, I believe there is) a linguistic level of representation for natural language in which quantifier scope ambiguity is resolved, for example. How such a level could circumvent our ability to express the nominalization of concept terms is obscure to me, but I suppose it is possible. It would involve a process by which such structures had to be de-nominalized before they could be represented at LF. In some sense this is how things worked for some versions of generative grammar in the 1960s and early 1970s. In some versions, the level of representation visible to the semantics (Deep Structure) was a level generated prior to operations like nominalization. Chomsky (1970) subsequently showed that not all nominals are derived. Suffice it to say that this line of investigation would be interesting, but orthogonal to our current concerns.

The problem comes in when we now imagine that the new special invented language gets to "call the shots" regarding ontology (a mistake that I do not attribute to Frege). Equally important is the language that was used in getting your reader to understand what you intended. And if your theory has some application, then the language that you use to explain how it is applied is no less important. Semantics has to account for more than the finished product of scientific and logical theorizing; it has to explain the language of how you got there and what you are supposed to do with the theory you have constructed.

Wittgenstein recognized this problem in the *Tractatus* (6.54) and immediately saw the implications, concluding that work with the famous passage about kicking away the ladder that got us there.

My propositions serve as elucidations in the following way: anyone who understands me eventually recognizes them as nonsensical, when he has used them - as steps - to climb beyond them. He must, so to speak, throw away the ladder after he has climbed up it.   (1961: 89)

What Wittgenstein presumably also understood was that the same admonition would hold not only for any talk about the framework of the *Tractatus*, but also for any talk about how and why the theory of the *Tractatus* was constructed, as well as for any claims about how the final theory advocated in the *Tractatus* was to be applied (including the admonition to throw away the ladder). Of course Wittgenstein eventually saw that this approach to theorizing was not viable, and at least as I understand the transition from the early Wittgenstein to the later Wittgenstein, the later Wittgenstein of the *Philosophical Investigations* is not trying to run away from natural language.[13] The moral for us is that you can't keep running away from the semantic commitments of your language. Sooner or later they catch up with you.

Here is a way to frame the issue from the point of view of scientific theorizing. Let's imagine that our complete and perfect theory of the physical world will have no perspectival contents (as we will see, this is probably false, but let's assume it for now). The issue is that we still needed perspectival language in the experimental setting that confirmed

---

[13] Although he perhaps did run away from claims about the syntax and semantics of natural language, since this would run into the teeth of his rule-following argument. I'll come back to this in Section 4.4.

this theory, and we likewise will need perspectival language in any attempt to apply the theory in the actual world. We will also need perspectival language in theory construction. For example, scientists should at least be free to entertain the possibility of a role for perspectival contents in scientific theorizing. Moreover, the acts of referring to and defending scientific theories and the norms governing that practice will require perspectival contents.

This is to say that there will be much language used in the discovery, construction, testing, revision, and application of physical science that will be perspectival. If this isn't obvious, think about a laboratory setting and the need to use indexicals to talk about experimental devices and their parts, materials that are the subjects of the experiments, meters, media for recording results etc. (see Section 8.2 for examples from online lab notes). The experimental setting is thick with perspectival contents, and semantics is not just a theory of the meanings of our finished theories, but of all our language, and this includes the language of the practice and application of science.

But semantics also has to account for the meaningfulness of our other linguistic practices as well. We engage in more than physics. One of the things we do, and actually we do quite well, is explain, rationalize, and predict the actions and emotions of other persons. We use language to describe our perceptual experiences. We use language to communicate norms and how those norms apply to us. We use language to state what rules govern us as individuals and how we, as individuals, ought to act. As we will see, the articulation of all these practices requires the deployment of perspectival contents.

Is there some reason why the semantics of these enterprises should have less ontological heft than the semantics of a finished, aperspectival physical theory does? It is difficult to see why it would. Whether we are providing the semantics for the language of physics or for the language of human action, the existential quantifiers we use are the same. Unless some good reason can be provided (for example, a clean reduction of perspectival contents to aperspectival contents in physical theory), it would seem that ontological pluralism would be the default position.

You might think that the language of physical theory is special because at the end of the day physics is the theory of everything, and thus everything must be reducible to the basic properties of physics. That would be reasonable had we some evidence that all of our explanations do in fact reduce to physics in its current form, but we really have no evidence that they do. We have robust theories that explain why people act as they do, but we have no idea how these explanations are to be reduced to quantum physics, for example. For that matter, Putnam (1975b) has argued that we don't even have an idea of how the basic properties of mid-sized earth-bound objects reduce to the properties of quantum physics. Can we explain at the quantum level why a square peg can't go through a round hole?

We may well discover that physics as we know it will have to change in robust ways in order to account for familiar macro-level properties. Just as physics had to change to account for the theory of valences in the elements we may find that physics may need to be revised to successfully ground our use of perspectival contents. For that matter, as we will see in Chapter 8, far from offering a path to the eliminative reduction of perspectival contents, basic physics may need to utilize them.

One can also argue that the language of physical theory may well be one part of our language that does *not* get to call the shots. Van Fraassen (1980), for example, has suggested that objects like tables and chairs have a claim to reality that the posits of our scientific theory do not. It is hard for me to see why this should be, apart from the sense that our scientific posits are fleeting, and apt to be revoked. But this amounts to a claim that such theories are going to turn out to be false, and not that the quantification in the semantics has no ontological bite. In other words, it would be ontologically committing if it were true.[14]

Nothing I say here leans on a particular semantic theory, or even on the assumption that semantic theory should be truth-conditional. I have elsewhere (2011: section 1.4) toyed with the idea of an expressivist semantics for all of natural language, so that the truth predicate would give way to the expression of an attitude (for example, Yay! or For!). It is hard for me to see that such a semantics is less ontologically committing

---

[14] One might suggest another gambit here—fictionalism about our discourse. Fictionalism has been applied in areas ranging from ethics to mathematics. Could we use it to escape ontological commitment about temporal discourse? While it is true that in my view, our discourse would not be ontologically committing should it turn out to be false, saying that all of our tensed language must be fictive is just another way to say that pretty much everything we say is fictive. In that case we need to replace talk of truth conditions with talk of "application conditions," and I have difficulty seeing that this move spares us from ontological commitment in any sense I intend here.

than a traditional truth-conditional semantics. Nor does it appear to me that such a semantics has less need of perspectival contents. That is to say, we can be Yay! the meeting is at 3:00, without being Yay! the meeting is now! It is my belief that my arguments in this book cut across a very broad range of semantic theories—basically any semantic theory that links language with the world, whether that connection is mediated by model theory or truth, expressive attitudes or application conditions.

If semantics incorporates our theory of everything one might ask why we bother with the linguistic formulations at all. Why not cut directly to the world itself? To put it another way, why talk about language when we can talk about the world instead and not lose anything?

The answer is that our language is a record of the things we encounter in the world. We may proudly offer a scientific theory in which perspectival contents play no role, but there often remain records of our discussions of the process of discovery, the process of experimentation, and the process of application of those theories, and those records illuminate our many encounters with perspectival contents in the practice of science.

So too our language records our encounters with perspectival contents in our explanations of human action and emotion, our normative actions, and, as we will see, even our theorizing about computation, informational states, and basic features of physical theory.

In other words, we attend to linguistic formulations and pay attention to their semantics because doing so keeps us honest. It prevents people from surreptitiously utilizing perspectival contents while at the same time denying the need for such contents. It is easy enough to wave a hand and say that the use of tense in language has no reflex in reality, but the semanticist is there to say, "wait a minute, slow down, you are deploying perspectival contents whether you admit it or not."

0.5 The Plan

The plan for this book is as follows. I will begin in Chapter 1 with a discussion of the Cappelen–Dever arguments against the need for indexical/perspectival content. I will go on to give some of the considerations that weigh in favor of perspectival content.

In Chapter 2 I will develop the idea of interperspectival contents. Key to this will be the idea that linguistic tense (and other perspectival language) is used to express interperspectival contents, and that interperspectival contents are expressed in different ways from within different perspectival positions. I will then try to sharpen up the notions of perspectival position and interperspectival content. I will also offer some thoughts about the different ways this general strategy might be executed with different metaphysical primitives. Then I will turn to some concerns that David Kaplan has raised about introducing perspectival contents into a semantic theory, and I will address whether we will get caught up in the kind of "sloppy thinking" that he warns against.

In Chapter 3, I will address the problem of how our semantics can come to grips with the expression of perspectival contents, and in particular how language can express the contents of utterances and thoughts of those in other perspectival positions (for example, an utterance of 'I am hungry now' as uttered by another person at another time). I will offer a theory of the cognitive dynamics of such cross-perspective reporting and suggest that it can serve as a theory of interperspectival contents. Then I will address problems such as Kaplan's Rip van Winkle case, in which we report on an agent that has lost track of her perspectival position.

In Chapter 4 I will address some alternative accounts of indexicality/ perspectival contents, including token-indexical theories, Kaplan's account, and David Lewis's account of *de se* attitudes. I will argue that all of these approaches share the feature of sweeping the key issue under the rug by keeping perspectival content free of the semantics, but I suggest that this strategy merely postpones the inevitable semantic account of perspectival content, and I show that this is a responsibility that cannot be ducked.

Our discussion in Chapter 4 will lead us into a discussion of the ways in which rule following leans on perspectival contents, and this in turn will lead us to a question, raised by Wittgenstein and Kripke, about the nature of computational states in physical systems. In Chapter 5 I will make the case that computational states too need to be understood as leaning on perspectival contents. More generally, informational states can and should be thought of as kinds of perspectival states.

In Chapter 6 I will make my case for A-series/B-series compatibility. I will suggest that given an approach to the lexicon (advocating dynamic word meanings) we can address puzzles like the "moving now." I will also make the case that this view also affords a natural account of the flow of time.

In Chapter 7, I turn to some objections that might be considered metaphysical in nature. The first objection—the truth-maker problem—we will see is defanged if there is no commitment to presentism. I will then take up the question of whether perspectival contents run afoul of Humean Supervenience and whether it should concern us if they do. Not surprisingly, I will argue that the allergic reactions to perspectival contents are not well grounded, considering the motivations that made Humean Supervenience attractive in the first place.

Finally, in Chapter 8, I will take up the compatibility of perspectival contents with current physical theory. I will argue that with respect to the theory of relativity they pose no difficulties that don't already exist in the reporting of contents across perspectival positions. I will then argue that B-theoretic temporal relations (before and after) don't have workable reductions to atemporal properties of physical theory. Finally, I will argue that physical theory and science lean heavily on perspectival contents, both in the context of scientific experimentation and observation and ultimately in base-level physics, which cannot neatly extract the context of observation from the theory itself.

The material on presentism could have been added as an additional chapter, but I wanted to make it clear that it is orthogonal to my central interest in this book—defending perspectival contents. Thus I move discussion of presentism into the Appendix.

1

Why We Need Interperspectival Content

In the Introduction we saw that there have been numerous arguments made for interperspectival content (perspectival content, for short), ranging from the role that it plays in the explanation of human action (the late for the meeting case) and human emotion (the "Thank Goodness" case), perception, consciousness, and normative action. In some sense, philosophers have leaned on the importance of perspectival content in almost every aspect of philosophizing about human nature.

Philosophers have disagreed about whether perspectival content is really a feature of the world, and they have disagreed about whether it is eliminable, but they have more or less been on the same page about one thing: Perspectival content, understood in a very weak sense of 'content' that includes narrow psychological states, is necessary for the explanation of human action, emotion, etc. (For the purposes of this chapter we can think of perspectival content in this weak way; as we move into Chapter 2 we will think of contents as being features of the world and not merely narrow psychological states.)

Cappelen and Dever (2013: 9) are not impressed by this rare point of convergence among a very broad range of philosophers. So many philosophers in agreement about something simply cannot be good! They may be right about that, but it is not entirely fair of them to object that the positing of perspectival (or, as they and most other philosophers call it, "indexical") content in this weak sense "is widely relied on without argumentation and there is hardly any critical examination of it." Philosophers have deployed perspectival content in order to make sense of the human enterprises they were trying to come to grips with—the theories of action, emotion, perception, ethical agency, etc. That is, they came to this view about the need for perspectival content via the product of deep philosophical analysis in a broad range of topics. They did not begin with the idea that there must be perspectival contents.

Still, there is no harm in examining this assumption more closely. Do we really need perspectival contents to explain our actions, emotions, features of human perception, etc.?

Let's take a look at Cappelen and Dever's principal reservation and their accompanying arguments, which focus on the first person perspective. As they view the situation, the case for the importance of the first person perspective in explanation is grounded in what they call the "Impersonal Incompleteness Claim."

Impersonal Incompleteness Claim (IIC). Impersonal action rationalizations (IAR) are necessarily incomplete because of a missing indexical component.

They then give two examples of explanations, each from an impersonal and a personal perspective. Consider the first case. (They use the expression 'IAR explanation' so I am going to treat these as explanations as well.)

Personal Action Rationalization (explanation) 1.
- Belief: François is about to be shot.
- Belief: I am François.
- Belief (Inferred): I am about to be shot.
- Desire: That I not be shot.
- Belief: If I duck under the table, I will not be shot.
- Action: I duck under the table.

Impersonal Action Rationalization (explanation) 1.
- Belief: François is about to be shot.
- Desire: François not be shot.
- Belief: If François ducks under the table, he will not be shot.
- Action: François ducks under the table.

In their view, the impersonal action rationalization is a perfectly good explanation for what François did. And to be sure, that explanation sometimes is (or at least appears to be) fine. But is it always? The first person perspective is motivated by cases in which, for example, François does not know who he is. Suppose, using an example inspired by Kaplan (1977), François sees someone in the mirror, about to be shot. He does not duck. Why? Because he does not know that he is the person who is about to be shot. Or to use an example from Perry (1979), suppose that

François has a bout of amnesia and does not realize he is François. He knows himself only as Frankie and takes himself to be a famous lounge singer. He is informed that François is about to be shot but does not duck. Why? Because he does not know that *he* is François. He lacks the appropriate perspectival knowledge.

In such cases there can be a similar explanatory failure when François ducks. Suppose, not knowing that he is François, François ducks when he is told that François is about to be shot. We might fairly ask under such circumstances, "why did he duck?"

Of course all this makes us wonder if there is something enthymematic about the *Im*personal Action Rationalization explanations in those cases when they do seem satisfactory. For example, the IAR explanation above may be hiding the premise that François realizes that he himself is François—that is, the premise that he has a thought that he would express as 'I am François'.

But there is something else odd about the allegedly impersonal action rationalization as an explanation. The initial belief—that François is about to be shot—is already loaded with a *temporal* perspectival content, for what it is saying is that François is about to be shot *now*. If there is to be any ducking, it needs to happen now! It is perhaps less obvious, but the same is true of the second premise as well. François may have been shot several times in the past. The desire is not that François' timeline be free of getting-shot events; it is too late to realize such a desire. You can't get unshot. His desire is that he not get shot *now*. Similarly for François' belief: His belief is that if he ducks under the table *now* he will not get shot now. And finally, if the action is to happen as described—the ducking is happening now.

The second example provided by Cappelen and Dever is similar. Again, they provide us with two rationalizations for the action—one from a first person perspective and one allegedly from a non-egocentric perspective. This example involves an agent Herman, who believes Nora is in danger.

Personal Action Rationalization (explanation) 2.
- Belief: Nora is in danger.
- Desire: That Nora not be hurt.
- Belief: If Herman closes the door, Nora will be safe.
- Belief: I am Herman.
- Action: Herman closes the door.

Impersonal Action Rationalization (explanation) 2.

- Belief: Nora is in danger.
- Desire: That Nora not be hurt.
- Belief: If the door is closed, Nora will be safe.
- Action: Herman closes the door.

On Cappelen and Dever's view, the second rationalization is entirely third person:

Our guiding question is thus whether there are any arguments to the effect that the IAR-explanations must be incomplete. We'll argue that there are none. First, it is not necessary for an indexical element to enter into the rationalization. Second, on our view the agent doesn't even need to be represented in a non-indexical way in an adequate action rationalization. Nor does any part of the agent's body need to be represented (indexically or not).   (p. 37)

Even conceding Cappelen and Dever's core position, Rationalization 2 suppresses some critical details. For example, we need to know whose beliefs these are. There are no beliefs independent of believers. To be sure, there are belief *contents*, which, let's say, are propositions, but the beliefs themselves are what are needed to rationalize and explain actions. We accordingly have something like the following.

Impersonal Action Rationalization (explanation) 2*.

- Herman's Belief: Nora is in danger.
- Herman's Desire: That Nora not be hurt.
- Herman's Belief: If the door is closed, Nora will be safe.
- Herman's Action: Herman closes the door.

But there is already something very off about describing Herman's action as 'Herman closes the door'. We feel some pull to give accounts of his action like the following.

- Herman's Action: his closing the door.
- Herman's Action: closing the door.
- Herman's Action: he himself closes the door.

What is the difference between expressing this action as 'Herman closes the door' and the other options? Well, describing his action as 'closing the door' is our third person perspectival way of describing Herman's action. There is a good reason it sounds odd to describe Herman's action using his name—in doing so we are giving up the device we have for expressing the perspectival nature of actions. Using the proper name makes it sound like he is bringing about the event of Herman closing the door from a distance—like there is a Herman 2 being manipulated like a puppet by Herman 1.

Again we get to the cases that originally motivated perspectival accounts of action explanation. If Herman doesn't realize he is Herman—suppose he thinks he is Hume—then the explanation offered by Cappelen and Dever is a peculiar way to describe how Herman came to act in the way that he did. If Herman doesn't know he is Herman then why does he bother closing the door? And if he does close the door not knowing he is Herman, well, why did he do that? There is something missing from the explanation.

Beyond this, it is really hard to make sense of Herman's beliefs and desires apart from some additional perspectival facts. There are billions of children in the world; why is it that Herman cares about Nora? Why does he desire that she in particular be safe? And why does he think that he, among all the adults in the world, is responsible for taking care of her? Well, one natural explanation is that she is *his* daughter. Note that it is not enough to say that she is the daughter of Herman. In the case when Herman thinks he is Hume, we lose the explanation for why he closed the door.

The creep of assumed perspectival contents does not end there. It seems that smuggled into Cappelen and Dever's rationalizations above are some of the key perspectival contents that this book is arguing for— the temporal ones. When we say that Herman's belief is that Nora is in danger, we are saying his belief is that she is in danger *now*. When we say that he believes that if the door will be closed she will be safe, we are obviously saying that if the door is closed *now*, she will be safe *now*. When we say that Herman's action is to close the door, we are saying that his action is to close the door *now*. All of these are temporal perspectival contents.

Even if we explain his behavior after the fact, we still locate Herman's action from a time-internal perspective. For example, we might give an account of his actions the following day.

Impersonal Action Rationalization (explanation) 2*-past.
- Herman's Belief yesterday: Nora was in danger.
- Herman's Desire (always): That Nora never be hurt.
- Herman's Belief yesterday: If the door were to be closed, Nora would be safe.
- Herman's Action yesterday: Herman closed the door.

Notice what happens when we strip the perspectival temporal contents from this.

Impersonal Action Rationalization (explanation) 2*-past-tenseless.
- Herman's Belief at t1: Nora be in danger at t1.
- Herman's Desire (for all t): Nora not be hurt at t.
- Herman's Belief at t1: If the door were to be closed at t1, Nora would be safe at t1.
- Herman's Action yesterday: Herman closed the door at t1.

With these two rationalizations we are back to a case that is similar to examples (1) and (2) from the Introduction—the examples about my meeting with the boss that got this whole business going (repeated below).

(1) I have a meeting with the boss at three o'clock.

(2) Oh no, I have a meeting with the boss *now*!

What if, yesterday, Herman knew that Nora would be in danger at t1, but did not realize it was then t1? For example, suppose that Herman knows it is only problematically dangerous during a full moon in Norway. Herman knows it will be a full moon at t1, but is busy locked away in his study, working so hard he does not realize that it is now t1. In such a case we have no explanation for why Herman closed the door. Even the so-called "Impersonal Action Rationalization" is larded with perspectival content.

On the Bratman (1987) hypothesis that action requires some minimal form of deliberation, this presumably holds for the rationalization/explanation of any action whatsoever. We would need perspectival contents for my deliberations are about what *I* should do, and whether I should do it *now* or later, and whether I should do it *here* or elsewhere.

As we saw in the Introduction, the use of perspectival content extends beyond simple action explanation. We also saw that such content has been claimed to be necessary for normative reasoning. Let's run an impersonal action rationalization for such an explanation to see exactly where the perspectival content comes into the picture.

Personal Responsibility Rationalization (explanation).
- Fact 1: Nora is in danger.
- Fact 2: If the door is closed, Nora will be safe.
- Responsibility 1: I am responsible for Nora's safety.

- Responsibility 2: I am responsible for closing the door.
- Obligation: I ought to close the door.

Impersonal Responsibility Rationalization (explanation).
- Fact 1: Nora is in danger.
- Fact 2: If the door is closed, Nora will be safe.
- Responsibility 1: Herman is responsible for Nora's safety.
- Responsibility 2: Herman is responsible for closing the door.
- Obligation: Herman ought to close the door.

Again, the Impersonal Responsibility Rationalization doesn't work if, for example, Herman believes he is Hume. In that case the impersonal rationalization confers no responsibility on him. However, even if he thinks he is Hume, under the right circumstances he can still know that it is *his* responsibility to take care of Nora. Notice too the implicit temporal element in this. It is his obligation to close the door now, not seven years from now.

Things need not be so dramatic. To use my linguistic example from the Introduction, if I feel an impending Ross violation in the sentence I am planning to produce, I will make adjustments to avoid the worst kind of rule violation. But notice that I will do that even if I do not know who I am. I can still know that the Ross Constraint is a rule *for me*.

There are many other ways in which these cases are fraught with perspectival content. This is perhaps true even in the use of the proper names 'Nora' and 'Herman'. The world is full of Noras and Hermans. Which ones are intended here? It is really hard to see that the referents of these terms are fixed without the aid of some perspectival help—the Herman that we met at that place and time or who teaches at that school we visited, the Nora that is his (that-guy-that-we-met's) daughter, etc.

Even if (following Kripke 1980) you believe that the name gets its content from a causal chain going back to an initial baptism, we can rightly ask how that baptism took place. And surely perspectival content is involved in the act of baptism; for example, it may have played out thus: "I hereby name *this* child 'Aristotle'" (said in Greek).[1]

---

[1] There are of course other options for the causal theory of names here. I'm just using the Kripke baptism story to illustrate that perspectival content gets smuggled into unexpected places, and whatever the semantic story, one cannot be cavalier in claims that the story is aperspectival.

Suppose you wanted to say that there is only one Nora and one Herman (and one door) *in the relevant domain*. Well then, we can rightly ask, how is the relevant domain fixed? Is it so clear that the domain-fixing device isn't some form of perspectival property?—for example, the individuals that *currently* are in *our* common ground? My point here is that attempting to regiment all perspectival content from our language is not a trivial exercise. Such content is deeply engrained in almost every aspect of our language and the mechanisms by which we interpret it.

It is exceedingly hard to construct even artificial cases in which there is no perspectival content in play. For example, Cappelen and Dever offer the following case, intended to show that the agent may not even be locatable in space, but could still act for all that.

> We think there could be a god, who can bring about states of the world just by intending them or maybe just by thinking them. The god thinks, "The door is closed," and straightaway the door is closed. On our view, this god's actions can be rationalized even if we don't specify any kind of de se state (or, indeed, even a de re representation of the god, or of his body parts).   (37)

But this certainly doesn't seem right from a temporal perspective. If there is a god bringing things about, closing doors and whatnot, then one would suppose that the god is closing doors and bringing things about *in time*. That is, the god must have thought, "I'll bring about the closing of the door *now*," and thereby closed the door (or as Cappelen and Dever put it above: "the god thinks, 'The door is closed,' and *straightaway* the door is closed." [My emphasis]).

You might object that Cappelen and Dever slipped up in their description of the case and argue that our door-closing god could sit outside time and bring about a B-series timeline in which the door is open at t1 and closed at t2. This raises the interesting question of when and where the god brought about the B-series timeline. Given that the god is nowhere and nowhen—would it reside in second-order Spacetime? And if so, what is that and why do we suppose the god doesn't need second-order perspectival thoughts to carry out its creation of the first-order timeline? Doesn't it require the god to have some thought to the effect of "I shall now (in second-order time) create a world having such-and-such first-order timeline?" Even if that question can be answered in a way that doesn't undermine Cappelen and Dever's thesis, there is the further question of whether the closing of the door would be, under the imagined scenario, the product of the god's action. At best, it seems like the entire history of this world has been brought about (in second-order

Spacetime) in a single creative action. After that (act of?) creation the god is no longer acting in time or in the world. It would be one of those slacker, abandon-its-creation gods.[2]

Furthermore, while, in the scenario envisioned by Cappelen and Dever, the god may not have a body, if it is *acting* it is nevertheless acting *in space* (shutting a particular door in a particular Spacetime location). As we will see when we take a closer look at perspectival properties in 3D video games, you don't need a body to have a perspectival position. Embodied or not, if a god is acting in space to close a particular door, it must somehow have a perspectival position with respect to that door. Even gods need to have perspectival access to the door they want to close.

To see this, consider a very bored god who has foolishly created a world with only ten identical doors standing in a circle. As the doors are identical, no definite description can distinguish them.[3] Can the god form the intention to close/open one of the particular doors? You and I could do this perceptually. We might focus our attention on one of the doors. We could locate the door relative to our egocentric position. Could the god do the same without the help of indexical thoughts? Do gods have other ways of forming intentions toward a particular object when a description will not suffice? What would it be?[4]

---

[2] You might think (one reviewer did) that the god could still have intentions like "door closes at time t2," but it isn't so obvious that these intentions are causally efficacious in the door's closing. To put it another way, once everything is set in motion, the door is closing whether the god has the intention or not. You might respond that perhaps the god's intentions formed the basis for the construction of the Universe so they must form the basis for the door closing at t2, although this raises questions about times existing before the Universe, and one can still ask whether the intentions actually play a role in individual actions like door closings, given that intentions would have to be located in second-order time. So, too, we might wonder if the perspectival content hasn't been pushed up into second-order time. Does the god, in second-order time, have thoughts of the sort "this will happen at *that* time"? If not, how is the god to determine which time is t2, for example?

[3] We are assuming here that the god has also neglected to create a Cartesian Spacetime coordinate system in which to place the doors. This is Leibnizian space. Even if a coordinate system were introduced, I submit that perspectival content would have to be smuggled in. Suppose, for example, that the god has a thought about the door closest to position 3–4–7. Does it not need to know that *that* location is location 3–4–7? Or at a minimum does it not need to know that the X axis lies thus, the Y axis thus, and the Z access so? It is hard for me to see a path in which even a god can establish and utilize these coordinates without the help of perspectival contents.

[4] You might think that gods, being gods, can think about individual things without having ways of thinking about them. So, for example, a god might be able to think about a particular door in the scenario above even though there is no way to perspectivally identify the door (even for the god). Note that this even denies the god the perspectival thought it would express thus: "I am thinking about that door." As one referee observes, a lot depends

For that matter, on some views of action—for example, as we noted earlier, Bratman (1987)—acting involves plans. Thus, on such views, if the god is acting, it is presumably acting on some plan, and in particular on a plan for itself. The god might deliberate as follows: "A world with doors opening and closing would be a good idea; it falls upon *me* to make it so." In other words, if the god is acting at all, it must have some first person perspectival property.

The subject of gods leads us to David Lewis' (1979) example of the two gods that are omniscient with respect to all nonindexical (aperspectival) facts. One lives on the tallest mountain and throws down manna. The other lives on the coldest mountain and throws down lightning bolts. Lewis observes that even if they are omniscient with respect to all the aperspectival facts, if they are denied indexical knowledge can either of them know which god they are? Presumably not. But then, we might ask, can either of them act? Again, meaning can they act in a way that is directed by their intentions. Gods without perspectival knowledge are feeble beings, it seems.[5]

Of course, while a broad range of philosophers have agreed that there is something special about perspectival contents, understanding 'contents' in very general terms, they have decidedly *not* agreed on the proper analysis of these contents. Is the heavy lifting being done by our mental states? By pragmatics? Or, is the work being done at the semantic level? Does our semantics reflect the phenomenon of perspectivalism, and if so, how does it do it? As I've already suggested, I'm going to make the case that tense and other perspectival phenomena are directly reflected in the semantics and that the key semantic elements are ineliminable perspectival contents, understood as features of the world. In the next chapter I will take a closer look at the semantics of tense and I'll show how we can elucidate this idea of perspectival contents.

here on what the rules for gods and their thoughts are, but even if gods can have such thoughts, they are so different from our own thoughts that it seems rash to argue backwards from their thoughts (or what we imagine their thoughts to be like) to our own. (And recall that this is what Cappelen and Dever are asking us to do.)

[5] We will return to a more detailed discussion of Lewis's two gods in Section 4.3.

2

Tense and Interperspectival Content

2.1 Tense

Is tense, as some contend, merely a feature of language (linguistic tense) or is it used to express some perspectival feature of the world? Many have argued that a proper analysis of linguistic tense would say that the tense operators in natural language express nonperspectival features of the world—that past and future *linguistic* tense are just used to express static universal relations between events or times.

As I am using the expressions 'tenser' and 'detenser', tensers and detensers are split on precisely this point: The tensers take tense to express an irreducible and real perspectival feature of the world, and the detensers think it is a superficial property of language or thought that refers to aperspectival contents. The detenser *may* allow that linguistic tense can express tensed thoughts, but will reject the idea that it can be used to express perspectival features of the world, because the detenser believes there are no such things (see, for example, Mellor (1981, 1998) and Oaklander and Smith (1994) for discussion).

How is tensism traditionally represented in the semantics of natural language? Consider a sentence like (3).

(3)   Theatetus flew.

Let's suppose that (3) has a very simple syntax, consisting of a base clause—[Theatetus flies] and a past tense morpheme that we can call PAST. Let's suppose that the simple syntax for (3) is as in (3s) (s for "simple syntax").

(3s)   PAST[Theatetus flies].

On the standard tenser's view, the morpheme is cashed out in the metalanguage as a tensed predicate (was true, is true, will be true) that operates on the contents of the clause 'Theatetus flies'. The truth conditions for (3s) could be one of the following options, where the double square brackets indicate the proposition expressed by 'Theatetus flies'[1] (t for "truth conditions").

(3ta)   'PAST[Theatetus flies]' is true iff it was true that Theatetus flies.

(3tb)   'PAST[Theatetus flies]' is true iff 'Theatetus flies' was true.

(3tc)   'PAST[Theatetus flies]' is true iff [[Theatetus flies]] was true.

Notice that I've used the past tense form 'was' in the metalanguage. That is not accidental; the tenser typically considers a move like this (using tense in the metalanguage) unavoidable. Tense is irreducible and there is no way to eliminate tense from the metalanguage of the semantics and still express the meaning of (3).

Another possibility, which I discuss in Ludlow (2012), holds that tense is not an operator, but rather that tense is expressed directly by verbal forms, and the morphemic analysis is not a correct way of approaching tense (it may be appropriate for other purposes). It also follows that the syntax of basic tensed sentences is simpler than we ordinarily suppose:

(3td)   'Theatetus flies' is true iff Theatetus flies.

(3te)   'Theatetus flew' is true iff Theatetus flew.

(3tf)   'Theatetus will fly' is true iff Theatetus will fly.

On such a view, the three forms are related, but they are related *analogically*. They are *not* constructed from a single verbal stem and three separate tense morphemes (typically PAST, PRES, and FUT).

I have used a T-sentence to state the semantics for tense (both with morphemes and without) because it has the virtue of being able to express or "display" (in the sense of McDowell 1980) perspectival contents. For McDowell the idea was that the T-theory can display the *sense* of expressions. I have no quarrel with this way of speaking if we take 'sense' as being a covering term for a publicly available fine-grained component of thought contents. This leaves the matter open as to whether the sense of tensed expressions is to be cashed out as abstracta

---

[1] Here we would take propositions to be non-eternal. See Brogaard (2012) for a worked-out version of such a view of propositions.

(as Frege thought) or psychological objects (which Frege rejected[2]) or perspectival features of the world (a view that I will be defending).

There is another way to state these options. A number of individuals might sign on to the idea that tense must be lifted into the metalanguage but nevertheless argue that this doesn't mean we need to be realists about tense. For, it could be argued, the metalanguage is only telling us something about the language of thought. Or, they might argue that the metalanguage here is only telling us something about a third realm of abstracta. My general view is that the metalanguage of the semantics must be grounded in the world and the contents that are expressed in the metalanguage are features of the external world. Even if this is wrong, however, there remains the fact that we have no vocabulary for explaining actions and emotions, perceptual states and informational states that does not employ perspectival language.[3]

Of course a semantics that lifts indexical/perspectival language into the metalanguage looks weird. To see this note that the tokening of a T-sentence, for example, is only effective if the person tokening the T-sentence (e.g. uttering it) is in the right temporal position. Presumably it was for reasons like this that Davidson (1967b), even while advocating homophonic T-theories, avoided treating indexicals disquotationally. Cases like (4) illustrate this point.

(4)   I am hungry now.

Suppose John utters this in the morning and I want to report what he said after lunch. It would be odd for me to say that the content of John's utterances is that I am hungry now. Accordingly, we might think that (4t) is a very bad idea if we are interested in giving the semantics of (4).

(4t)   'I am hungry now' is true iff I am hungry now.

---

[2] I believe Frege was thinking of psychological objects as Husserl sometimes (but not always) seemed to—as being individualistically individuated and thus not available to a public audience. I don't want to get derailed by possible moves here, but given an externalist psychology as an alternative, Frege's opposition might have softened.

[3] Might one argue that the metalanguage, despite apparently being tensed, is actually untensed? In principle this would be possible if some acceptable reduction were offered—one that played the necessary role in our explanations of emotions and actions, etc. However, as this book attempts to show, no such reduction is on offer.

And of course the theorem as stated in (4t) would fail under many circumstances. It wouldn't fail if it were used by John at the time of his utterance, but this isn't sufficient if *we* are interested in giving the semantics for what John said.

This concern is expressed as follows by Cappelen and Dever.

One problematic feature of the view is that it implies that the true semantics of language can only be stated in the right context. In particular, the full semantics of the language can't be said at one time, or in one place, or by one person. Prima facie it is bizarre to be told the following: Let me tell you our best scientific theory of how English works. I'll have to go stand on the other side of the room to tell you part of it. There are of course moves that can be made here (maybe a theory of cognitive dynamics works for moves between "yesterday" and "today," but it is hard to see how to extend it to "here": there's no automatic replacement the way we have for "today"), but we won't explore those moves here.   (2013: 80, fn 10)

There are actually two concerns being raised by Cappelen and Dever here. The first concern is that you can't have a scientific theory of the semantics for natural language given perspectival contents expressed in (4t) above. The second concern is that we are unable to express what another person expressed unless we are in the same time and place that they were when they said what they did.

The first concern can be dispatched in short order. If it were true that the meaning of an utterance couldn't be expressed from the other side of the room, that would not be a problem for the theory, because "our best scientific theory" can certainly allow that some meanings are not expressible under certain circumstances. There is nothing wrong or unscientific about that. A scientific theory of semantics is not supposed to express all meanings everywhere—it is simply supposed to give a theory of how we build meanings and meaningful sentences in a way that is sensitive to our surroundings and linguistic stimulus.

You might think that Cappelen and Dever have a response here, which is that their concern is not merely that some meanings can't be expressed; their real concern is that the semantic theory itself can't be expressed in certain places. But this response confuses the idea of a particular semantics consisting of a set of axioms and rules with the idea of an object of scientific investigation, which is the system by virtue of which humans construct semantic theories. The latter can be expressed everywhere. A scientific theory of the semantics of natural language doesn't require that we should always be able to express everything that might ever be expressed. To the contrary it is a theory of *how* we are able to express what we do and *how* what we express is understood when it is understood.[4]

The second concern is more compelling. Cappelen and Dever are saying something along the following lines: There is a meaning I am expressing with the use of the term 'here', but I wouldn't be able to express that meaning if I was on the other side of the room. Similarly there is a meaning I am expressing with the use of the term 'now', but I wouldn't be able to express that meaning at another time. More concerning, when I express something using 'here', unless you are here with me you won't know what I am saying, and if I leave a message using 'now'—for example, in your voicemail—you won't be able to understand what I am saying at a later time.

We will explore this concern in detail in Chapter 3, but for now suffice it to say that Cappelen and Dever are being overly pessimistic here.

As they themselves note, some theory could be deployed in explaining how a belief expressed using 'today' on day 1 can be expressed using 'yesterday' on day 2. But as I will argue, this strategy can be generalized. For example, if we *now* want to report what John said when uttering (4) at an earlier time, we need something like (4t').

(4t')   'I am hungry now' as uttered by John at t is true iff John was hungry then (at t).

We need to recalibrate the T-sentence to account for different temporal and personal positions.

Similar considerations apply to the spatial indexical case that Cappelen and Dever raise as an objection. If someone over there says 'It is draughty here', we don't need to go over there to express what they said. We say 'It is draughty there', using some gesture to indicate where. This serves the purpose of not just referring to a location, but also locating the state of affairs from within our perspectival position. More generally, it serves to locate the state of affairs within an interperspectival space. The interperspectival content is that shared locating information.

I will go into more detail developing this idea in Chapter 3, but looking ahead a bit we can explain the core idea as follows. When we engage in a conversation with someone, we sometimes communicate across

---

[4] Some (e.g. Larson and Segal (1995)) would say it is a theory of the *knowledge* we have that allows us to express/understand the utterances we do.

temporal and spatial positions.[5] So, for example, if there is an object nearby from your perspectival position but farther away from my perspectival position, we have different ways of expressing where it is relative to our perspectival positions. I say "it is there" and you say "it is here." But in doing so we are not expressing different thoughts—we are expressing the same interperspectival thought from different perspectival positions.

2.2 Perspectival Position and Interperspectival Content

The content of a single utterance does not supervene on the perspectival position of any one person, but rather (and in part) upon the perspectival positions of multiple individuals. Individuals find themselves in different perspectival positions and an interperspectival content is a content that is expressed from across those perspectival positions. To develop this idea, then, we need to get clear on two questions: What is a perspectival position, and what is a perspectival content?

One helpful way to think about perspectival position is to take a leaf from Schein (2017) and what he calls "cinerama semantics." As Schein observes, a proper account of the semantics of natural language (for example in treating plural constructions, conjunctions, and anaphora) requires that we not only identify points of reference but that we also think of individuals *mise-en-scène*. We need to think of more than who stands where, but we want to think of the situation as being storyboarded from a participant's perspective, so that the perspectival position of the participant is presented. But recall, importantly, that the perspectival position of a participant is also externally anchored, so that that storyboard for the participant would include an external location (their mark on the stage, as it were).

To illustrate, let's consider my encounter with John Perry in the supermarket after he has come to realize he is making a mess. On my view, there are (at least) two perspectival positions: John Perry's and mine. There is a storyboard panel that locates me in the store and

---

[5] Relativistic effects will matter here, given the possibility of conversations across inertial frames. We will go into this in detail in Chapter 8.

represents things from my point of view, with John Perry before me saying "I am making a mess," and a storyboard panel that is anchored in John Perry's position and which represents Perry's point of view—one in which I am represented as before him saying "You are making a mess." Each of these anchored storyboard panels represents a perspectival position.

Continuing with our storyboard illustration, the *interperspectival content* consists of this collection of storyboard panels (one for me and one for John Perry) and a theory of how the panels in the storyboards are related. If you like, you can imagine a dramaturge that has the whole picture, and can pair the panels of John Perry saying "I am making a mess" and me saying "you are making a mess," and also has a theory of how those utterances are related in those paired panels, and how that entire picture expresses the beliefs of the characters in a way that might motivate their actions and emotions.

A similar thing could be done for cross-temporal situations. If in Act 1, Scene 1 John Perry says "I am making a mess" and in Act 2, Scene 2 he says "I *was* making a mess" the panels representing John Perry's perspectival positions are related, again by a theory understood by the dramaturge—a theory that constitutes the interperspectival content for those two scenes.

In Chapter 3 I will talk about attitude reports as involving the construction of a (local) theory of the mental life of the agent(s) we are reporting on. We can also think of these storyboards as illustrating theories of what is happening, why it is happening, and what might happen next. They are representing local theories.

Obviously we are using metaphors here, and we can hardly do more, given that on my view perspectival contents are primitive. We aren't going to be able to break them down until smaller, tidier components. However, we can use these metaphors to help us come to grips with the ideas in play, and we can use multiple metaphors to triangulate a better understanding.

In this vein, let's reflect a bit more on perspectival contents and see if we can't sharpen up the idea by introducing a new metaphor. I find it helpful to think of perspectival positions in terms of video games. Consider the difference between old school 2D games like *Pac-Man* or *Space Invaders* and "3D" first person shooters like *Halo* or virtual worlds like *Second Life*. In a first person shooter you are immersed in a virtual space and certain virtual objects and agents are represented as being before you.

Perhaps the following can illuminate the contrast. Suppose we have a simple video game in which a red avatar fights a blue avatar.[6] In the 2D game you need to know which avatar you are—red or blue—in order to play. (Embarrassingly, I've found myself in more complex 2D video games, losing track of which is my avatar.) In the first person shooter version of this game, however, there is no losing track of who I am. If I see a red player I know that is the enemy.[7] Perhaps I see a hand floating before me with a weapon. I immediately know that that is my weapon. This knowledge rests upon the (simulated) perspectival position that the video game has afforded me.

I want to be clear that perspectival position is not identified with the phenomenology of my experience. Here, I believe, I part company with Recanati (2007: part 8) and Noë (2012: chapter 3). There are any number of ways my perspectival position might be represented by the video game—down to rendering it with nothing more than lines. For that matter, in playing a first person shooter game, I may encounter a situation in which "the lights go out." Despite me now having a black screen, my perspectival position has not vanished, for the game still represents me (and I represent myself) as being in a certain location and a certain time with certain things before me (even if the visual information has gone black).

Notice that my perspectival position is likewise not exhausted by the simulated physical orientation of my avatar in the virtual space. In three-dimensional video games like Second Life I can create a perfectly spherical avatar and move in that virtual environment with absolutely nothing determining what is in front of me other than what is oriented as before me. For that matter, I can enter the video game with what amounts to a point-sized avatar. Something being before me is largely a matter of my primary direction of attention. (I may glance to the side from time to time, and still say that the thing I glance at is not in front of me.)

---

[6] Yes, I am thinking of the video game *Halo* here.

[7] Unless, of course, the game designer has thrown us a curve and placed "mirrors" in the virtual space. If I see myself in a virtual mirror, I will find myself in the position of Ernst Mach's shabby pedagogue; I may see a blue avatar and thereby think I am the red one, and I may think that I am blue, but I still, for all that, know which player I am in the game (I simply don't know my color).

You might think that we could reduce this perspectival position to relational properties, since in the case of a simple machine you could define "in front of" as "in the direction of sensors." This gets us quickly into some very deep waters that I will revisit in the discussion of rule following and computation in Section 5.1, but for now suffice it to say that whether something is a sensor, and what direction it is sensing, and whether that is the principal focus of interest of the machine depends upon the information-theoretic architecture of the machine, which in turn depends upon perspectival contents.

The important thing to keep straight is that my perspectival position can be represented graphically in any number of ways, but it is ultimately not a matter of how things appear. It is not a matter of phenomenology; it is a matter of how things are oriented from the perspective of my avatar.

I have used talk of video games and avatars to illuminate the idea of perspectival position, but obviously what can be said for video games and the perspectival positions of avatars should apply to persons that are out and about in the world as well. My perspectival position is a matter of how things are oriented relative to me as I am anchored in some external position.

Summing up so far, interperspectival contents are expressed in different ways from different perspectival positions. Perspectival contents, when expressed, do not supervene on the state of a single individual, but they rather supervene (at least partly) on multiple individuals in multiple perspectival positions. Perspectival positions, in turn, need not be understood phenomenologically, but rather should be understood in terms of location and how things are oriented in the agent's egocentric space.

Perspectival position underdetermines phenomenology, and there are cases where different perspectival positions can have the same phenomenology.

You might be tempted by the idea that the interperspectival content could just be the referential content—it is a content that is stable across perspectival positions, after all. Why not say that the interperspectival content is (for example) that John Perry is making a mess, and that this is expressed in different ways across different perspectival positions ("I am making a mess," "You are making a mess," "I was making a mess," etc.)? Unfortunately this won't work.

Whatever the interperspectival content is, we know that it can't be the referential content, for that content (as we saw in Chapter 1) is not explanatory content in many critical cases. Nor can referential content, conjoined with perspectival vocabulary, fare any better, for the vocabulary by itself has no more explanatory power than the referential contents. By itself, it is just syntax. Coupled with referential contents it is just syntax coupled with referential contents. There is a missing part of the story.[8]

There is, perhaps understandably, some desire to have an all-purpose description for what a given interperspectival content is, but there can be no such description! Interperspectival contents, by their very nature, are perspective sensitive. There is no aperspectival way to describe them, nor even some core or kernel element of them. They are points in conceptual space, got at only by triangulating from multiple perspectival positions.

If another metaphor can help make this idea clearer, we can go back to the storyboards in the possession of the dramaturge. Let's say that the dramaturge collects these storyboards in a binder—let's say each binder consists of panels that represent a single event. Or, for our purposes, each bind of interest would correspond to some content-involving mental event or situation—let's say my encounter with John Perry in the supermarket. There is a page that illustrates John Perry's perspectival position with him saying "I am making a mess" and there is one that illustrates my perspectival position with me saying "You are making a mess." Let's say there is a third page that has an aperspectival account—just a claim that John Perry is making mess. What is the interperspectival content in this metaphor? Well, if it is anything, it is the binder itself. There is no perspective-free description of this content, nor can there be.

None of this is to say that what the binder represents in our metaphor is ineffable. In Chapter 3 we will cash out the metaphor with robust theory of cognitive dynamics—the theory that shows how the different expressions of the interperspectival content hang together.

---

[8] One might object that elsewhere in this book I have argued that the contents of attitudes are interpreted logical forms (ILFs) or that-clauses with referential contents attached. And this is true, but in Chapter 3 I point out that to serve as a theory of attitudes such an account needs some theory that allows different ILFs to express the same belief content. As we will see, that theory will inform our understanding of interperspectival contents.

2.3 The Varieties of Perspectivalism

Given the story I have told regarding perspectival position and inter-perspectival content, there is a lot of room to maneuver if you are interested in executing the idea within a particular metaphysical framework. For example, one might opt for perspectival properties or perspectivally true propositions or perspectival situations, etc. My goal is not to endorse one of these approaches but to offer some cautionary notes about how one would proceed.

Let's start by thinking about my general proposal in terms of property theories. While I am on record as being dubious about the value of properties, I don't see anything about the theory of properties that is inconsistent with my position about perspectival contents. However, as I said, cautionary notes are definitely called for.

The first thing to understand is that perspectival properties cannot be tied to modes of expression in a one-to-one mapping. To put it another way, perspectival properties can be expressed, but they don't have stable names.[9] Take, for example, what John Perry believes when he believes he himself is making a mess. Let's continue to suppose that the real action is not in the indexical pronoun, but the predicate. Let's use angled brackets to indicate a Russellian proposition and square brackets to indicate a semantic content. Is this the property-theoretic account of what John Perry believes?

(P1)   <JP, [[am making a mess]]>

If so, what happens when we encounter Perry and tell him he is making a mess by saying 'You are making a mess'. Is this what we are saying?

(P2)   <JP, [[are making a mess]]>

But aren't these supposed to be the same contents in the case I am imagining? When Perry says "I am making a mess" and we say to him "you are making a mess" aren't we saying the same thing? (Yes, this is disputable, but I will defend the idea in the next chapter.) Obviously one needs to proceed with caution here. The danger comes in thinking that 'am making a mess' and 'are making a mess' always express the same properties. Rather they would express different perspectival properties

---

[9] Thanks to an anonymous reviewer for very helpful discussion here.

from different perspectival positions. Accordingly, the formalism might look something like this, where we use *persp* (for perspectival position) instead of *c* (for context):

(P3)   <JP, [['are making a mess']]*persp*>

That little *persp* subscript is doing important work here. Because of it, 'am making a mess' expresses a different property in John Perry's mouth than it does in David Kaplan's mouth. And because of the little *persp*, the predicate also expresses a different property when said today than it will tomorrow. (It may also express a different property here than it does there.) In the next chapter we will get into *how* it does all this. For now I simply want to highlight that the perspectival property itself will be an interesting animal.

One might think it wouldn't *have* to be *so* interesting if we allowed people to take the perspective of others when we encounter perspectival claims.[10] Perhaps, when John Perry says 'I am making a mess', we grasp what he says by adopting or simulating his perspectival position—like the movie *Being John Malkovich*, only this movie is called *Being John Perry*.

I am dubious about such strategies. The first problem here, as I see it, is in the situation where I encounter John Perry and say 'You are making a mess'. By parity of reasoning he would have to enter my perspectival position or simulate it to understand what I am saying. Which, let's say, is possible, and let's suppose that Perry believes me. But then Perry is entertaining two propositions.

(P4)   <JP, [['is making a mess']]*persp1*>
(P5)   <JP, [['are making a mess']]*persp2*>

So we are back where we started. Maybe you want to argue that the first person perspective takes priority (and so, presumably, do the properties expressed by 'now' and 'here'). This is an option we will consider in more detail in Chapter 3, but I'm going to pursue a strategy in which both utterances can express the same interperspectival content.

If I am granted leave to pursue this bolder project for now, then we need to think carefully about the nature of these properties. They are

---

[10]   Here I am thinking of proposals by Recanati (2004) and Brogaard (2008) in which the perspectival positions of others can be taken.

more complicated than relational properties, obviously, because they reflect perspectival positions and not merely relative locations. But given that perspectival contents can be shared we want to say that these properties also encode shared contents. If I say "I am here" and you say "you are there" the shared content we are expressing is one about a picture we have of our relative perspectival positions and where those positions lie with respect to each other. It is a complex property involving you, me, where we are, where we know we are, each of our perspectival positions, etc.

I don't mean to suggest that the players in these conversations shake hands and agree to a picture of how things lie. We can see this with the help of temporal distance. I write in my diary 'I am hungry today' and a year later I read my diary and say to myself 'I was hungry that day'. In doing so I express an interperspectival property that involves my diverse temporal perspectival positions.

Now, obviously, a detailed story needs to be told about how we accomplish keeping track of properties of this nature, and to be honest I am a little bit unclear about how we keep track of *any* properties, much less these.[11] I suspect the answer will involve something very much like the story I tell in the next chapter about the cognitive dynamics of attitude reports. But as my goal here is not to defend properties, I'm not going to dot the i's and cross the t's, for such a project—I'll leave that up to property theorists. My more immediate concern in this section is to show that matters proceed in pretty much the same way for most if not all accounts of perspectival contents.

For example, suppose you didn't want to talk about perspectival properties but you want your core properties to be stable and you want to talk about *propositions* being perspectivally true (for example, we say that a given proposition was true or is true, or is first person true or is second person true[12]). In that case, we need to lift the tense elements out

---

[11] This follows from a more general concern I have about abstracta. I tend to be attracted to Charles Parsons's (1984) views about our epistemic access to abstracta, which involves having something like a linguistic structure mediating that access. If that story is right, then the story I tell in Chapter 3 about cognitive dynamics might be thought of as part of, or at least consistent with, an account of our epistemic access to perspectival properties/propositions, etc.

[12] I suppose we could gloss the idea of something being first person true as something like "true in my mouth," and second person true as "true in your mouth."

of the verb and make it an operator (let's say it is a tense morpheme, or some inflection for person—thus a "personal tense" in the sense of A. N. Prior). So, to stay with our example of John Perry in the supermarket, we have the following two expressions of propositions:

(P6) $<[['am']]_{persp1}<JP, [[making\ a\ mess]]>$
(P7) $<[['are']]_{persp2}<JP, [[making\ a\ mess]]>$

If you prefer, we can decompose the English expressions into explicit morphemes, thus yielding the following:

(P8) $<[[PRES]]_{persp1}[[1st\ Pers]]_{persp1}<JP, [[making\ a\ mess]]>$
(P9) $<[[PRES]]_{persp2}[[2nd\ Pers]]_{persp2}<JP, [[making\ a\ mess]]>$

In this case the propositional operators 'am' and 'are' combine with untensed (gerundive) propositions to express different perspectival contents from different perspectival positions.[13] As before, when we encounter Perry in the grocery store and see him spilling sugar, *persp1* and *persp2* are aligned so that Perry and I express the same thing when he says 'I am making a mess' and I say 'You are making a mess'.

Similar considerations would apply to perspectival facts or events or situations. We could build perspectival facts/events/situations by introducing perspectival properties, or introducing perspectival facts into those semantic objects. Obviously it won't be business as usual in any of these cases, but on the other hand I don't see any problems that arise in those projects that would not already arise in the Truth-theoretic semantics I am offering throughout this book. If there are problems, they should be the same (or similar) problems for everyone.

One such problem that everyone will have is the task of making sense of interperspectival contents. This will be true whether we think of those as properties or operators, or just T-theoretic disquotational contents; we will want to know how those perspectival contents work.

In Chapter 3 I'll go into more of the gory detail about how the cognitive dynamics of that picture works. First, however, we should pause and heed warnings that David Kaplan has issued about "sloppy thinking." Are we in danger of that?

---

[13] I believe operator theories are more problematic than we ordinarily suppose and this gloss is a bit quick. I take up this worry in Ludlow (2012).

2.4 Sloppy Thinking?

The idea of deploying perspectival contents in our semantics for tense and other indexicals has not had much consideration in the philosophical literature, and I believe that part of the reason for this is Kaplan's (1977: 533ff) admonition that doing so (or at least using indexical sense in an account of indexicals) amounts to "sloppy thinking." That is, you wouldn't just be wrong to consider such a strategy, but would be defective ("a sloppy thinker") were you to do so.

Kaplan discusses a number of concerns, and I've taken the liberty of spelling each of them out below. As we will see, a lot turns on what one is asking perspectival contents to do. Philosophers have envisioned no end of roles for perspectival contents, from fixing reference to exhausting perceptual content, and Kaplan is perhaps right to suppose that this is too much to ask of such contents. As his admonitions show, it is entirely possible to trip ourselves up if we are not careful. Let's walk through Kaplan's concerns, and see why this is so.

2.4.1 Concern (i): Perspectival contents can't exhaust the agent's experiential picture

Kaplan's point of departure for this argument is the following passage from Frege (1956: 298).

Now everyone is presented to himself in a particular and primitive way, in which he is presented to no one else. So, when Dr. Lauben thinks that he has been wounded, he will probably take as a basis this primitive way in which he is presented to himself. And only Dr. Lauben himself can grasp thoughts determined in this way. But now he may want to communicate with others. He cannot communicate a thought which he alone can grasp. Therefore, if he now says 'I have been wounded', be must use the 'I' in a sense that can be grasped by others, perhaps in the sense of 'he who is speaking to you at this moment', by doing which he makes the associated conditions of his utterance serve for the expression of his thought.

Kaplan then goes on to approve the core point of this passage, thus:

What is the particular and primitive way in which Dr. Lauben is presented to himself? What cognitive content presents Dr. Lauben to himself, but presents him to nobody else? Thoughts determined this way can be grasped by Dr. Lauben, but no one else can grasp *that* thought determined in *that* way. The answer, I believe, is, simply, that Dr. Lauben is presented to himself under the character of 'I'. (1977: 534)

I'm not convinced that Dr. Lauben has a thought which cannot be expressed and that he therefore defaults to some weaker claim which he expresses as 'I have been wounded', but I'll get to that issue in Chapter 3. I also want to emphasize that my interest is more in the perspectival nature of the way contents are expressed by the predicates (using 'I am wounded' vs. 'is wounded', for example) than in the first person pronoun, but I believe that is a side issue at the moment. What I'm more concerned with now is where the sloppy thinking comes in. Kaplan continues.

A sloppy thinker might succumb to the temptation to slide from an acknowledgement of the privileged *perspective* we each have on ourselves – only I can refer to me as 'I' – to the conclusions: first, that this perspective necessarily yields a privileged *picture* of what is seen (referred to), and second, that this picture is what is intended when one makes use of the privileged perspective (by saying 'I'). (533–4)

Now a lot depends on what Kaplan means by privileged *picture* here, but obviously there are ways in which we experience things that are not and perhaps cannot be shared when we give our first person reports.[14] I have no idea of what it is like to be shot, so I have little grasp of whatever experience gave rise to Dr. Lauben saying 'I am wounded'. For that matter, even if I too had been shot, I have no reason to believe it was the same experience for me as it was for Dr. Lauben. But by the same token, if Dr. Lauben says 'guns are dangerous' I don't necessarily have full insight to whatever experience gave rise to that utterance either. In my view, cashing out the experience is not the job of the semantics for the utterance.

You might be persuaded by McDowell (1996) and Byrne (2005) that perception is propositional and hence that it must be possible to give a semantics for perceptual experiences. I am agnostic on whether this is so,

---

[14] Notice I am not saying there are things *thought* which cannot be shared, just that perhaps there are things experienced which cannot be shared. Of course it is always possible to pack a reference to an experience into the expression of a thought, so we might get something like this: 'I'm having this experience which I just can't convey.' But it seems to me that this is no more bizarre than saying 'I saw something which you cannot see' (for example, a past solar eclipse). I suppose we still have referential access to the experience just as we do to the eclipse, although it needn't follow that we know what the experience was like (just as we may not know what the eclipse was like).

but if it is so, it need not follow that the semantics for an utterance that is occasioned by a perceptual experience must reconstruct the semantics of the perceptual experience.

My point here is that perspectival contents are no different than contents like being green or being a father. There are a zillion ways we can experience these contents (perhaps no two people experience them in the same way!). That doesn't undermine the case for deploying them (without the trappings of perceptual experience) in the semantics. I don't see that perspectival contents are on any worse footing than any other contents here.

You might think that I fell into giving something like a "picture" relating to perspectival contents when I used the illustration of a first person shooter video game or with my metaphors of cinerama and storyboards, but the virtue of the storyboard metaphor is that storyboards are (or at least can be) quite minimal in terms of the perceptual information they carry. Stick figures are more than enough to convey perspectival positions, for example.

So I suppose that so far Kaplan and I are on the same page, or almost the same page. We agree that there are some things that a semantic theory is *not* supposed to do (cash out the perceptual experience giving rise to the utterance), and there are things that a semantic theory is *supposed* to do (at a minimum provide referential contents).

2.4.2 Concern (ii): Perspectival content can't uniquely determine a referent

Kaplan continues.

The perceptive reader will have noticed that the conclusions of the sloppy thinker regarding the pure indexical 'I' are not unlike those of the Fregean regarding true demonstratives. The sloppy thinker has adopted a *demonstrative theory of indexicals*: 'I' is synonymous with 'this person' [along with the appropriate *subjective* demonstration], etc. Like the Fregean, the sloppy thinker errs in believing that the sense of the demonstration is the sense of the indexical, but the sloppy thinker commits an additional error in believing that such senses are in any way necessarily associated with uses of pure indexicals. The slide from privileged perspective to privileged picture is the sloppy thinker's original sin. Only one who is located in the exact center of the Sahara Desert is entitled to refer to that place as 'here', but aside from that, the place may present no distinguishing features. (534–5)

You may be surprised to hear that I believe that Kaplan and I are still on the same page here: There is no picture associated with the indexical (perspectival) content. *Perhaps* Frege thought there was, but it is certainly not my claim. Nor is it my claim that perspectival contents give a complete picture of whatever might be running through someone's head when they deploy such content.

Kaplan doesn't mention the Fregean doctrine that sense determines reference here, but perhaps now is a good time to address it. First, this doctrine is detachable from any motivation to introduce sense content. Furthermore, is it at all clear that the doctrine, once spelled out, comes to the claim that, starting from a single sense content, one can identify some unique individual determined by the sense? That would surely be a magical property for senses to have. If I were to adopt the sense determines-reference-doctrine, I would probably endorse a version like that given by Heck (2002: 3): "On the weakest interpretation of [the doctrine that sense determines reference], it speaks of 'determination' only in a mathematical sense: it claims only that senses are related many-one to references." I certainly don't have a need for a stronger notion than that.

2.4.3 *Concern (iii): Perspectival content can't resolve Twin Earth cases*

Kaplan also makes the point that perspectival properties are not sufficient to distinguish attitudes. This, I take it, is the point of his example involving Castor and Pollux—an example that amounts to a Twin Earth thought experiment.

We raise two identical twins, Castor and Pollux, under qualitatively identical conditions, qualitatively identical stimuli, etc. If necessary, we may monitor their brain states and make small corrections in their brain structures if they begin drifting apart. They respond to all cognitive stimuli in identical fashion. Have we not been successful in achieving the same cognitive (i.e., psychological) state? Of course we have, what more could one ask! But wait, they believe different things. Each sincerely says,

My brother was born before I was

and the beliefs they thereby express conflict. In this, Castor speaks the truth, while Pollux speaks falsely. This does not reflect on the identity of their cognitive states, for, as Putnam has emphasized, circumstances alone do not determine extension (here, the truth-value) from cognitive state. Insofar as distinct persons can be in the same cognitive state, Castor and Pollux are.   (Kaplan 1977: 531)

But whoever said that any form of *narrow* content would be sufficient to distinguish the cognitive states of two individuals? I assume that, as perspectival contents are kinds of relational contents, when expressed by Castor and Pollux they express different contents—relational contents anchored by different individuals but also different external locations. Their cognitive states are not "the same" (any more than, for Putnam (1975a), water beliefs and XYZ beliefs are the same, or Burge's (1979) Oscar and Twin Oscar have the same beliefs).

In the previous section I used the idea of video games to illustrate a first person perspectival position. Let's now imagine a very boring video game in which two different players with identical avatars "rez"[15] in different spots in a completely flat, monochromatic, virtual world. What each of the players "sees" is the same, no matter what direction they turn and how far they walk (so long as they do not encounter each other). Still, they have different perspectival contents, because they are in different locations in their world. At this point the discussion mirrors that in discussion of Twin Earth thought experiments. We could play switching experiments to cross up the players. They would not notice if they were switched. But so what? Why should they?

Kaplan seems to be warning us against making two assumptions, neither of which I have made here. The first assumption is that the introduction of perspectival content is supposed to be a way of avoiding referential content. The second assumption is that perspectival contents do not have referential components. I see no reason we are compelled to endorse either assumption, nor do I see how the assumptions are related to the positive thesis for perspectival contents.

2.4.4 Concern (iv): It is a mistake to think that perspectival content provides acquaintance with our thought contents

Kaplan (p. 545) addresses another possible source of the sloppy thinker's conclusions.

Failure to distinguish between the cognitive significance of a thought and the thought itself seems to have led some to believe that the elements of an object of thought must each be directly accessible to the mind. From this it follows that if a singular proposition is an object of thought, the thinker must somehow be immediately acquainted with each of the individuals involved.

---

[15] 'Rez' for resolve or resurrect—a way to describe an avatar appearing in a video game.

I don't have strong objections to the idea that we are acquainted with the constituents of our objects of thought, but I don't believe that my position depends one way or the other on whether we enjoy such an acquaintance relation. Furthermore, and more importantly, it would never occur to me that perspectival contents or indexical sense contents are the sole route by which that acquaintance is secured. It may not be any sort of route at all. It is possible, for all I know, that only proper names are routes to securing acquaintance. This would not diminish the need for perspectival content in explaining actions and emotions, normative facts, and perceptual content.

John Perry might assent to 'that person I am following is making a mess', and not assent to 'I am making a mess' as he doesn't realize he is following his own trail of spilt sugar. But I have no reason to doubt that Perry is appropriately causally acquainted with that person who is making the mess and is therefore acquainted with the constituents of a singular thought. However, when Perry learns that *he* is that mess-making person it does not make him more acquainted with that guy/himself, but it does give him additional perspectival knowledge that leads him to stop and repair the broken bag of sugar at the bottom of his shopping cart.

Finally, I do not know who endorses the idea that perspectival content is motivated by the need to establish an acquaintance relation and Kaplan does not say. Perhaps he has in mind an early incarnation of Bertrand Russell (i.e. Russell (1910–1911)), who once held that we are only directly acquainted with egocentric particulars. I don't know that Russell thereby thought that egocentric particulars were the route by which acquaintance was achieved, but if he thought this I don't see any reason why the advocate of perspectival content should be compelled to follow suit.

2.4.5 Concern (v): Semantics shouldn't give accounts of cognitive significance

The fifth complaint is not directly offered by Kaplan in the section on "sloppy thinking" but it seems to be running in the background, and it has been clearly endorsed by philosophers like Wettstein (1986). According to this complaint, the problem is that a semantic theory should not attempt to account for cognitive significance period.

My view of the role of cognitive significance, when it is deployed in the semantics, is that it must provide content sufficient to explain actions and emotions. In this vein, my understanding of cognitive significance is precisely in accord with that of Perry (2001) in the following passage:

> I cannot accept that a semantic theory can be correct that does not provide us with an appropriate interface between what sentences mean, and how we use them to communicate beliefs in order to motivate and explain action. A theory of linguistic meaning should provide us with an understanding of the properties sentences have that lead us to produce them under different circumstances, and react as we do to their utterance by others.   (2001: 8)

I share this view with Perry. Perry would no doubt disagree with me that a correct theory must deploy perspectival properties (I'll address a recent iteration of his view in Section 4.1). Of course, I fully understand that this shared view of semantics and cognitive significance is controversial. Some believe that semantics has rested on a mistake—and precisely the mistake of thinking that semantics should be in the business of accounting for the cognitive significance of our utterances. Admittedly, there are apparently good reasons to think that semantics should not be in this business—most of those reasons having to do with the conundrums one gets into while handling perspectival content in the semantics. But if those reasons prevail then the position is at worst wrong—I don't see sloppy thinking as being in play here. But I don't think that the position is wrong and I believe that the concerns can be addressed. I will take up those concerns in the next chapter.

3

Communication Using Interperspectival Contents

The problem we soon encounter with any semantic theory that expresses perspectival content is that when we engage in communication, we of necessity communicate with people in other perspectival positions. So, as noted earlier, we often speak with people in different physical locations. Sometimes, we communicate across time, e.g. by leaving messages, and we often report on thoughts and comments made at an earlier time. Unless we are talking to ourselves, we also communicate with other persons, who are, obviously, in different perspectival positions.

Earlier I suggested that a semantics, given for someone at a different time and place, calls for a readjustment of the semantics. So, for example:

'I am hungry today' as uttered by you yesterday is true today iff you were hungry yesterday.

So, to express the semantics of what you said, I must deploy a different set of expressions than you did. Or as we put it earlier, the same interperspectival contents are expressed in different ways from different perspectival positions.

In this chapter, the goal is to understand how this works. I'll first try to situate the core idea within discussions about the role of sense since Frege, and try to sharpen the resulting thesis. Then I will go into some detail on the mechanics and nature of these cross-perspective communication abilities and the resulting picture of the role of perspectival content that emerges.

3.1 Sense and Interperspectival Content

The notion of interperspectival content we have been working with bears certain similarities with the idea of sense introduced by Frege. Indeed,

I am tentatively inclined to consider this a possible execution of Frege's program, although I'm not at all prepared to argue with Frege scholars who might disagree with that. But I am confident that there are instructive similarities between the Fregean notion of sense and our notion of interperspectival content, in particular in the problems that are encountered. Let's begin with this famous passage from Frege (1956).

If someone wants to say the same today as he expressed yesterday using the word 'today', he must replace this word by 'yesterday'. Although the thought is the same, the verbal expression must be different so that the sense, which would otherwise be affected by the differing times of utterance, is readjusted. The case is the same with words like 'here' and 'there'. In all such cases the mere wording, as it is given in writing, is not the complete expression of the thought, but the knowledge of certain accompanying conditions of utterance, which are used as means of expressing the thought, are needed for its correct apprehension. The pointing of fingers, hand movements, glances may belong here too. The same utterance containing the word 'I' will express different thoughts in the mouths of different men, of which some may be true, others false.

Perry (1977) argued that Frege erred by trying to identify the sense of a sentence (utterance) with a thought. Perry's thinking was that because 'yesterday' and 'today' have different senses, it follows that 'Today is a fine day' and 'Yesterday is a fine day' must have different senses (since they are *composed* of different senses). But if I can express the same thought today with an utterance of 'yesterday is a fine day' that I expressed yesterday with an utterance of 'today is a fine day' then thoughts cannot be associated with senses. Different senses are deployed in expressing the same thought, so thoughts are not in a one-to-one correspondence with the senses of sentences.

This is the concern about indexical sense/perspectival content. Our next step in understanding the problem is to lay out some of the responses to Perry's argument. As we will see, the best response (and the one that I believe Frege favored) has largely slipped through the cracks. Here, it will be useful to begin with an outline of the Fregean project as laid out in Heck (2002).

According to Heck, Frege was committed to the following doctrines (using Heck's numeration).

1a) There can be different Thoughts that I cannot accept concerning the same object and ascribing the same property to it. For example, the

Thought that Superman flies and the Thought that Clark Kent flies are different, even though Superman is Clark Kent.

2a) Sentences of the form 'N believes that a is F' and 'N believes that b is F' can have different truth-values, even if 'a' and 'b' refer to the same object.

3) Sense determines reference.[1]

4) The sense of a sentence is what one grasps in understanding it.

5) The sense of a sentence is a Thought.

In Heck's view (and I believe this is also the crux of Perry's argument) not all of these doctrines can be maintained. Heck has a proposal about which doctrine needs to be given up, but different philosophers have rejected different doctrines.

Many referentialists, for example, reject doctrines (1a) and (2a). They argue that if 'a' and 'b' refer to the same object, then 'N believes that a is F' and 'N believes that b is F' must have the same truth-value. Similarly, the thought that Superman flies is, strictly speaking, the same thought as the thought that Clark Kent flies.

Alternatively, Heck proposed that we reject (4)—the idea that there is a single thought associated with the understanding of a sentential utterance. Here is how Heck sets out his idea.

But why do we want to find something to call the meaning? What we (relatively) uncontroversially have are speakers who associate Thoughts with utterances and restrictions upon how the different Thoughts they associate with a given utterance must be related if they are to communicate successfully: to put it differently, we have the fact that utterances have cognitive value for speakers, and we have communicative norms determining how the cognitive values a given utterance has for different speakers must be related if we are to understand them.   (p. 31)

I take it that Heck's point is that even if we end up entertaining different thoughts (e.g. the speaker has one thought and the hearer comes to have another thought) there are cases in which we might say that is good enough for us to claim that the speaker successfully communicated with the hearer. The view bears some similarity to Davidson's same-saying relation. In this case, same-saying is replaced with the idea of "appropriately related" contents.

---

[1] As noted earlier, Heck (2002: 3) allows that this may be understood in a weak way: "On the weakest interpretation of (3), it speaks of 'determination' only in a mathematical sense: it claims only that senses are related many-one to references."

Segal (1989), however, diagnosed a problem with same-saying accounts of attitude attribution, and his objection is applicable here. In Segal's view, it won't do to say that 'Fred believes that P' is true if and only if Fred believes something similar to [[P]], where [[P]] is some propositional content, because the relevant relation to [[P]] would not be a belief relation, but something else: belief*. And what is that?

Similarly, one might gloss Heck's solution as follows: 'Fred communicates P to Barney' is true if and only if Fred communicates something similar to [[P]] to Barney. But strictly speaking one should say "Fred communicates* something similar to [[P]] to Barney." And then we get to ask "what does it mean to communicate*?" As with belief*, it is difficult to see what the communicate* relation comes to. Segal concluded that one is better off folding the flexibility of the meaning of 'believes' (and 'says-that' and 'communicates') into the relations themselves.[2]

Another possibility is to reject doctrine (5)—we could break the link between senses and thoughts. This way we could say that different senses are expressed on different occasions (yesterday and today) but the thoughts are still, somehow, the same. This is clearly a repudiation of a core doctrine of Fregeanism, and one wonders what purpose senses would then serve, if any.

I don't intend to go into more detail discussing these options because it seems to me that Heck has left out a critical sixth doctrine, unremarked and unquestioned by both Perry and Heck in their critique of Frege, and when we make that doctrine explicit we will see a very clear alternative solution path. We can state that doctrine as follows.

6) A sense is intimately tied to its manner of expression, so that the senses expressed by 'today' and 'yesterday' remain constant across uses of those terms.

Clearly this additional doctrine is needed to generate the Perry argument, for Perry assumes that the senses of 'today' and 'yesterday' must remain constant. But it is clear that for Frege this simply cannot be the case. Consider the first sentence of the above passage from Frege again, this time with key points emphasized.

---

[2] Segal (1989) thus serves as the point of departure for Larson and Ludlow (1993). Readers are referred to the latter paper for a more detailed discussion of Segal's argument.

If someone wants to say the same today as he expressed yesterday using the word 'today', he must replace this word by 'yesterday'. *Although the thought is the same, the verbal expression must be different* so that the sense, which would otherwise be affected by the differing times of utterance, is readjusted.

In other words, the same thought/sense will be expressed in different ways (using different words!) at different times, in different places, and in different mouths. For example, indexical expressions like 'today' can be used to express or display senses, but they do not express the same sense on each occasion of utterance. The sense expressed by the words must be realigned. Branquinho (2006) puts the idea as follows.

Cases where one is dealing with indexical contents are problematic because they often involve some realignment in the linguistic means of expression of a thought—on the part of a given thinker—as time goes by. In other words, there are situations in which the verbal expression of an indexical thought entertained by a thinker at a given time must, at a later time, be readjusted in a certain way by the thinker in order for the thought in question to be then entertained; so that one could presumably say that some attitude held at the earlier time towards the thought in question has been retained by the thinker at the later time, the very same thought being the object of the attitude on both occasions. Naturally, such readjustments are to be thought of as being operated in the linguistic means employed for the expression of the thoughts. It does not make much sense—at least in the light of the picture of content we are assuming—to think of the thoughts as being themselves subjected to any sort of change or realignment.

Evans (1996) appears to be making a similar point, although without the explicit reference to expressions.[3]

Frege's idea is that the same epistemic state may require different things of us at different times; the changing circumstances force us to change in order to keep hold of a constant reference and a constant thought—we must run to keep still. From this point of view, the acceptance on *d*2 of 'Yesterday was fine', given an acceptance on *d*1 of 'Today is fine' can manifest the *persistence* of a belief in just the way in which acceptance of different utterances of the sentence 'The sun sets in the West' can.   (308–9)

In the foregoing discussion, the talk was about senses, but the same point applies to perspectival contents. The idea is that the same perspectival content will be expressed in different ways on different occasions of utterance—indeed it must be.

---

[3] It could be that Evans is rejecting doctrine (3)—the relation between senses and thoughts, so the senses must change to retain the thoughts, although this seems unlikely.

Given that we can express the same content in different ways, there is an interesting question as to whether one form is more basic. There are several choice points here. First, you might think that the core case is the first person perspective, and that when we use the second or third person perspective to describe a situation, we are simply describing a first person attitude from another perspectival position. Let's call this option *First Person Fundamental*.

I might express a first person thought as "I am hungry now" and I could give the semantics for what I was saying as I said it, so that I could express the solipsistic truth conditions as follows.

(5)   My utterance now of 'I am hungry today' is true iff I am hungry today.

But the problem with this alleged exclusively egocentric thought is that (*pace* Heck's rejection of doctrine 4 above) I can always choose to recall that thought, and moreover, I can always tell you what I was thinking. For example, the following day I could say to you 'I was hungry yesterday'. Assuming that you can understand what I said, then there is a semantics for what I said (deployed by you), which looks like this.

(6)   Your utterance now of 'I was hungry yesterday' is true iff you were hungry yesterday.

One possible conclusion that can be drawn is that cases like (6) show that first person thoughts can have the semantics of second person thoughts, which thereby suggests that they *are also* second person thoughts. This is a fairly radical idea, and it is admittedly difficult to get a grip on it. Here is one, I believe flawed, way to put the idea, from Rödl (2007).

We found that, in suitable cases, "Today..." said yesterday and "Yesterday..." said today express the same act of thinking. These cases are fundamental in that, without them, there would be no such thing as an act of thinking expressed by either phrase. And when "...today..." yesterday and "...yesterday..." today express the same *act of thinking*, then they express the same *thought*. Therefore, it would be misleading to contrast "yesterday"-thoughts with "today"-thoughts; in the fundamental case, a "yesterday"-thought is a "today"-thought. What holds of "today" and "yesterday" holds of "I" and "you"... My thinking second personally about you and you receiving my second person thought, thinking back at me second personally, is one and the same act of thinking, an act of thinking for two. But you receive my thought thinking an unmediated first person thought. Hence my "You" addressed at you and your "I" that receives my address express the same act of thinking. This case is fundamental in that, without it, there would be no such thing as thoughts expressed by "You..." and, consequently, by "I...". As "You..." said by me to you and "I..." said by you in taking up my address, express the same *act of thinking*, they express the same *thought*. Therefore, it is wrong to oppose second person thought to first person thought. This is a difference in the means of expression, not in the thought expressed. Second-person thought is first-person thought. It is thought of the self-conscious.

(196–7)

I believe it is clearly an error to call these two events "the same act of thinking," but I think it is at least plausible to say that they are acts that involve *the same thought* or same thought contents (I don't understand why Rödl thinks he needs to collapse the distinction between thoughts and *acts* of thinking).

Rödl might have also noted that my first person thought could also be a third person perspectival thought. For example, I overhear David Kaplan say 'my pants are on fire' and I report the content of his belief to you by pointing at Kaplan and saying 'he realizes his own pants are on fire'. This seems to be the point made by McDowell (1996: 102).

The wider context makes it possible to understand that the first person, the continuing referent of the "I" in the "I think" that can "accompany all my representations", is also a third person, something whose career is a substantial continuity in the objective world: something such that other modes of continuing thought about it would require keeping track of it. That is a way of putting the gist of Gareth Evans's brilliant treatment of self-identification, which builds on P.F. Strawson's brilliant reading of the Paralogisms.

Let's call this option *Perspectival Pluralism*: first person thoughts are not exclusively first person thoughts; they are also second person thoughts and third person thoughts.[4]

Applied to tense, Perspectival Pluralism would say that present tense thoughts are also past and future thoughts. However attractive this view might be for the case of person, it leads to some strange consequences in the case of tense. In particular, it suggests that tensed utterances are all

---

[4] Some caution is necessary here. It does not follow that having the same thought entails acting in the same way. Consider a case in which A thinks "I am being attacked by a bear," and B thinks "You are being attacked by a bear." A curls up into a ball and B runs away. What this shows is that the same thought can yield different behaviors, obviously. The same is true for more mundane thoughts, like the thought that it is snowing. A might stay indoors while B goes out and makes snowmen.

simultaneously past, present, and future, and that seems to lead either to contradiction (as McTaggart argued) or to a view like Fine's (2005) fragmentalism—the idea that, to avoid contradiction, reality itself must be fragmented.[5]

The third option—let's call it *Perspectival Relativization*—would be to try and relativize the perspectival contents to a context or frame, so that a single thought would be first person from one perspectival position, but second or third from another (it is never all of them simpliciter). Similarly, a tensed thought might be future tensed from one perspectival position but present or past from others. For example, you could say it was future at t1 but past at t2.

There is a concern with this view that is parallel to one raised by Williamson (1999) with respect to modals. On Williamson's view, if you think that contingency is variation in truth value relative to varying assignments to world variables you are betraying a failure to understand what contingency is. Hawthorne (2015) has extended this point to tense: If you think that change in truth value (e.g. future to present) can be characterized as truth values indexed to times, you don't have a handle on what change is. If this is right, then genuine tense (and genuine perspectival properties) can't be indexed in this way.

On option 4, the perspectival semantics I deploy gets to call the shots, so that whether something is first, second, or third person depends upon the semantics I use. It would follow that *I* have first person thoughts, *you* have second person thoughts, and *they* have third person thoughts. Let's call this idea *Perspectival Chauvinism*. The crux of the option is that the correct characterization (first, second, or third person) of the perspectival thought depends upon the semantics *I* give. Full stop. It still follows that other people have thoughts with the *form* of my first person thoughts, but those thoughts are in fact second or third person thoughts. The view isn't solipsistic, for it concedes that other people exist and that they share thoughts with me; however, I get to call the shots on the perspectival characterization of the thoughts (person, place, and time). The same is not true for you, sadly, but should you read option 4 out

---

[5] That is, reality is broken into pieces and each piece gets its own truth predicate, as it were. So 'I am hungry' is true in one fragment of reality and 'I was hungry but am not now' is true in another.

loud, it will be true in your mouth. It will mean something different in your mouth than in mine, however.

This view is obviously weird. Suppose that John Perry utters, 'I have first person thoughts'. There are two options here for me, the chauvinist semanticist. I can either say that what Perry says is false, because the reality is that only I have first person thoughts. Or I can say that 'first person thought' means something different in his mouth than it does in mine. Perhaps in Perry's mouth, 'I have first person thoughts' means that he has second and third person thoughts.[6]

If you don't find these first four options particularly attractive, that is good, because I prefer a fifth option—one I introduced in the previous two chapters.

Let's call option 5 *Expressive Pluralism*: Perspectival contents are expressed with the use of different expressions in different perspectival positions. This is different from option 2—Perspectival Pluralism—in that there is no claim that the same thought is both first person and second person in character. It is rather the case that the same thought can be got at with first person and second person vocabulary.

It is different from option 3—Perspectival Relativization—in that there is no indexing of tenses to particular times (future at t1, past at t2). The perspectival content itself is not indexed in any way; it is simply expressed in different ways.

It is different from options 1 and 4—First Person Fundamental and Perspectival Chauvinism—in that there is no privileged mode of expressing perspectival contents.

What all of these options have in common is the idea that the semantics for perspectival properties are not homophonic, and that the expressions in the metalanguage will often have to be different from those in the object language if we are to correctly characterize the perspectival character of our utterances.

Of course matters are not always as simple as the substitution of 'you' for 'I', 'yesterday' for 'today', and 'was' for 'is'. Sometimes descriptions of tensed thoughts (and other perspectival thoughts) appear to be radically different even though they are expressing the very same thought. Other times very different tensed thoughts can be expressed using exactly the

---

[6] Thanks to an anonymous referee for discussion here.

same language. In many of these cases there is no obvious rule for modifying the description (e.g. substituting 'yesterday' for 'today'). What is going on in these cases? Getting at the answer will require that we first take a detour through the theory of attitude attribution.

3.2 The Cognitive Dynamics of Attitude Attribution

We will find it useful to step back from perspectival contents for a moment, and consider fine-grained contents more generally, as well as the role that they play in a theory of the attitudes. I intend to lean on joint work with Richard Larson (in particular Larson and Ludlow (1993)) and subsequent work including Ludlow (2000). In Larson and Ludlow (1993) we offered an account in which the objects of attitude reports are "Interpreted Logical Forms" (ILFs) or structural descriptions of that-clauses along with the semantic contents of the components of that structural description. To keep matters informal, I'll speak of "that-clauses" going forward, understanding them to be structural descriptions annotated with contents.[7]

In our (1993) paper we faced the puzzle of explaining our ability to know when two that-clauses attribute the same attitude or can count as saying the same thing. The puzzle was to show how using different words in a that-clause at different times could count as attributing the same attitude to an agent. For example, sometimes (not always, but *sometimes*) 'Fred believes The Morning Star is beautiful' and 'Fred believes the Evening Star is beautiful' can attribute the same belief to Fred. Similarly, sometimes using the very same words 'Fred believes Paderewski is a pianist' at different times can attribute very different beliefs to Fred.[8] How is this possible?

---

[7] For the record, this usage is not innocent. The problem is that the complement clauses of attitude reports are often not that-clauses (they could be infinitivals, for example). It is also important to keep in mind that we are talking about that-clauses as interpreted, but this is a peculiar way to talk, given that clauses are interpreted within the context of a sentence as a whole and would be uninterpretable in isolation (infinitivals again). Still, I'm going with the "that-clause" locution to be more user friendly.

[8] For example, following Kripke's (1979) example, Fred mistakenly believes that there are two different Paderewskis—one a famous pianist and the other a famous Polish statesman.

The answer we gave was that when we proffer an interpreted that-clause in a report on someone's attitude (e.g., belief), we are not offering it because we have special insight into some internal state they are in. We are offering it to our audience as a contribution to our shared theory of the agent's mental life. The shared theory is one we construct for each other that, given our interests, will enable us to predict and understand the behavior of the agent we are talking about.

For example, let's suppose that a speaker S and a hearer H are discussing an agent A. If H is interested in information that A has about the world (for example, the distance to Venus), then the referential component of the that-clause will be of primary importance to the goals of belief ascription. H will therefore be indifferent to the choice of 'The Morning Star' versus the 'The Evening Star' (or 'Hesperus' versus 'Phosphorus') in an attitude ascription concerning Venus. By contrast, if H is interested in explaining or predicting (or understanding) A's behavior (for example, whether A will assent to an utterance of 'The Morning Star is the Evening Star', or whether A will act in a way compatible with the knowledge that the Morning Star is the Evening Star) then H may well be interested in the syntactic expressions that S uses to characterize A's belief.

In cases of the latter kind, where prediction or explanation of behavior is the goal, we envisioned the speaker's choice of syntactic constituents in a that-clause to involve two components. Let's call these the *Modeling Component* and the *Expression Component*.

The Modeling Component determines how S and H model A's belief structure. The Expression Component is how S "negotiates" with H the expressions to be used in speaking of the components of that model. Both components theoretically involve complex subprocesses. For example, in the Modeling Component, where S and H model A's belief structure, S and H would appear to draw at least on all of the following:

(a) S's knowledge of H's interests;
(b) general principles of common sense psychology that S supposes that H believes;
(c) knowledge that S knows H to have about A.

Suppose S knows H to be interested in the behavior of A—for example, in whether A will use her telescope to look at a particular region of the morning sky. Then by (b)—the general principles of common sense psychology, which S supposes H to share, S may infer that H will deploy a *fine*-grained model of A's psychology—one that distinguishes Morning Star beliefs from Evening Star beliefs. S may also rely upon information supplied directly by H or some other source. For example, S may learn that H knows that A is unaware that the Morning Star is the Evening Star.

In the Expression Component for selecting a that-clause, S and H must (tacitly) agree on expressions used to speak of the components of H's model of A's belief structure. Expressions used in attitude ascriptions will be tacitly "negotiated" by participants in the discourse, following general principles holding of discourses of all kinds. The general process by which discourse participants negotiate a way to speak of objects (sometimes called "entrainment" by psychologists) has been the subject of considerable research in psycholinguistics (see Brennan and Clarke (1996), Brennan and Schober (1999), Clarke (1992) for discussion).

I used this entrainment idea in my (2014) book *Living Words*. There the idea is that when we sit down with a conversational partner we don't come to the conversation with fully complete languages, but rather we build microlanguages by using bits and pieces of our overlapping linguistic backgrounds, but also by introducing new terms and modulating the meanings of existing terms. Sometimes that process of modulation is tacit, and sometimes it is explicit, but it is an ongoing process sensitive to the contexts in which we find ourselves, and to the interests of the discourse participants. Applied here, the idea is that the product of our tacit negotiations and entrainment may be that 'The Morning Star' and 'The Evening Star' sometimes have different contents, sometimes the same, and sometimes we may leave the matter open.

This idea is naturally extended to the study of the way states of mind come to be described, and explains why subtle differences in expression will have great consequences for the truth of the attitude ascription. The words we use to describe the conceptual apparatus of an agent can vary greatly across microlanguages.

Consider Kripke's Paderewski case to illustrate this idea. In some microlanguages (for example, one constructed after attending a concert with Fred, who thinks there are two Paderewskis), we may introduce the term 'Paderewski' to invoke Fred's concept of Paderewski-qua-pianist. In other microlanguages (for example, constructed after watching the news with Fred), we can introduce the term 'Paderewski' to invoke Fred's concept of Paderewski-qua-statesman. In still others, where we know that Fred knows they are one and the same person, we may be invoking Fred's statesman-pianist concept. In contexts where Fred does not know there is only one Paderewski and we want to explain the manifestation of the knowledge deficit in Fred's behavior, we need to expand our micro-language by introducing terminology to reflect the two guises under which Fred knows Paderewski. For example, we may explicitly introduce terms 'Paderwski-1' and 'Paderewski-2', or we may use definite descriptions or we may avail ourselves of the philosophical device of qua-talk: 'Paderewski qua statesman' versus 'Paderewski qua pianist'.

Thus, when Kripke asks, does Fred or does he not believe that Paderewski is a pianist, the answer is that it depends on which concept is being invoked in our current microlanguage. There is a kind of error of equivocation necessary to generate the paradox—the error being the thought that the meaning of 'Paderewski' is stable across microlanguages and a correlative error in thinking that we can conjoin formally similar expressions from different microlanguages to try and generate a contradiction ('Fred believes that Paderewski is a pianist and Fred does not believe that Paderewski is a pianist'). This is equivalent to leaning on the different meanings of 'chips' in British and American English to try and generate a contradiction ('Gabriel likes chips and Gabriel does not like chips').[9]

3.3 Microlanguages and Local Theories

One helpful feature of microlanguages is that they can be constructed to aid in an account of someone's psychological states (or of what they said); in this way microlanguages thereby help us express theories, constructed on the fly, of the mental life of agents we encounter. But these are special kinds of theories. They are not theories like the theory of gravity is a theory. These theories are *local*. They are theories that involve particular individuals at particular times. They also involve local interests (i.e. the interests of the discourse participants).

The phenomena we are explaining include why a particular individual does or does not take their telescope out on a particular morning, why a particular person does or does not attend a particular piano concert, etc.

---

[9] The British English term 'chips' would translate as 'French fries' in American English. 'Chips' in American English would translate as 'crisps' in British English.

It is natural for us to talk of having theories that explain why individual people do what they do, even though we have no general covering theory. Even folk psychology is not local, and the theories I am talking about, to the extent they lean on folk explanation, are offered against a background of general folk theories. For example, above I pointed out that general principles of folk psychology would play a role in our construction of our more local theory.

You could, of course, say that given this story you may not need the abstract objects—belief contents, thoughts, senses. Can't we replace these abstracta by talk of expressions being used at different times and places to characterize local theories about other agents? I don't know that there is anything to be gained by this strategy, and I'm not sure this theory offers new ammunition to the nominalist. Theories (local or otherwise) are abstract objects, after all, as are expression types—the words we use to characterize attitudes.[10] And ultimately, it may be that our ability to express attitudes in different ways from different perspectives is simply a way of giving us epistemic access to those abstracta (this is an idea pursued in Parsons (1984: chapter 1, 2008)).

Everything I have said about the theory of attitude attributions would apply *mutatis mutandis* to accounts of what is said and what is meant. So, for example, if I report what Fred said on one occasion by uttering 'Fred said that Paderewski is a pianist', I may use different expressions to report Fred's same statement on another occasion. In each case, I am constructing (with my interlocutor) a local theory of what it is that Fred said. It can be used to make predictions about what he might say or do next, about what he agreed to having said, about what he might be held culpable for having said, etc. Similarly for the meaning of a sentence: The content of what is said needs to be characterized in different ways on different occasions, and in particular as we shift between different microlanguages.

3.4 The Cognitive Dynamics of Indexicals and Interperspectival Contents

In the previous section I talked about vanilla attitude contents, and did not take up the issue of perspectival contents. Do these pose difficulties

[10] These are notoriously difficult to treat nominalistically, as I argued in Ludlow (1982).

not already entailed by attitude contents? The answer is that sometimes they do.

In some cases, adjusting talk about perspectival contents across perspectival positions is automatic. Consider again the way it is done in English. If I am in a conversation with you and say "I am hungry," you can report this back to me with the words 'you are hungry'. The following day, you can report what I said the previous day by using the words 'you were hungry yesterday'. Thus, some expressions have fairly regular rules for tracking indexical contents—rules that we might, following Branquino (2006), call *natural realignment* rules.

Thinking of attitude reports and content reports as being theories, the natural realignment rules give us established ways of expressing the same local theory from different (even if nearby) temporal and spatial positions. For example, if you sincerely utter 'I am thirsty', then the realignment rule yields 'you are thirsty', which in my mouth expresses the same local explanatory theory you originally expressed with the first utterance. Embedded in a larger theory, it might explain why you poured yourself a drink.

However, as Branquinho notes, this natural realignment is not always possible. One example of this would be third party perspectival reports. A person eavesdropping on my conversation with John Perry might report the content of what Perry said by uttering, 'John realized that he himself is making the mess', thus expressing the same local theory that Perry and I expressed with our brief conversation in the supermarket. But how did the eavesdropper construct that report? There are also cases, which we will discuss shortly, that can confound the natural realignment rules governing our uses of 'I' and 'you', 'today' and 'yesterday'. There are cases that do not afford natural realignment—or at least they don't appear to.

So the idea of these content reports is to express theories in a way that preserves their explanatory power across perspectival positions. As we saw in Chapter 1, stripping the perspectival content from these theories neuters them, and typically renders them nonexplanatory. In Chapter 2, we used the idea of multiple storyboard panels to illustrate multiple perspectival positions in a conversation. We also talked about coordinated storyboard panels as offering something like theories (or parts of theories) that could help explain the actions and emotions of the discourse participants.

Let's take that basic idea/metaphor and knit it together with our account of attitude attribution as initially developed in Larson and Ludlow. Here again we lean on the distinction between the Modeling Component and the Expression Component. In this case, we can think of the storyboards as illustrating the Modeling Component. The overarching theory of content attribution combines the perspectival information (illustrated by the multiple storyboards), coordinates its expression across the agents represented, and combines that with fine-grained contents as in the Larson and Ludlow ILF theory (distinguishing Morning Star beliefs from Evening Star beliefs, etc.). The resulting local theory is your interperspectival content.

None of this is to say that the Modeling Component is in some sense temporally prior to the Expression Component. These two components work in parallel, so that establishing expressions for contents is an integral part of the modeling process.

Recall that, among other things, the Expression Component coordinates ways in which we express contents from different perspectival positions. In this case, given a speaker S and hearer H, and some number of agents A_1 to A_n (we can now include S and H among A_1 to A_n), S and H do not necessarily set a single vocabulary for the model of a given agent A_i, but rather tacitly agree to different ways of expressing the model from different perspectival positions (e.g., 'you are hungry' from one perspective and 'I am hungry' from another).

In Section 2.2 I offered the idea that we could think of perspectival contents in terms of the storyboard panels collected in a binder. One panel represents the perspectival position of John Perry as he utters, 'I am making a mess'. Another represents my perspective as I utter, 'you said you are making a mess'. The question we left open earlier was what the binder itself is representing in this metaphor. The answer is that it is the local theory, constructed on the fly by the discourse participants, to express the contents, utilizing the Modeling Component, the Expression Component, etc.

You might pause at this point and offer the following challenge. If the theory of how expressions for contents are chosen can be executed successfully, doesn't this put my project out of business? Wouldn't such a theory replace the need for perspectival contents? The answer is that it does not and cannot, for the theory (deploying the Modeling Component and the Expression Component) itself relies upon perspectival contents. Indeed the elements of that theory are perspectival from top to bottom (tacit agreements could be of the form "I'll use this expression to refer to that thing..."). There is no harm in this. The theory was not intended to be reductive, after all. It is hopefully illuminative, however, in that it addresses how interperspectival contents are selected, labeled, and deployed in our construction of local theories for the explanation of actions, emotions, normative judgments, etc.[11]

Still, one might want to press an objection raised earlier. Perhaps all we need is a theory of how we express a referential content in different ways, so that the interperspectival content is nothing more than the referential content (a standard Russellian proposition, for example). The problem is that the expressions in isolation are simply patterns of electrons on a computer screen or ink on paper or perhaps sound waves. They are not explanatory of anything, nor can they be until they are coupled with an explanatory theory of how those expressions are related, and this is where the perspectival contents enter the picture. Coupling the expressions with referential contents does not advance our understanding of the explanatory part of the local theories.

Of course all of this assumes that the local theory that underwrites the cognitive dynamics of our tracking abilities can be constructed. And in point of fact there are serious questions about whether the project can be executed in certain critical circumstances—in particular, circumstances in which the agent we are reporting on has lost track of information that appears to be critical to the tracking of thought contents. This brings us to Kaplan's case of Rip van Winkle.

3.5 Rip van Winkle

In a thought experiment offered by Kaplan (1977: 538), Rip van Winkle takes a nap one day, saying to himself as he falls asleep, "today is a fine day." He wakes thirty years later, thinking that only a day has past. He attempts to express his earlier thought by uttering, 'yesterday was a

---

[11] Here we bump up against a theme that will recur throughout this book—the idea that you don't eliminate a content C by giving an analysis that relies on content C. Creating a regress in this way does not free us up from an ontological commitment to C. Nor, I might add, does this make the analysis less interesting. The goal of the analysis of C is not always to eliminate C. Sometimes the goal is to better understand C.

fine day'. Clearly something has gone amiss, and one idea is that the simple realignment rule no longer successfully allows him to express his earlier thought. But if he wasn't expressing his earlier thought, what was he doing? As Kaplan (1977) noted, these cases present serious difficulties for stand-alone sense-based accounts of indexicals (and thus, we would add, perspectival accounts).[12]

Evans (1996) thought that this showed there was a bullet that needs to be bitten.

> I see no more strangeness in the idea that a man who loses track of time cannot retain beliefs than in the idea that a man who loses track of an object cannot retain the beliefs about it with which he began. (311, n.21)

I believe that Evans gave up too easily here. Recall that on the Larson and Ludlow approach to attitude attributions, belief attribution takes place between a speaker S and a hearer H, regarding an agent A (or group of agents, possibly including S and H). But the theory isn't just a theory of belief *attributions*; it must of necessity also be a theory of *belief*, for on balance our belief attributions are true.[13] Accordingly, the question of whether Rip or anyone has retained an earlier belief does not depend so much on what he may be able to report but depends also upon what in-the-know third parties are in a position to report.

Let's suppose that S and H are "in the know" about Rip's long nap. Let's suppose further that they have evidence that Rip sincerely uttered 'today is a fine day' just before his thirty-year nap. When Rip wakes up, he may try to report his earlier belief by saying, 'Yesterday was a fine day', but we are not constrained by that report. S and H shall want to report his earlier belief in a very different way—something akin to 'Rip was thinking *that day*—thirty years ago—to be a fine day'. On the face of it, that report is also completely true. S and H are attributing the same belief to Rip that he had thirty years earlier. Since their belief attribution is true, it follows that Rip has retained his belief.

But something has gone wrong, obviously. It was not Rip's failure to retain his belief, however; it was his characterization of his earlier belief. Has Rip lost his *ability* to express that earlier belief? Presumably not, for

---

[12] See also Perry (1979) for discussion of these cases.
[13] In some respects they are remarkably accurate. I can attribute to hundreds of philosophers the belief that an important talk will be held at a certain time in a certain place, and sure enough, they will be there at the appointed time and place.

Rip still has the ability to say things such as 'That was a fine day—just before I fell asleep, however long ago that was'. And that is a perfectly fine characterization of his earlier belief (recall there are many ways of expressing that belief). The belief attribution correctly characterizes the belief from his current perspectival position, and it correctly attributes to him the belief that he himself was having a fine day.

Evans might object that you can only retain a belief if you successfully track it, and this is connected to Evans' view about the importance of tracking in reference relations. To use one of Evans' own examples (from Evans (1982)), if I drop a ball bearing in a bucket of ball bearings and shake up the bucket I may lose my ability to find that ball bearing. For Evans, this meant that I could no longer refer to the ball bearing or even entertain singular thoughts about it. But I'm inclined to think this is an excessively restrictive understanding of thought retention. I believe I have memories of that very ball bearing even though I am in no position to recover or identify the ball bearing itself. Whether my memory is preserved via a causal chain (an option rejected by Evans) or some other mechanism,[14] I want to say I remember it (not just that there was a single ball bearing in my hand, but also that that particular ball bearing was in my hand). Rip's ability to recall his earlier thought is no stranger than our ability to recall the ball bearing that I tossed into the bucket.[15]

I've been suggesting that we can think of indexicals as playing a role in the expression of interperspectival contents, and I've offered a proposal in which we think of interperspectival contents as local theories that we express in different ways from different perspectival positions. But are there better stories to tell? There are plenty of accounts of indexicals available and few of them claim to utilize perspectival contents. Perhaps the correct analysis does not lean on perspectival contents, but rather keeps the semantics clean and moves the perspectival nature of things up into the psychology. Or maybe we can skirt this reification of perspectival

---

[14] For example, the more liberal account of reference in Hawthorne and Manley (2012).

[15] See Branquino (2006) for a similar memory-based account. Branquino puts the idea like this:

> The demonstrative phrase 'that day' would be here taken as expressing in the context a memory-based demonstrative mode of presentation of d, i.e. a way of thinking of a certain day anchored upon a memory demonstration of the day in question.

contents and opt for some type of use theory. Or perhaps Lewis' account of the *de se* can give us an alternative. We will examine all of these options in the next chapter, beginning with an account that keeps the indexical content in the semantics but attempts to tame it by treating it as token-reflexive content.

4

Some Alternative Accounts of Interperspectival Content

Let's go back to examples (1) and (2)—repeated here.

(1)   I have a meeting with the boss at three o'clock.
(2)   Oh no, I have a meeting with the boss *now*!

Pace Cappelen and Dever, there is something more to my utterance of (2) than there is to my utterance of (1) but the big question now becomes whether this "something more" is something *semantic* as we argued in Chapters 2 and 3, where we explored the idea that the semantics can deploy perspectival contents to account for this something more.

Prima facie, there is quite a bit of pull to suppose that semantics should reflect this something more. John Perry (2001), in a passage we quoted earlier, put the idea this way:

I cannot accept that a semantic theory can be correct that does not provide us with an appropriate interface between what sentences mean, and how we use them to communicate beliefs in order to motivate and explain action. A theory of linguistic meaning should provide us with an understanding of the properties sentences have that lead us to produce them under different circumstances, and react as we do to their utterance by others.   (2001: 8)

Perry then offered the following "cognitive constraint on semantics":

If there is some aspect of meaning, by which an utterance u of S and an utterance u' of S' differ, so that a rational person who understood both S and S' might accept u but not u', then a fully adequate semantics should say what it is.   (2001: 9)

Of course, plenty of philosophers have argued that this aspect of meaning content has no place in a semantic theory.

For example, *referentialists* would hold that this extra bit of perspectival content does not make it into the truth conditions. On their view, the truth conditions for (1) and (2) would fundamentally look the same:

(1r)   An utterance u, by s, at t, where t = three o'clock of 'I have a meeting with the boss at three o'clock' is true iff s has a meeting with the boss at t.

(2r)   An utterance u, by s, at t, where t = three o'clock of 'I have a meeting with the boss *now*' is true iff s has a meeting with the boss at t.[1]

What about the difference in cognitive significance between (1) and (2)? As noted earlier, Wettstein (1986) argued that it is a mistake to think that the something extra is semantical. In this chapter we will look at a number of attempts to exorcise perspectival content from the semantics (and thus, presumably, from our metaphysics). First, there is an account of indexicals that keeps something extra in the semantics, but a something extra that does not involve perspectival contents. Perhaps, as suggested by Casteñeda (1967, 1989), Perry (2001), Higginbotham (1995, 2009), and others, we can make do with token indexical (token reflexive) content, give the account of human action and emotion that we needed, and avoid the use of perspectival contents.

4.1 Token Indexical Theories

In Chapter 1 we saw that indexical or perspectival language was critical to an account of human action and emotions. I held that this means that some extra content is needed in the semantics. But does that something extra really involve perspectival content like that proposed in Chapters 2–3? Could we not get all the content we need using resources that don't involve perspectival content? The token indexical theory is one way to try and do this.

In rough form, the idea of a token indexical theory is that you can do all the work that perspectival content is supposed to do by leaning on the relation between the event you are talking about and the utterance event (or thought event). So, to take our example (2) from above, we might have an analysis like (2x) ('x' for reflexive).

(2x)   The utterance u, at three o'clock, of 'I have a meeting with the boss *now*' is true iff the utterer of u has a meeting with the boss at the time u is uttered.

---

[1] Here I am assuming that variables do not display sense content. If Heck (2002) is right this assumption may not be so innocent.

This is supposed to have the advantage of providing sufficient perspectival content by situating events in the future or past (or present) with respect to an utterance event.

Now, including the utterance event in the semantics is not a new idea. Reichenbach (1947) used it to give tenseless truth conditions for tensed language. What is novel is the idea that by incorporating a reference to the utterance itself, one can also account for the perspectival nature of tense. But as we will see, it is far from clear that token-reflexive truth conditions can accomplish this.

Before we get to the question of whether token-reflexive truth conditions can account for perspectival content, we need to come to grips with a recognized problem that these approaches must deal with—the modal profile problem. Consider (7).

(7)   There are no utterances now.

We surely don't want (7) to have an analysis like (8), because (8) appears to be a necessary falsehood while (7) does not.

(8)   There are no utterances at the time of this utterance.

In any possible world in which there is an utterance of (8), that utterance of (8) is going to come up false.[2] And of course it doesn't really solve the problem to talk about mental tokenings instead of utterances, because the example could be changed to 'There are no tokenings now'.

This observation is often attributed to Kaplan, but as Kaplan notes, the point was originally made by Casteñada (1967: 87):

Reichenbach, for instance, claims that the word "I" means the same as "the person who utters this token." This claim is, however, false. A statement formulated through a normal use of the sentence "I am uttering nothing" is contingent: if a person utters this sentence he falsifies the corresponding statement, but surely the statement might, even in such a case, have been true. On the other hand, the statements formulated by "The person uttering this token is uttering nothing" are self-contradictory: even if no one asserts them, they simply cannot be true.

---

[2] Here we need to assume that the meanings of the expressions are held constant, or, if you prefer, we only evaluate utterances of (8) in worlds in which the word meanings are held constant. If you think about it, that assumption can't possibly be innocent, since we are in the middle of telling a story about word meanings. There are also issues about the modal profile of expressions themselves. We set all of these concerns to the side for the time being.

Higginbotham (1995) and Perry (2001) have both argued that the token indexical solution should not be abandoned in the face of this objection. As Higginbotham (1995: 248) put it, "The quirks of modality should not .... be allowed to undermine the thesis that what we say and think is literally and robustly expressed by the words that we use." But what then do we say about the modal profile of indexical sentences? Both Perry and Higginbotham have explored the possibility of using "modal discards" to keep the token indexical content while saving the modal profile.

One way to develop this idea would be to say that there are multiple semantic contents (for example, a referential content and some additional token reflexive content) and specify that only the former is relevant to the evaluation of the sentence in other possible worlds. Perry (2001) developed this idea by suggesting that utterances have at least three kinds of content:

The *indexical content* (sometimes he calls this *content-M*) of an utterance corresponds to the truth-conditions of the utterance given the facts that fix the language of the utterance, the words involved, their syntax and their *meaning*.

The *referential content* (sometimes he calls this *content-C* and sometimes the *official content*) of an utterance corresponds to the truth-conditions given all of these factors, plus the facts about the *context* of the utterance that are needed to fix the designation of indexicals.

The *designational content* (sometimes he calls this *content-D*) of an utterance corresponds to the truth-conditions given all of these factors, plus the additional facts that are needed to fix the *designation* of the terms that remain (definite descriptions in particular, but also possessives, etc.).

Let me say a little bit about the natures of indexical content and referential content (designational content won't concern us here). Referential content (or "official content") suggests that we are only talking about the objects referred to in the semantics (e.g. the referents of names and the referents of predicates) and nothing more. So, for example, the official content of (2) is as given in (2r). Strictly speaking, however, a perspectivalist could argue that perspectival content is also perfectly good referential content, assuming realism about perspectival properties. This is technically right, but doesn't follow in the spirit of what Perry is doing, so I am going to add an amendment to Perry's gloss of referential content.

The *referential content** of an utterance corresponds to the nonperspectival truth-conditions given all of these factors, plus the facts about the *context* of the utterance that are needed to fix the designation of indexicals.

Indexical content is a modified version of Reichenbach's token-reflexive theory of content. Perry's formulation (2x) departs from Reichenbach's in that it is not the utterance *tokens* that are constituents of the descriptions in (2x), but rather the utterances themselves are—that is, the acts of uttering.[3] Perry could have called his theory "utterance-reflexive" or more generally "act-reflexive," but I will follow his usage and simply call it *reflexive*.

Returning to the idea of modal discards, since we have (at least) two kinds of contents, we can rely upon the reflexive content to give us an account of the cognitive significance of the utterance, but we don't need to keep the reflexive content around all the time. In fact, when we want to consider the modal profile of a sentence (i.e. when we want to evaluate it in a counterfactual situation) we can simply discard (ignore) the reflexive content and rely on the referential content. This is the sense in which we can have our cake and eat it too. We can account for both the cognitive significance and the modal profile of an utterance if we simply get clear that these involve different contents of the same utterance!

Of course, having your cake and eating it too is supposed to be impossible, and my concern here is that we don't get to eat cake and we don't get to have it either. First, it seems to me that the notion of reflexive content deployed both by Higginbotham and Perry is not sufficient to the task. But second, I think that close inspection will show the modal discard strategy is not sufficient to solve the modal profile problem either. I'll take up these concerns in order.

4.1.1 Is reflexive content too thin?

What's wrong with reflexive content? Consider the following version of the classic case for tense from Prior.

(9)   I am thankful that my root canal is over with.

According to Perry's theory, for an utterance u, of (9), at time t, by Ludlow, we have a reflexive content akin to the following (again using x to indicate "reflexive").

---

[3] Actually Reichenbach is unclear on this point. He might well have endorsed Perry's formulation.

(9x)   The utterer y, of utterance u, is thankful that the event of y's root canal is earlier than the time of u.

And a referential content as in (9r).

(9r)   Ludlow is glad that the event of Ludlow's root canal is earlier than u (at time t).

The first thought is, well, is (9x) really something to be glad about? In the first place why do I care about y's root canal? And who is y, other than the utterer of u? Suppose I believe that I didn't utter u or suppose I don't realize that y's root canal is my root canal. The analysis is already missing badly needed first person perspectival content.

But there is another problem even if we ignore the problem of first person content; why should I care about the relative ordering of my utterance and my root canal? One might respond that this objection has no force, because at a minimum my utterance of (9), by having (or being associated with) the reflexive content in (9x), temporally situates me with the time of that very utterance and therefore places me well after the root canal.

But of course it can and has been argued that the contents expressed by (9r) and (9x) do no such thing, either individually or in concert. Famously, Prior in his (1959) "Thank Goodness" paper concluded that token-reflexive theories do not capture what I express with my utterance of (9). The question is, why did Prior consider reflexive content (or at least Reichenbach's token-reflexive content) to be inadequate?

For a four-dimensionalist, my location just is my Spacetime worm and while that includes my utterance of (9) as a temporal segment, there are still big chunks of my Spacetime worm that are eternally situated earlier than that root canal. The only thing that an utterance actually claims to be safely situated later than the root canal is the utterance itself (utterance *event*, for Perry) and the part of my Spacetime worm that overlaps with the utterance. The problem is that we still want to know why *that* utterance and the corresponding part of my Spacetime worm are supposed to be special and why I should be glad about the fact that *that* utterance and worm segment are a safe temporal distance from the unpleasant event.

It is open to detensers like Perry to argue that explaining why I am glad is not really part of the goal here. Lots of facts could explain my being thankful; perhaps I am delighted that I now possess free samples of mint-flavored floss or perhaps I enjoy having fresh memories of the smell of dental gauze. Perry presumably will say that all this is very fine, but the reflexive content of my utterance is what makes my utterance of 'I'm thankful that's over' true. It doesn't do more than that and it isn't supposed to do more than that. The reflexive content certainly isn't supposed to *explain* why I am relieved.

We can refine Prior's objection, however, by introducing explanatory talk directly into the crucial utterance, as in (9e).

(9e)   I'm thankful *because* my root canal is over with now.

Someone who utters (9e) clearly isn't talking about mint-flavored floss or the smell of dental gauze, but they do seem to be offering an account of the reason for their thankfulness, and that appears to be that they are thankful *because* the root canal *is past*, quite independently of whatever other reasons they may have for being thankful. More to the point, isn't (9e) basically what I am saying when I utter (9)? So isn't the explanatory part of (9) somehow crucial to a proper analysis of it?

Is it plausible to say that this is illusory and what makes (9) and (9e) true is that the state of affairs described by the *reflexive* content of 'my root canal is over with now' is what causes me to be thankful? Well, presumably that is an option for Perry, but now one has to worry about the stability of Perry's position; precisely what amount of explanatory role is semantic content supposed to play? For many direct reference theorists, the answer is simple: none. But for Perry, accounting for cognitive significance is a very important part of semantics. Recall his cognitive constraint on semantics, from above:

If there is some aspect of meaning, by which an utterance u of S and an utterance u' of S' differ, so that a rational person who understood both S and S' might accept u but not u', then a fully adequate semantics should say what it is. (2001: 9)

Given such a constraint, how can Perry reject the idea that perspectival content should be part of the semantics? Wouldn't the consistent strategy be to try and augment the theory with additional perspectival content so as to account for Prior's "thank goodness" case? Here is a possible amendment: just add a new kind of content to the mix.

The *perspectival content* (we can call this the *content-P*) of an utterance corresponds to the perspectival contents expressed (or displayed, if you prefer) by the truth-conditions of the utterance.

This would result in a very ecumenical theory. We would now have the "official" referential content, the reflexive content, and perspectival content, among others.

One might think that Perry's reflexive content is more austere than it needs to be—indeed, more austere than other token-reflexive accounts have been. Would the situation be better if we jazzed up the reflexive content of (9)? For example, we could take Higginbotham's proposal to be that the reflexive content of (9) is actually much closer to (9xx) ("xx" for "extra reflexive").

(9xx)   The utterer of this utterance u is thankful that the event of his root canal is earlier than the time of u—*this very utterance!*

That is, maybe it would help if we added some reflexivity in the way that we describe the utterance u. Perry avoided this strategy, and I think I understand why. The problem comes in with the way we go about identifying (reflexively) an utterance. In (9xx), for example, we used the phrase 'this very utterance'. Question: just how innocent is that indexical 'this'?

Arguably, the appearance of the indexical in the metalanguage is not innocent at all, for it amounts to smuggling in a disquotational treatment of indexicals, which is to say that it smuggles in an appeal to perspectival contents. Or at least it certainly appears to. Later in this chapter we will see that the appearance is not deceptive and that the commitment to perspectival contents cannot be dodged here.

But are we really giving away the store just because we are deploying 'this' in the metalanguage? It is true enough that the kinds of indexicals being deployed in the metalanguage (e.g. 'this') may be different than those found in the utterance of the object language sentence (we have, in the case of (9xx), traded in a 'now' for a 'this'), but this isn't much of a victory. Furthermore, on closer scrutiny even this small victory may be chimeral, since the 'this' being deployed in the metalanguage doesn't look much like the indexical we use when pointing to nearby objects; we aren't pointing at anything, there is no act of indicating, and we don't appear to have any relevant referential intention. What is going on when we use 'this' in (9xx)? It seems as though in cases like (9xx), when one utters 'this very utterance' one is really saying "the utterance happening now," or more accurately, "the utterance I am producing now."

This may look like a technical objection, but in fact it points to a very deep problem with the token-reflexive response. The deep problem is that when the aperspectivalist attempts to smuggle an indexical expression (like 'this utterance') into the right-hand side (RHS) of a theorem, the aperspectivalist is breaking from the usual path of keeping the literal truth conditions free of such elements. If the use of the indexical on the RHS is to make any sense at all, then it looks like 'this' has to be treated as invoking a perspectival content. But if perspectival contents are possible in this case, why not allow them in the case of temporal indexicals?

I've spoken at some length about the limitations of token-indexical contents. The contents are just too thin to properly account for the phenomena that motivated our positing of perspectival content to begin with—the explanation of human action, emotion, perception, etc. But too thin as it may be, it could be that it is also too thick, in that it introduces contents that blow up the modal profile of sentences containing such token-reflexive contents.

Reviewing, the key advantage of Perry's proposal is supposed to be that by having two kinds of content, we can utilize one sort of content for the modal profile of the utterance and the other kind of content to get the cognitive significance right (now setting aside the worries just raised as to whether his reflexive content is sufficient to do the job). To illustrate, consider an utterance of a sentence like (10).

(10)   You are the addressee of this utterance.

Suppose, for example, that I utter (10), addressing John Perry; in that case we would have the following two contents (again ignoring designational content):

(10r)   JP is the addressee of this utterance.
(10x)   The addressee of this utterance is the addressee of this utterance.

Now it is clearly metaphysically possible that Perry might not have been in front of me when I spoke, or even in the neighborhood. This is OK because on Perry's view (10x) is supposed to play no role in the modal profile of my utterance. Good thing, too, because (10x) is true in every possible world in which the utterance is made. We're safe, because what we evaluate in other possible worlds is simply (10r), and of course there are worlds where Perry is not my addressee.[4]

I don't think this works, however, and the problem has to do with cases where we need the reflexive content in another possible world. In the previous section I argued that reflexive content is not enough to give the cognitive content of temporal indexicals. For now, let's set aside that objection and suppose that reflexive content gives us all we'll ever need to account for the cognitive significance of temporal indexicals. Now, what are we to do with an utterance of (11), said after I didn't need a root canal after all, and the time of the initially scheduled root canal had passed?

(11)   By now I would have been relieved that it was over.

We want to evaluate the nonmodal portion of this in another possible world (that is, we want to evaluate 'I'm relieved that's over' in a possible world in which I had a root canal), but we can't exactly discard the reflexive content when we do so, because we need it in that world of evaluation—obviously so, if we want to explain why I'm relieved in that counterfactual situation.[5]

There is a kind of "hacky" response that is possible here. One can say we don't always discard the reflexive content; we only do so under certain circumstances—like when the reflexive content messes up the modal profile of the utterance. But this hack won't work, since it is possible to find examples where we need to keep some reflexive content *and* discard some reflexive content, lest the modal profile goes haywire. This requires some stage setting, but bear with me.

Imagine that we are entertaining a possible state of affairs in which you have an evil doppelganger. In this possible state of affairs, if I unknowingly address the doppelganger today I shall be subjected to

---

[4] There are, of course, assumptions being made here about how utterances are individuated. I'm assuming here that utterances are individuated by sound producing activities and nothing more. You could imagine a story about utterances in which they are individuated by their actual addressees.

[5] An anonymous reviewer has observed that this point is similar to the nesting arguments against two-dimensionalism, discussed in Soames (2005), Dever (2007), and Forbes (2011). Accordingly, and taking a leaf from Soames, we could try to make things worse for Perry with utterances like the following that want both the reflexive and referential content: 'It could have been that I was happy about the contingent fact that I was speaking'. Here we need the reflexive content to account for the happiness, but we also need to jettison it to account for the contingency of the utterance.

five hours of Milton Babbitt music and a root canal operation on the following day. Suppose you ask me what, under such circumstances, my reaction would be on the day after tomorrow, having entirely avoided the root canal and the Milton Babbitt music. I respond by uttering (12).

(12) By then I would been relieved that you had been the addressee of this utterance.

Clearly there would have been no relief in the fact that the addressee of the utterance had been the addressee of the utterance. One needs to go with the reflexive content for the tense, but the referential content is what is crucial for the evaluation of the indexical 'you'.

Well, it might be objected that reflexive content need not be discarded across the board, and in fact may be deployed for some indexicals, yet discarded for other indexicals—all within the same utterance. This solution strikes me as even hackier than what we have been considering up to now, but here again we can find counterexamples to the proposal.

To set this one up I need to introduce a stock objection to token-reflexive theories, show how Perry's theory could handle that objection, and then go on to consider some more complex cases where I think the theory founders. The stock objection (similar to the one from Casteñada above, and developed in Smith (1993) and Craig (1996)) revolves around the possibility of utterances of (13).

(13) There are no utterances now.

Pretty clearly, reflexive content all by itself is not going to fare well in an analysis of (13).

(13x) There are no utterances at the time of this utterance.

Whatever we might want to say about (13) it is clearly not necessarily false, so (13x) cannot be what we carry to other possible worlds for evaluation. So far this is not a problem for Perry, since he can simply employ his referential content:

(13r) There are no utterances at t.

The problem comes in when we consider more complex cases that combine the 'no utterance' argument with the 'thank goodness' argument.

Imagine the following case. You ask me to consider a counterfactual situation in which utterances are excruciatingly painful to me. Not just my utterances. Not just your utterances. Any utterances. If someone is talking somewhere on planet Earth I am in pain, and the pain is worse than getting a root canal *while* listening to Milton Babbitt. You then ask me to consider the possibility that at some time everyone in that world goes mute. There are no more utterances and I am no longer in pain. You ask me what I would think then. I respond by uttering (14).

(14)   I would be relieved that there were no longer any utterances.

Now we are in a real jam. We need to keep the reflexive content to deal with the "thank goodness that's over" problem, but we need to discard it because of the "no utterance" problem.

But Perry (pc) offers a way out. We needn't suppose that my relief be earlier than the time of the utterance. It might be enough to say that it is earlier than the time of the corresponding thought token, so that the theory is not really utterance-reflexive (as I suggested above), but rather thought-reflexive (or more precisely, act-of-thinking-reflexive). This is now similar to a proposal made by Higginbotham in his paper "Tensed Thoughts," although augmented with the possibility of multiple kinds of contents. Here is Higginbotham's (1995) thought-reflexive proposal:

If e is the event of my affirming to myself with a sense of relief, 'My root canal is over' (or: 'over now'), then the thought that I think is indicated in [(A)].

[(A)] ($\exists$s) s is the situation of my root canal's being over & the time of s includes (the time of) e. (p. 228)

The thought that I have when I affirm with a sense of relief that my root canal is over is a thought whose very existence depends upon the existence of a certain episode in my mental life: it contains that episode as a constituent, and could not exist without it. (p. 229)

Does Perry want to go there? That is, does he want to be committed to the view that our (tensed) thoughts contain themselves as constituents? Even if he does want to go there, the objection can be recast with thought tokens. Consider a scenario in which not merely utterances are excruciatingly painful to me but the mere tokening of representational thought is. If someone is thinking that the cat is on the mat I am in pain. I am then asked to consider a scenario in which no such thoughts obtain. On this scenario there are still mental states, but let's suppose they are states like relief and pain. You might consider these to be representational states as well, but we can carve out an exception for such states if necessary.

Now, what happens? You ask me to consider the possibility that at some time everyone in the world ceases to have representational thoughts; there are no more representational thoughts and I am no longer in pain. You ask me what I would think then. I respond by uttering (15).

(15)   I would be relieved that there were no longer any representational thoughts.

You might think that this is all very well but all it is saying is that in such a world I am relieved that my state of relief (or some other tokened psychological state) is later than the time when representational thoughts obtained. But wait, it isn't even saying that, for what is it that makes it *my* state of relief? On that account, my relief is simply over the fact that representational thoughts preceded some particular tokened psychological state. Even assuming we can identify that state without the aid of perspectival content (a difficult task in itself), it is hard to see where the relief is supposed to come from. Surely I am not relieved that my tokened psychological state is later than a particular temporal interval in which representational thoughts obtain. This is just another version of Prior's "Thank Goodness" case.

4.2   Tense as a Mere Psychological Content

There are a number of people who might agree that tense is ineliminable, but object that while tense is very much necessary and in some sense ineliminable, it is for all that a mere psychological content and not a feature of the physical world.

I've addressed this move in Ludlow (1999) but perhaps not in sufficient depth, so maybe now is the time to develop the core idea, which basically is that psychological states (and contents) in general are grounded in the physical world. What I say here about tense generalizes to other forms of perspectival content—that is, perspectival contents cannot be construed as illusory or ungrounded psychological states.

To be sure, there are illusions. For example, in the Müller-Lyer illusion, two lines of the same length can appear to be of different lengths, but notice that this illusion, like other illusions, trades on actual physical properties. We can be wrong about the relative length of two lines, but length is, for all that, a property that things have in the physical world.

Similarly, a white wall trickily illuminated with a red light may appear to be a red wall, but redness is for all that a property of surface reflectance. We are just wrong about saying that the property red applies to our trickily illuminated wall.

More generally, following work by Burge (1986) and many others, we have reason to believe that our desires and other psychological states are anchored in the physical world. My desire for a glass of mineral water can be characterized as a relation between me and mineral water—that liquid that consists of H_2O and many minerals and some amount of impurities. If such liquid never existed I would not be able to have a desire for it, unless of course I came to have that desire by the study of chemistry and I imagined that such a liquid would be refreshing. In that case my desire is still anchored in important micro-level properties of our physical world.

Accordingly, what is it that people are saying when they claim that tense is a mere psychological content? Well, clearly what they mean is that it is an individualistically individuated content, not an externally anchored content. A tensed thought is a tensed thought without there being a corresponding tensed content (or contents) in the external world.

Does this make any sense? Can the mind be a theater of magical contents with absolutely no basis in external reality? Sure, we can imagine unicorns, but we can do this by virtue of there being horses and horns. What is it that tensed thoughts (and other perspectival thoughts) are built out of?

It might be supposed that tense is like a persistent illusion. Here is an example of a persistent illusion. It appears that the sun rises every day, but we know it does not. The Earth rotates. So we have the experience of a rising sun but in point of fact it only looks this way because the Earth is turning.

I tend to believe that from one frame of reference (Earthbound) there is nothing wrong with saying the Sun rises, but even if Sunrise is across the board illusory how is tense like this? We know what it looks like for objects to rise, because they do rise. Most of us rise out of bed most days. Balloons rise. People on escalators rise. Things rise in our world. It *appears* that the sun does too. That may or may not be an illusion, but it does not involve imaginary contents. At worst, as in the case of the white wall under red illumination, it involves the misattribution of a content that is perfectly well anchored in the world. At worst, rising should not be applied to the sun. But tense can't work like this. The detenser isn't saying tense is applicable to some things but not others, she is saying that tense is across the board illusory.

Here is another candidate for such a content: free will. When we make choices we often experience those choices as the product of our free agency. Well now, let's suppose that we live in a causally closed world. There is no agency. We only have the *illusion* of agency.

So, not only is there the illusion of agency when we say we chose to do something, there is also the illusion that this happened in our perspectival past. It is something else—it is simply a nonagentive mental state that is earlier than the time of utterance.

I don't know if the phenomenology of free agency is illusory or not, but at least we can see why it might be. If you think of the world in causally closed terms then what could free agency possibly consist in? You can have free agency and you can have causal closure, but you can't have both. So too, the detenser can argue that we don't merely live in a causally closed world, we live in one without perspectival contents.

The problem with this line of reasoning is that there are important differences between a claim that free will is illusory and a claim that perspectival contents are illusory. In the former case we can anchor enough of the phenomenology in uncontroversial features of the world. For example, we can say that the belief that one has free will is anchored in the belief that our actions are not causally determined and that they are the product of our internal deliberations and our intentions. In that way the phenomenology of free will might be illusory but it is for all that anchored in contents that are well attested in the external world.

The argument that perspectival contents are illusory does not work that way. We cannot define the experience of egocentric properties negatively (as we did in the "not causally determined" case). It is not adequate to say: Our experience of egocentric contents is anchored in our belief that reality is not B-theoretic. Tense is not simply the negation of the B-theoretic picture.

There is thus something odd about the claim that tense is a psychological property and hence a kind of illusion. Usually, when people construct illusions, they can explain the source of the illusion. If it is an illusion that the Earth rises we can explain the illusion (by pointing to the Earth's rotation, for example). If the stick looks broken in the water we can again explain why (water refracts light). But if time is an illusion, what is the explanation? Here, there is little on offer.

One attempt at grounding the experience of time in the physical world is offered in Atkins (1986), who suggests that our time consciousness is simply our experience of entropy.

> We have looked through the window on to the world provided by the Second Law, and have seen the naked purposelessness of nature. The deep structure of change is decay; the spring of change in all its forms is the corruption of the quality of energy as it spreads chaotically, irreversibly, and purposelessly in time. All change, and time's arrow, point in the direction of corruption. The experience of time is the gearing of the electrochemical processes in our brains to this purposeless drift into chaos as we sink into equilibrium and the grave. (p. 98)

This is a beautiful passage, but what does it actually mean? In Chapter 8 we will discuss the relationship between thermodynamics and the direction of time and we will see that attempted reductions of temporal order to thermodynamics are problematic, but in the meantime, supposing that this is coherent, the question is why do we experience the second law of thermodynamics in this way? (Or any way?)

For example, why should the direction of greater entropy be experienced as the future? Why not past? How and why are our brains "geared" to a process that was not discovered until the nineteenth century? What was the selectional advantage of that? But in any case, why is the brain, which for much of our lives is a thermodynamically isolated system with *fluctuating* entropy, geared to the usually, but not always, increasing entropy of our local region of the external world?[6]

Questions like this can be asked for any account of the psychology of time. And the question isn't merely how we account for the "hard problem" of the experience of time. The question is: how does the brain (or any system) manufacture a (nonveridical) representation of time out of nontemporal states of the world?

Note also that the Atkins passage is fraught with temporal language. Time is not supposed to be real, but the "gearing of...processes," "purposeless drift," "sink[ing] into equilibrium," "decay," and the "corruption of the quality of energy as it spreads" are supposed to be nontemporal physical alternatives. The problem is that these are nothing

---

[6] See MacDonald (2016) for an informal discussion of frequent fluctuations in brain entropy.

if not temporal descriptions of physical processes. As we will see in Chapter 8, even calling on the Second Law of Thermodynamics is suspicious, since the Second Law packs temporal direction into its definition.

Attempts to eliminate this temporal language and replace it with an alternative (for example Sider's (2001) at-at account of change[7]) are not trivial, but once such nontemporal accounts are explicit, the claim that an account of the psychology of time is available seems even less plausible. This is what we get when we make such B-series substitutions in the Atkins passage.

The experience of time is a function of the electrochemical states in our brains at times t1, t2, ... tn, where this sequence of states represents a sequence of physical states in the world, each successive state having higher entropy.

As I noted earlier, there are a lot of problems with this account, not least the question of how successive states in the brain, which may or may not be increasing in entropy, can represent a sequence of physical states in the world which, if they are local states, may or may not be a sequence of greater entropy. But even if there is a perfect isomorphism between these mental states and the physical states, why are the successive states of the brain supposed to be representing time and not a sequence of atemporal physical states? That is, why would the brain be representing time and not just physical states organized by level of entropy?[8]

You might think that this whole mess could be avoided if we stop trying to think of psychological states as being representational. Perhaps tenses supervene on pairs of times and behaviors. So, for example, representing something as present comes to <t, act!>, representing something as future comes to <t, plan!>, representing something as past comes to <t, remember!>.[9] There are lots of ways to develop this basic idea, but I don't think any of them can achieve airspeed. Can we really understand an act of remembering without some prior notion of the past? Or can we construct plans without some notion of the future? And going way back to examples (1) and (2) in this book, it is hard to see

---

[7] So, for example, change could constitute being red at time t1 and not red at time t2, or being location L1 at t1 and location L2 at t2.

[8] Here setting aside all the worries about whether entropy itself can be defined without recourse to a prior notion of temporal order.

[9] Thanks to an anonymous reader for this idea.

how there could be a state of acting without an understanding that one is to act now! The point is that even nonrepresentational mental states require perspectival contents. You cannot manufacture psychological states (representational or nonrepresentational) out of thin air.

4.3 Lewis on the *De Se*

Maybe kicking the analysis of perspectival content into psychology is not the way to go. Maybe something deeper is going on. That is the view of a number of philosophers who have taken a leaf from David Lewis's (1979) account of the *de se*.

Lewis's view, in short form, is that the *de se* involves the self-ascription of properties, here construed as centered possible worlds. Here is the longer form. On a standard possible worlds account of propositions, you could think of a proposition as a set of possible worlds—intuitively the worlds in which a sentence is true or in which a state of affair holds. There are well-known limitations to naïve versions of this account of propositions, not least of which is the discrimination of beliefs that are co-extensional (for example, distinguishing the belief that grass is green from the belief that grass is green and 2 + 2 = 4). Solutions to this problem have long been on the table (for example, you might build additional structure into the proposition), but another question has to do with the representation of first person belief.

Lewis's account begins with the idea of centered worlds—sets of possible worlds in which each world contains a counterpart of the same individual. So, for example, there are many possible worlds, and in some of those worlds my counterparts do not exist. Let's take a set of worlds where I or one of my counterparts do exist, and call that a centered world.

The result is a more fine-grained object than we get with a simple set of possible worlds, but is it fine grained enough to characterize first person states? Sometimes philosophers and linguists talk as though centered worlds are sufficient to characterize first person (perspectival) thoughts, but Lewis did not make this mistake. Here Lewis draws on his example of the two mountaintop gods discussed in Chapter 1.

Imagine that there are two gods, each omniscient—or at least each knowing all the nonperspectival facts. One lives on the tallest mountain and throws down manna; the other lives on the coldest mountain and throws down thunderbolts. The problem is that each god can have complete knowledge of all the aperspectival facts, but that would not be sufficient to know which of the two gods they are.

To see this, consider the god on the tallest mountain and consider the type of knowledge available to it. It knows there is a god on a tallest mountain. It knows what is visible from the tallest mountain. It knows that the god on the tallest mountain throws down manna, but it could know all of that and not know *of itself* that it is the god on the tallest mountain. It would have to know, for example, that it, itself, is the god on the tallest mountain, or that it, itself, is perceiving what can be perceived from the tallest mountain, or that it, itself, is throwing down manna.

What is the solution? Lewis argues that the missing ingredient here is that the god on the tallest mountain must self-ascribe the property of being the god on the tallest mountain.

There is a lot to unpack here. First, what exactly is self-ascription and what does it involve? Is it supposed to involve an actual mental act of ascribing a property to oneself? If so, then it must be a cognitively inexpensive mental act, for (on Lewis's view) some form of self-ascription is taking place in every assertion we make—even in straight-up vanilla propositions like the proposition that grass is green.[10] It must also be a mental act that is not transparent to us, for surely it comes as a surprise that this sort of self-ascription is going on with every assertion we make. For that matter, there are people that don't believe in proper-ties yet have first person (perspectival) knowledge. Such people might insist that they are not ascribing *de se* properties to themselves because they do not believe in such things. Let's set this concern aside, for I (unlike Searle 1995) have no trouble with the idea of mental processes that are opaque to us. I'm more concerned about the acts of self-ascription. The concern I have is that the talk of self-ascription carries this very intuitive imagery that makes us think we know what Lewis is talking about, but on closer inspection the central thesis is not so clear at all.

To see the problem let's think about temporal indexicals like 'now'. On Lewis's view it isn't exactly we that do the self-ascription, but rather our

---

[10] This is because we are attributing to ourselves that we are inhabitants of a world where grass is green.

stages that do. Presumably, our time-slices self-predicate the property of being in a time-slice centered world in which the meeting is happening.

Similarly, when I utter 'I am hungry', this gets us a set of centered worlds, worlds centered on stages of me being hungry. That set of centered worlds is what my time-slice ascribes to itself.

What does this mean? When we think about cases involving temporal indexicals ("Oh no, the meeting is now!") we usually think of some cognitive achievement having taken place. (I came to realize that the meeting was now. Perhaps I came to realize it slowly.) But on Lewis's story, what happens is that some time-slice of me self-ascribes. What is left when we sweep away the cognitive act metaphor, which no longer seems apt? There is a time-slice of me that stands in some undefined relation R to a set of centered worlds—worlds centered on time-slices. We don't know what kind of relation that is, exactly. It can't really be a cognitive relation because it is instantaneous. All we are told is that it is a relation that, whatever it is, will do whatever is necessary to provide the missing ingredient necessary to explain the role of indexicals (perspectival content) in human action and emotion, perception, and normative action.

As we noted earlier, calling R a self-attribution relation is metaphorical at best because there really isn't any sort of cognitive achievement or process or cognitive much of anything that a time-slice of me engages in, when it bears R to some property (set of centered worlds). Is R simply the predication relation? It can't be that—that is too thin, for merely predicating sets of centered worlds is not sufficient to enable the gods to know which gods they are.

My thought is that R comes to something like this: the content of R is whatever my time-slice needs to make it such that I know that the meeting is now. That might sound like a petty shot, but I don't think it is. I think the entire self-ascription relation is riding piggyback on our understanding of a full propositional perspectival claim. I'll get back to this point, but first I want to circle around and examine some other problems with the account, and I want to begin with this idea of time-slices being self-ascribers.

Imagine that I am working in my office, oscillating between remembering that I have an important meeting today and forgetting that I have an important meeting today. Each time I recall the meeting I suffer a mild panic, shuffle some papers around, think about what I will say in the meeting, and then become distracted and forget the whole thing. However, let's say that later in the day, around three o'clock, I recall the meeting for the third time that day and utter the following:

(16)   This is the third time today I've forgotten and then realized I have a meeting today.

How is this to work? It can't mean that there are three time-slices of me that self-ascribed a meeting. There are an infinite number of such slices. Perhaps we need to bundle these slices together into chunks of time-slices. So, we form the chunks and find that there are three chunks in which the slices are self-ascribing (whatever that means) the property of having a meeting today (said property being a set of centered worlds, where the worlds are centered around a particular meeting that obtains today).

But how does this chunking work? What determines whether a slice makes it into a particular chunk? Suppose the first time that I became aware of today's meeting was at 10 a.m. During that initial period of awareness, I ponder the importance of the meeting and what I shall say for five minutes before I become distracted by an online video of a hamster eating a tiny burrito, after which the meeting slips my mind completely for several hours. Was every slice of me in that roughly five-minute period self-ascribing the relevant property? Not necessarily. There may have been nanoseconds where the slices did not have the proper relation R. It's hard to say, really, because we have no idea what R is. Well, actually, we have some idea.[11]

We know that the slices constitute a chunk just in case they are time-slices of me during the period in which I realized I had a meeting today. Once again it seems that R is just some magical property that does whatever it is that needs to be done to make it so that R holds precisely when I realize I have a meeting. To put it another way, there is no independent grounding for the self-attribution relation or the relation R that time-slices must hold to properties, other than the prior

---

[11] An anonymous reviewer observes that this looks like a standard problem for "slicers," which is true, but saving the Lewisian position isn't as simple as giving up time-slice theories of persons and objects. The time-slices are used to get the right sorts of centered worlds to explain why I get up and go to my meeting *now*. Give up time-slices and the centered worlds will be too coarse grained to model temporal indexicals.

understanding of the first person claim Lewis is trying to offer an analysis of. I submit that the perspectival propositional knowledge is all we have. The talk of self-ascription is just an attempt to hide the perspectival character of that knowledge.

But even if this was all wrong—even if we had a perfectly good understanding of what it is for time-slices to self-attribute properties (or for whole individuals to self-attribute properties), this would still be an attempt to disguise what is going on. The use of the phrases 'self-ascribe', 'self-attribute', 'self-predicate' is deceptive as well. What we are being asked to imagine is that they are perfectly legitimate two-place relations that hold between an agent and a property. But these claims have truth conditions, and when we provide these truth conditions we again reveal the propositional structure of our first person (perspectival) claims.

Let's consider again the case of the two gods. One of them self-ascribes the property of being the god on the coldest mountain. The other god does so as well. Which is right? Well, one of them might say, "but I'm the god who throws down lightning bolts," but the second will say, "that is just to say that you self-ascribe throwing down lightning bolts, but I do the same. I too self-ascribe that I am on the coldest mountain." Which god is right?

Presumably, some self-ascriptions are true, and others are false. We might even give a T-theory for such things (now ascribing truth to self-ascriptions rather than sentences or properties—recall we can do this because for Lewis all forms of propositional knowledge are species of self-ascription).

(17) My self-ascription of being the god on the coldest mountain is true iff I'm the god on the coldest mountain.

Can there be any other way to do this? Notice that it will not do to use the self-ascription language on the right-hand side of the T-sentence.

(18) My self-ascription of being the god on the tallest mountain is true iff I'm self-ascribing the property of being the god on the tallest mountain.

Both gods can self-ascribe that property. What about this?

(19) My self-ascription of being the god on the tallest mountain is true iff I'm correctly self-ascribing the property of being the god on the tallest mountain.

But this T-sentence is now tautological—or nearly so. It comes to this: A self-ascription is true iff it is correct.

One might object as follows: You think you are so clever by forcing my truth conditions to have propositional structure—<I, [[unique god on the tallest mountain]]>—but this propositional structure is illusory. In point of fact the locution 'I'm the god on the tallest mountain' is standing proxy for a self-ascription! But now we are right to wonder if we aren't back where we started. Is the self-ascription correct or not?

You might think that this objection is hardly fair, since on a standard T-theory we get regresses as well, so for example we can take a T-sentence for a true object language sentence and insist that the right-hand side describe a *true* state of affairs. But the problem is not with the regress; the problem is with trying to hide unwelcome contents. Semantic theory is a lens that makes clear our semantical commitments, and that lens shows that kicking matters up to the next level does not mitigate our use of unwanted contents.

Suppose we try to play with the notion of self-ascription so that self-ascriptions aren't acts of volition in any sense but they just happen. They are facts. What is it to self-ascribe the property of being the god on the tallest mountain? The god on the tallest mountain stares down and cannot help but self-ascribe the property of being in the perceptual state that the god on the tallest mountain would have. That is, you don't have a theater of perceptions and then wonder if it belongs to you; you are just wired to know that it is yours. In this way the god on the tallest mountain has enough automatic self-attribution to deduce that it is the god on the tallest mountain.

In talking about these automatic self-attributions I am more or less describing a phenomenon that Shoemaker (1968) and Evans (1982) characterized as "immunity to error through misidentification."[12] For example, I can't be wrong about a self-attribution of pain.

Does this provide a way out? Let's imagine that the god on the coldest mountain is known to have migraine headaches and the god on the tallest mountain has none. Both gods insist that they are self-attributing the property of being the god on the coldest mountain, but the immunity to error through misidentification tells us that one of those gods is

---

[12] See Pryor (1999) for a detailed discussion of kinds of error through misidentification.

wrong. Only the god on the coldest mountain can self-attribute headaches, and this is enough information to deduce that he is the god on the coldest mountain.

(20)   My self-attribution of being the god on the coldest mountain is true iff I'm self-attributing being the god on the coldest mountain, and this attribution is immune to error through misidentification.

If the god on the tallest mountain tries to utter this T-sentence we can say there is a presupposition failure—that god isn't making such a self-attribution, nor could it. If Evans is right, the gods might also be immune to some forms of proprioceptive error. One god has the proprioceptive experience of throwing down lightning bolts and can't be wrong about its doing so.

One problem with this strategy is that we can revise the two-gods example so that the gods are distinguished only by properties that *can* be misidentified. Imagine, for example, that they live on opposite sides of a very boring world, on phenomenologically equivalent mountains. One mountain has a piece of diamond at its core and the other does not. Although the gods are omniscient with respect to nonperspectival properties, neither knows whether it is the god on the mountain with a diamond at its core.

But there is a bigger problem. Even if the gods boast experiences that are immune to error through misidentification, we are still talking about the correctness of these attributions. Even if the god on the coldest mountain can't be wrong about its headaches or its throwing lightning bolts, there is a propositional truth doing the work—not propositional in Lewis's sense (e.g. a set of possible worlds) but rather a proposition more akin to a Russellian proposition. Such a proposition might be a structured object consisting of ordered contents. On my view, some of those contents will be perspectival.

At one point Lewis (p. 536) strikes an ecumenical note regarding sentential or propositional accounts of content.

Some philosophers would favor sentential objects, drawn either from natural language or from some hypothetical language of thought. Others would favor sentence meanings, entities enough like sentences to have syntactic structure and indexicality. If you are one of these persuasions, my advice to you is by no means new: do not limit yourself to complete, closed, nonindexical sentences or meanings. Be prepared to use predicates, open sentences, indexical sentences, or meanings thereof—something that can be taken to express properties rather than propositions.

Lewis can only be so ecumenical here, however. He can afford to be forgiving of those of us who have sentential accounts of propositions or Russellian accounts of propositions, but what he cannot countenance are perspectival contents themselves. The game is to keep the self-attribution out of the semantics proper, for that entails a metaphysical commitment to perspectival contents. The semantics can introduce contents all it wants—it can even introduce properties construed as centered propositions or hyperintensional objects of some sort, but the self-attribution part needs to happen elsewhere.

The game is fairly clear. But is the game rigged? Is it a cheat? What exactly does it come to, to self-attribute a property or to self-satisfy an open sentence? In the case of the open sentence it is pretty clear what is amiss. If self-attribution is a cognitive act of some form one is in effect saying "I hereby assert that I satisfy this open sentence." The gloss in the property case can't be much different. I assert that I, myself, satisfy this property. Or, I hereby ascribe this property to myself.

These are all ways of describing what the act of self-ascription comes to. And we need to know what self-ascription comes to because we need to know what Lewis is talking about. Lewis knew that we needed to know this, so he told us. In language. And given that the words he used to describe what happens were meaningful, there must be a semantics for the language that he used to describe what happens. And here is the thing: Every description that Lewis used—every description that any of us would use to get the point across—is fraught with perspectival content.

Just to highlight the point, we can put it this way: if any of these self-attributions or ascriptions or satisfyings are to be true, then we shall want to give a semantics and when we do, some perspectival content seems to be necessary to give the truth conditions.

You might defend Lewis like this: Sure, we can talk about self-attribution in the meta-language, but we treat that exactly the way we treated it in the object language. When in the meta-language I say I am self-attributing a property, I am self-attributing the property of self-attributing a property. This defense, however, is problematic. The property of self-attributing can't have perspectival content built into it. It has to be a safely nonperspectival property. This means, among other things, that the property can't be built out of perspectival properties.

Furthermore, this meta-metalinguistic account would have its own semantics and the semantics would never result in a level with a perspectival property. It would be self-attribution all the way up.

I have to say that I'm suspicious of a theory that is forever kicking the meaning up a level, and frankly it seems counter to an argument given by Lewis (1972). In that paper ("General Semantics") Lewis argued that you couldn't account for the meaning of a sentence in a purely syntactic language of thought (he called it 'Markerese'), because that in turn would stand in need of interpretation. The target of that criticism might have responded "fine, we give the meaning of the language of thought in a language of thought for the language of thought, and on we go. It's languages of thought all the way up." I had always thought that the moral of Lewis's story was that to be interpreted, language had to be anchored in the world. Infinite regresses hardly seem like a solid anchoring. In the case of self-attribution I feel I am never being told what the analysis comes to. I'm being asked to keep running up the ladder.

One wonders. If this kick-it-upstairs strategy actually works for perspectival contents is it good for all contents? Suppose we didn't like thermodynamic properties. We could easily say we aren't referring to such things; we are simply speaking thermodynamically about systems. Maybe we don't like objects like sets. Well, then we can say we are speaking set-theoretically without ontological commitment. In fact, why not say that everything we say is just a *facon de parler* and be done with it? This has, of course, been proposed by "quietists" like Horwich (1990). As much as I am not a fan of quietism, I am even less a fan of *selective* quietism.

There is something else amiss in the attempt to talk about the self-ascription of properties (or any contents). In contemporary generative linguistics, an infinitival is taken to be a clause that contains an unpronounced pronominal subject, typically indicated as PRO. So, for example, the linguistic structure of a sentence like 'I am self-attributing the property of being the god on the coldest mountain' would be something like the following.

(21) I am self-attributing [PRO being the god on the coldest mountain].

If this is right, there is a sense in which natural language doesn't allow you to self-attribute properties simpliciter. What it allows you to do is assert propositions in which you predicate things of yourself.[13] Lewis would want to deny this of course, but if PRO appears in every self-attribution it is impossible to avoid.

One feature of the unpronounced PRO subject in natural language is that it can be either *arbitrary PRO* (or PRO$_{arb}$ linked to no one in particular) or it can be the subject of control (in which case, in the example, it would be linked to a syntactically specified individual). Some verbs induce what is called obligatory control. 'Regret' is a case in point.

(22)   Max regrets [PRO being a shabby pedagogue].

PRO has to be controlled by 'Max'. Notice that this is stronger than saying PRO stands in for 'Max'. If Max sees a shabby pedagogue, not realizing he is seeing himself, he may regret that that fellow (he, Max) is a shabby pedagogue, but we cannot, in that case, express Max's regret by saying 'Max regrets being a shabby pedagogue'. Obligatory (controlled) PRO is one device that natural language has for expressing perspectival properties from a third person perspectival position. And here is the thing about predicates like 'self-ascribe': They would call for control of PRO not arbitrary PRO.

There are, by the linguistics textbooks, five tests for something being under obligatory control of PRO. The first test is that PRO must have an antecedent, as in example (23), where the star (*) indicates ungrammaticality.

(23)   *It was expected **PRO** to shave himself.

The problem here is that 'It' is not an antecedent (it is a pleonastic pronoun, like that used in 'It is raining'). The self-ascription construction shares this property.

(23')   *It was expected **PRO** to self-ascribe being the god on the coldest mountain.

Second, in English the antecedent for PRO must be local. It cannot be distant (for example outside of the immediate clause containing PRO).[14]

---

[13] You can even see this in the etymology of ascribe—"to write." So you are, to some extent, not gluing yourself to a property but rather writing of yourself as having a property, or, to put it another way, predicating something of yourself.

[14] This rule does not hold in all languages. Scandinavian languages would be an exception here.

(24)   *John thinks that it was expected **PRO** to shave himself.

This appears to be the case in the self-ascription construction as well.

(24')   *Thor thinks it was expected **PRO** to self-ascribe being the god on the coldest mountain.

Third, PRO must be c-commanded by its antecedent. This means that in the syntax of natural language, PRO must stand in a particular geometric relation to its antecedent in the linguistic structure. If you think of the syntactic structure as being a downward branching tree, then the relation between the antecedent and PRO must be roughly this: Go up one node in the tree; everything below that node is c-commanded by the antecedent.[15]

(25)   *John's campaign expects **PRO** to shave himself.

This can only have the weird sense of the campaign (not John) doing the self-ascription. The reason 'John' does not c-command PRO is that if you move up the tree one node from John you only get to the noun phrase 'John's campaign', which would thus be the limit of the c-command domain for 'John'. So, what happens in the self-ascription construction? We get a similar effect.

(25')   *Thor's campaign expects to self-ascribe being the god on the coldest mountain.

The fourth test is that under VP ellipsis, PRO can only be construed with a sloppy reading. The best way to explain this is by giving the example.

(26)   John expects **PRO** to win and Bill does too.

This only has the sense in which Bill expects Bill to win, and not the sense in which Bill expects John to win. It is called "sloppy" identity because when the ellipsed VP is reconstructed it doesn't pull along 'John to win', but allows the expected winner to shift to whoever the reconstructed VP is predicated of (in this case Bill). What happens when we extend this test to the self-ascription case?

(26')   Odin expects to self-ascribe PRO being the god on the coldest mountain and Thor does too.

---

[15] This is the definition from Reinhart (1976). Subsequent definitions do not differ in ways that affect the facts we are interested in.

As is expected with obligatory control, we have a case of sloppy identity—Thor too expects to self-ascribe being the god on the coldest mountain.

Fifth and finally, obligatorily controlled PRO may not have split antecedents. Again, the best way to explain this is via an example.[16]

(27) *Fred$_i$ told Barney$_j$ **PRO**$_{i+j}$ to wash themselves/each other.

PRO cannot have both Fred and Barney as antecedents in this case. Similarly for Odin and Thor in (27').

(27') *Odin$_i$ told Thor$_j$ PRO$_{i+j}$ to self-ascribe PRO$_{i+j}$ being the gods on the coldest mountain.

The construction scores five out of five in tests for the presence of an obligatory PRO construction. I conclude that we have a canonical case of a mandatorily controlled PRO element—in effect the principal device our language has for expressing perspectival contents from third person perspectival positions. To put it another way, closer examination of the language of self-ascription suggests that it always involves propositional structures having perspectival contents.

To be sure, there have been proposals that avoid propositional accounts of infinitival clauses—Gennaro Chierchia's (1984) dissertation for example—but thirty-four years later there has been plenty of development of linguistic theory and the PRO analysis of gerunds and infinitives is not only deeply sedimented into linguistic theory, but is intertwined with some of the deepest and most fundamental principles. The PRO analyses of these constructions are canonical.

Let's recap this section, because I don't want to lose the forest for the trees. The idea is that if we try to cash out perspectival contents as the self-attribution of nonperspectival contents, we can rightly ask what we are being instructed to do. But the problem is that any such attempt to articulate what is to be done (for example, to self-ascribe the property of being the god on the coldest mountain) is an instruction that has a syntax and semantics, and by the doctrine of Semantic Accountability, we cannot duck this. On inspection, there is strong linguistic evidence that any attempt to articulate some self-attribution relation amounts to a

---

[16] This example is from Hornstein (1999: 73).

disguised version of a propositional structure ascribing perspectival content. It thus appears that the attempt to duck perspectivalism has failed.

All of this has been critical of Lewis, but none of it touches the deep point in Lewis' paper, which is that *de dicto* and *de re* knowledge is a species of *de se* knowledge. This point seems spot on to me.

I've already alluded to cases where we might think the *de se* intrudes even in cases of *de dicto* utterances. Cases of quantifier domain restriction arguably get cashed out in terms of indexical (perspectival elements). So consider (28).

(28)   There is a book on the table.

There is more than one book and one table in the world; we can agree on this. The question is, how does the domain get fixed? One possible answer is that the domain is fixed by perspectival contents, so that what we are saying is that the book in *our* domain is on the table in *our* domain, or, if you prefer, *this* domain.

If this sounds forced, consider the difficulty of coming up with an indexical-free description that can do the same job. We can't say "the table in the common ground" because the relevant common ground is *our* current common ground. The description has to be something on the order of the common ground shared by Peter Ludlow and his interlocutor at time such-and-such and Cartesian coordinates such-and-such. But even this is problematic. Our world does not come tagged with Cartesian coordinates. We would have to index the world to the coordinates, which is to say we would have to index a place (stipulated by an indexical) to a coordinate position (say the intersection of the X, Y, and Z axes).

What gets done for place has to be done for time as well. There are many clocks in the world. We have to stipulate (by use of an indexical) one of those clocks, or some group of clocks of which one is representative, as the relevant measures of time.

Even the most general scientific claim has to have indexical content. On Lewis's picture, you have to self-locate yourself in a set of centered possible worlds. But we don't need possible worlds to make this point. Suppose we had a perfect scientific theory laid out in exquisite detail. We could marvel at it all day long and understand perfectly well the predictions it made, but there is one critical piece of information we need to understand that it is a scientific theory—we need to know that it is the theory of *our* world!

Having a scientific theory without the use of perspectival contents to anchor it (at least in the most general sense of knowing it is a theory for our world) is like having a perfect map without knowing it is a map for the territory where we stand. We need to know that it is a map for *this* place.

4.4 Kaplanian Character and Its Deployment

In the previous section we saw the limitation of David Lewis' account of the *de se* (and thus perspectival content). Would we fare any better with the theory of indexicals offered by David Kaplan in his work on demonstratives and indexicals? As we will see in this section, Kaplan's theory comes up short in a way that is similar to the way in which Lewis's proposal does. He moves the indexical content out of the semantics proper, and (as we will see) must ultimately lean on an application or use theory to do the heavy lifting, shifting the perspectival content elsewhere but not eliminating it.

4.4.1 Character and its application

Here is the idea. Kaplan's theory differs from token reflexive semantics for indexicals in that it is a theory of expression-type meaning rather than a theory of utterance meaning. That is to say, it is not the utterance that is true or false, it is the sentence type—construed as an abstract object. This helps Kaplan avoid some problems that afflict token indexical theories (problems we examined in Section 4.1). In particular it avoids any problems involving the modal profile of the semantic contents, while at the same time affording an account of cognitive significance—not in the semantic content, but in what Kaplan calls the "linguistic meaning" of the sentence.

As we will see, however, this move to abstract expression types comes at a cost, which is that when we consider the actual deployment of indexical expressions (utterances) it will leave us short of our goal, for we need some way to hook up those abstract rules of interpretation with the world. To put it another way, if we think of Kaplan's semantics for indexicals as expressing interpretive norms, then we need some story about the application of those norms in the production and comprehension of individual utterances.[17] And it is here, I submit, that the perspectival content will be snuck in.

This point is perhaps obscure, so some more detailed exposition is called for. I'll begin with a review of Kaplan's theory of demonstratives and then bend back around to my objection.

The guts of Kaplan's theory is to distinguish referential content and character. To illustrate the difference consider the following sentence.

(29)   I am hungry.

The character of 'I'—the linguistic meaning—is a function from contexts to individuals, where a context is an agent, a time, and a location. If you take the meaning of 'I' and place it in different contexts it will yield different contents—perhaps me in a context where I am the agent and you in a context in which you are the agent. The "content" or what we might call the semantic content (Perry has called it the "official content") would be the individual picked out in a context. So, for example, if I, Peter Ludlow, utter (29) at a time t, then the content is that Peter Ludlow is hungry at time t.

As I said earlier, the move to an expression-type-based analysis avoids the troubles that token reflexive theories had with the modal profile of the sentence. The character of an indexical like 'I', for example (something we might gloss as 'the speaker of S'), never makes it into the semantic content. The only apparent cost is rejecting the Fregean idea that thoughts are composed of senses (they are presumably just Russellian propositions). The theory is elegant, and an impressive philosophical achievement. However, as noted earlier, there is something missing in the story.

The problem becomes apparent when we put this theory in action. Suppose, speaking to a friend, I utter the sentence 'You are looking prosperous'. With knowledge of Kaplan's theory I know quite a bit about this sentence. I know by virtue of the character that the claim is being made of the addressee. I also know that the context will fix the referent of the indexical 'You', and I know the context will also fix the time t at which looking prosperous holds. The question is, however, how do I know that the rule applies to me the speaker in this moment or for that matter, that it applies to *this utterance* that just happened? Moreover, I know that the context fixes the reference of the indexical

---

[17] You might balk at thinking of the semantics as expressing norms. We will get to that concern shortly.

and the time, but *which* context? Notice it is cheating to say 'my context' or 'our context' or 'the current context' or 'the local context'. Furthermore, even if I knew which context is to do the fixing of the referent, how do I know the admonition to make these connections is an admonition *for me*? That is, *if* we think of Kaplan's theory as a kind of normative rule, then, as noted in the Introduction and Chapter 1, doesn't its being a norm for me require perspectival content as it does with all other normative rules?

There is a lot to unpack here, but let's take the temporal case just to begin. As I am working at my desk someone rushes into my office and utters 'The meeting is now!'. Following Kaplan, I know that for the expression type 'The meeting is now', the character of 'now' (the expression type) is going to take us from a context (type of context) to a particular time (time type, presumably). But does that apply to the utterance I just heard? I know it applies to *instances* of the expression type, but I need to know that *that* utterance was such an instance. This isn't an issue about the ancient problem of participation or the relation between types and tokens. It might be trivial to identify instances (utterances) of an expression type, but it is only trivial given the identification of a particular utterance. That is, perhaps I can tell you for a given token whether it is an instance of a type, but you first have to identify the token (that token, or this token, for example) before I can say whether *it* is a token of a particular type.

I also need to know that the rule for interpreting the indexical 'now' *applies* to that utterance. How is this a different problem? We can imagine a theory of expression types in which expression types come with their tokens attached (think of a type as being a collection of tokens, for example). We can also imagine that the collection of tokens is ordered, with the most recent token being at the top of the stack and thus made salient. In this case perhaps the identification of the applicable token is trivial, but I need more than a rule and a salient token. I need to know that the rule is applicable to *that* salient token.[18]

---

[18] You might be wondering why the rule isn't simply a matter of universal instantiation. Why does it have to be understood normatively? We will get to that idea in the next section, but peeking ahead the idea is that even systems that are hardwired to operate in a particular way require perspectival contents. This also follows from more general facts about the perspectival nature of computation and information states (as we will see in Chapter 5).

This isn't just a problem for the token. Even if there was some nonperspectival way to identify a salient utterance token and even if I knew the rule applied to that token, there remains the question of whether the rule for interpreting indexicals applies *to me*. This is the point from the Introduction and Chapter 1 about me needing to know that something is a rule *for me*. Another way to put it: How do I know that *I* am guided by or that it is a rule that *I* ought to apply to salient tokens of speech (salient to me)?

The questions don't end there. On Kaplan's theory the character of 'now' is a function from a context to a time. But which context is relevant here? One is tempted to say, "my current context" or "this context" or something of that nature, but obviously this won't do. This is cheating by using indexical content to identify the context.

It doesn't help to unpack the context as a triple of person, time, and place, because then I am entitled to ask which person (me, presumably), which time (now), and which place (here). Fixing each component of the context leans on perspectival contents.

Kaplan seems to have anticipated this argument in a passage quoted earlier.

The perceptive reader will have noticed that the conclusions of the sloppy thinker regarding the pure indexical 'I' are not unlike those of the Fregean regarding true demonstratives. The sloppy thinker has adopted a *demonstrative theory of indexicals*: 'I' is synonymous with 'this person' [along with the appropriate *subjective* demonstration], etc. Like the Fregean, the sloppy thinker errs in believing that the sense of the demonstration is the sense of the indexical, but the sloppy thinker commits an additional error in believing that such senses are in any way necessarily associated with uses of pure indexicals. The slide from privileged perspective to privileged picture is the sloppy thinker's original sin. Only one who is located in the exact center of the Sahara Desert is entitled to refer to that place as 'here', but aside from that, the place may present no distinguishing features.

(534–5)

Earlier we took this passage to be a claim that Kaplan's "sloppy thinker" supposes that sense involves a privileged picture, and we noted that perspectival theories of indexicals need not concern themselves with privileged pictures at all—in fact why would they? But perhaps Kaplan is here also objecting to the idea that indexical sense must involve (or just be) some form of indexical reference. But that isn't what is being claimed here. I am not claiming that the theory of linguistic meaning for indexicals offered by Kaplan is synonymous with a story involving demonstratives (and subjective demonstrations). What I am claiming is that the *application* of the theory—putting it to work in the interpretation of individual utterances—relies upon demonstratives and indexical, which is to say perspectival, content. This is no more remarkable than the claim, made by Velleman (2006), that moral laws involve such content.

To be sure, Kaplan can keep the indexical reference (this utterance, rule for me, etc.) out of the semantics for a significant fragment of English, but he can't keep it out of the language used in the application of the theory of indexicals. And this is the problem. We have this beautiful and elegant theory of indexicals and demonstratives, but we need to be able to deploy it, both for the production and comprehension of meaningful speech. But deploying it seems to require understanding how it is to be applied by me, here, and now, and to what.

Here is another way to put the problem. If Kaplan's account of character is to be applied by some agent for the comprehension of a particular utterance of an indexical 'I', then the character of 'I' is presumably deployed as a rule for that act of interpretation. But if it is a rule, then it is a normative rule (at a minimum an individual norm) and as we have seen, normative rule following too relies upon first person perspectival properties.

4.4.2 Wittgenstein to the rescue?

Perhaps the solution for the Kaplanian is to take a leaf from the later Wittgenstein and reject the idea of normative rule following (or at least tame it). Perhaps we just act in accord with community practices. It is part of our form of life. In that case, we don't actually follow a rule in applying the rule for indexical interpretation to particular utterances. We just do it, but in so doing we act in accord with our community's linguistic practices.

If we exorcise the bit about first person rule following, then maybe we can eliminate the need to introduce indexical reference to utterances and individuals and times and places in the application/use of the theory.

This may be a bit of wishful thinking for the Kaplanian that wants to go down this route. Even if Wittgenstein's rule-following argument holds up (and I don't think it does—see below) it is hard for me to see how any of this allows us to dispense with perspectival contents. If I'm to act in a way consistent with some rule I am acting in accord with *my* linguistic community, for example. Forms of life, too, would seem to be perspectival, in that my form of life depends upon *my* surrounds. I am acting in accord with a form of life for *my* community or *my* task or some such thing.

These remarks cut to Wittgenstein's positive proposal, and the question of whether it avoids the need for perspectival contents (I don't think it does). As we will see, when we follow Wittgenstein and Kripke down the rabbit hole that is their negative argument we will see just how deep perspectival content runs.

Before I dig into the issue of Wittgensteinian rule-following arguments, we should probably get clear on the exact nature of the rule following we are talking about when we think about using character as a rule. Using character isn't garden-variety conscious rule following; it would have to be unconscious for the most part, as we use indexicals without reflection for the most part. And the question is, how can there be unconscious rule following?

I don't think there is anything peculiar at all about being normatively guided without having conscious access to this normative guidance. In Ludlow (2011) I talked about this phenomenon in the context of our being normatively guided by linguistic rules to which we do not have conscious access. But I also noted that these cases are also attested to in the case of ethics.

Railton (2006) and Arpaly (2003) have both drawn attention to what I will call *The Huck Finn case*. As the story goes, while traveling on the Mississippi with the escaped slave Jim, Huck has the opportunity to turn Jim in at some point, but does not do so. He believes that turning in Jim is the right thing to do, as Jim is legally someone's property, but Huck just cannot do it. On Railton and Arpaly's view, Jim consciously flouts a public rule (turn in escaped slaves) but is still normatively guided by an unconscious rule—treat persons as ends in themselves perhaps.

How does this work? How can normative guidance be unconscious? Railton proposed the following:

Unconscious rule following (Railton): Agent A's conduct C is guided by the norm N only if C is a manifestation of A's disposition to act in a way conducive to compliance with N, such that N plays a regulative role in A's C-ing, where this involves some disposition on A's part to notice failures to comply with N, to feel discomfort when this occurs, and to exert effort to establish conformity with N *even when* the departure from N is unsanctioned and nonconsequential.

What this means is that there is some (unconscious) representation of a normative rule, and this rule plays a regulative role in the agent's behavior. In particular, failure to comply with the rule leads to a feeling of "discomfit" by the agent, and a resulting attempt to correct her behavior so as to avoid discomfit. In other words, the rule serves as a kind of set point regulator, which will set off an alarm bell of discomfit when the agent doesn't comply. This is the case even when the agent faces no external sanction for violating the rule.

In the case of Huck, it works like this. Huck has an underlying representation of a rule (let's say, *show respect for persons*). Consciously, he acknowledges other norms (escaped slaves should be returned), but flouting the unconscious rule (or contemplating doing so) leads to discomfit. Huck adjusts his behavior so as to avoid this discomfit. He thus does not turn in Jim.

In Ludlow (2011) I extended this analysis to the case of individual linguistic norms. To illustrate, consider the case from Lawler (discussed earlier) of the agent who anticipates a violation of a Ross Constraint (also called the *Complex Noun Phrase Constraint* and *Subjacency*) but acts so as to avoid doing so. In this case, the discomfit is perhaps minimal, but it is certainly possible to say that the agent is not for (is Against!) violating the constraint.

Now, getting back to Kaplan, the application of Kaplan's theory of demonstratives to particular utterances would work in a similar way. There is a norm involved: The utterance should comply with the character of the word 'I' or 'You' etc., as given in Kaplan (1977, 1979, 1990). Although we may not be conscious of such a norm, we nevertheless represent such a rule and it plays a regulative role in our behavior in the moment.

Of course, if it is a normative rule, it is a normative rule *for me*. In acting in compliance with the rule I am doing precisely that: *I* am acting so as to bring myself in conformity with the rule so as to avoid *my* discomfit, even though *I* will not be sanctioned if *I* fail to do so.

But what about the Wittgensteinian argument against rule following? As I argued in Ludlow (2011), Wittgenstein—or at least the Kripke (1982) version—has several points of attack, and I maintained that none of them are particularly compelling. Two of the points of attack involve questions that are worth consideration here.

i) The normativity question
ii) The determination question

Here is the normativity question: What is the fact that makes it true that an agent is rule guided? Kripke, in a frequently cited passage, puts the point like this.

What is the relation of this supposition [the supposition that I mean addition by "+"] to the question how I will respond to the problem '68 + 57'? The dispositionalist gives a *descriptive* answer of this relation: if '+' meant addition, then I will answer '125'. But this is not the proper account of the relation, which is *normative*, not descriptive. The point is *not* that, if I meant addition by '+', then I will answer '125', but if intend to accord with my past meaning of '+', I *should* answer '125'. (1982: 37)

The question might be a stopper for some accounts of normativity, but let's consider the Railton proposal and see how it holds up. On that proposed account of normative action someone might act in a way consistent with the rule, but not be rule guided. That is because had they failed to follow the rule for some reason they would not have felt discomfit for having done so. This is the extra ingredient to rule following that makes rule following more than a disposition to act in a way conducive to compliance with a rule.

But the Wittgensteinian has a second argument, which, I believe, cuts straight to the question of whether there is a fact of the matter about there being an unconscious representation of the underlying rule N. Railton helped himself to that, but on the basis of what?

One natural response is to say that obviously there *is* a fact of the matter whether an agent represents a rule N, and that is whether N corresponds to a data structure in the computational state that the agent is in. Here is how Fodor (1975) expresses the idea:

The physics of the machine thus guarantees that the sequences of states and operations it runs through in the course of its computations respect the semantic constraints on formulae in its internal language. What takes the place of a truth definition for the machine language is simply the engineering principles which guarantee this correspondence. (66)

... it is worth mentioning that, whatever Wittgenstein proved, it cannot have been that it is impossible that a language should be private in whatever sense the machine language of a computer is, for there *are* such things as computers, and whatever is actual is possible. (68)

The problem is that Wittgenstein anticipates this move, and suggests it will not fly. Wittgenstein's idea is that there is no fact of the matter about the states of a computational system in isolation. It is just a pile of silicon, metals, and rare earth minerals unless we have some idea about the intentions of the programmer.[19] Here is how Kripke explains the response.

I cannot really insist that the values of the function are given by the machine. First, the machine is a finite object, accepting only finitely many numbers as input and yielding only finitely many as output—others are simply too big. Indefinitely many programs extend the actual finite behavior of the machine. Usually this is ignored because the designer of the machine intended it to fulfill just one program, but in the present context such an approach to the intentions of the designer simply gives the skeptic his wedge to interpret in a nonstandard way. (Indeed, the appeal to the designer's program makes the physical machine superfluous; only the program is relevant. The machine as physical object is of value only if the intended function can somehow be read off from the physical object alone).   (p. 34)

You might think that, no, we could open a sufficiently simple computer and study the logic gates of the computer and determine what it was programmed to do. But Wittgenstein (1991) anticipates this response too.

The machine as symbolizing its action: the action of a machine—I might say at first—seems to be there in it from the start. What does this mean?—If we know the machine, everything else, that is its movement, seems to be already completely determined.

We talk as if these parts could only move in this way, as if they could not do anything else. How is this—do we forget the possibility of their bending, breaking off, melting and so on?   (*Philosophical Investigations*, § 193)

Kripke (1982) develops this idea in more detail.

Actual machines can malfunction: through melting wires and slipping gears they may give the wrong answer. How is it determined when a malfunction occurs? By reference to the program of the machine, as intended by the designer, not simply by reference to the machine itself. Depending on the intent of the designer, any particular phenomenon may or may not count as a machine 'malfunction'. A programmer with suitable intentions may even have intended to make use of the fact that wires melt or gears slip, so that a machine that is 'malfunctioning' for me is behaving perfectly for him. Whether a machine ever malfunctions and, if so, when, is not a property of the machine itself as a physical object but is well defined only in terms of its program, as stipulated by its designer. Given the

---

[19] Of course Wittgenstein predated silicon chip computers; he spoke of mechanical machines, but same idea.

program, once again the physical object is superfluous for the purpose of determining what function is meant. (pp. 34–5)

At this point, the appeal to the physics of the system has come full circle. One cannot determine what program a system is executing until one is clear on whether it is functioning properly, but one cannot determine if the system is functioning properly until one has the program that the system is executing.

The point can be extended to any information-processing system or device, no matter how simple. Consider a simple toggle switch, for example. We might think that it clearly represents two distinct binary states, but does it? As Chomsky (pc) has observed, it might be designed to test finger strength up to a certain threshold, after which we are uninterested. Or perhaps it is a design flaw—the designer didn't foresee such strong fingers. Even for something that merely encodes a 1 or a 0, whether that is its function will depend upon the intentions of the designer.

One problem with this kind of skepticism is that, as I argued in Ludlow (2011), it can be extended to any system that relies on information-theoretic properties. In biology, this means that it could be used to raise doubts about coding sequences in DNA. If you hold an information-theoretic view of physics, it means the skepticism can be pushed all the way down to the micro level.

But there is another problem with the skeptical argument. It really doesn't matter if we don't know what the anchoring conditions are for rule following. All that really matters is that there *be* such anchoring conditions. This is a point that Soames (1997) addresses, in the context of a discussion of the rule for addition.

Would the result change if we enlarged the set of potential meaning-determining truths still further to include not only all truths about my dispositions to verbal behavior, but also all truths about (i) the internal physical states of my brain, (ii) my causal and historical relationships to things in my environment, (iii) my (nonintentionally characterized) interactions with other members of my linguistic community, (iv) their dispositions to verbal behavior, and so on? Is there a possible world in which someone conforms to all those facts—precisely the facts that characterize me in the actual world—and yet that person does not mean anything by '+'?

I think not. Given my conviction that in the past I did mean addition by '+', and given also my conviction that if there are intentional facts, then they don't float free of everything else, I am confident that there is no such world. Although

I cannot identify the smallest set of nonintensional facts about me in the actual world on which meaning facts supervene, I am confident that they do supervene. Why shouldn't I be?   (p. 229)

I believe that this argument is spot on, but there is also a second argument not taken up by Soames: Why do we have to restrict ourselves to nonintentional facts? Let's step back a bit and consider the rule-following argument in broader form—here as reconstructed by Soames.

P_1)   If in the past there was a fact about what I meant by '+', in particular, if there was a fact that I meant addition by '+', then either:

(i)   this fact was determined by nonintentional facts of such-and-such kinds—facts about my past calculations using '+', the rules or algorithms I followed in doing calculations involving '+', my past dispositions to respond to questions 'What is $\underline{n}$ + $\underline{m}$?', the totality of my past dispositions to verbal behavior involving '+' etc.

or

(ii)   the fact that I meant addition by '+' was a primitive fact, not determined by nonintentional facts.

P_2)   Nonintentional facts of type (i) did not determine that I meant addition (or anything else) by '+'.

P_3)   What I meant by '+' was not a primitive fact.

C_1)   Thus, in the past there was no fact that I meant addition (or anything else) by '+'.

C_2)   By parity of reasoning, there never was a fact about what I, or anyone else, meant by any word; *ditto* for the present.

So far we have been going after premise P_2, but what about premise P_3? Why should it be given a pass here? I understand the resistance to primitive intentional facts, but a lot of the resistance extrudes from the fact that intentional facts involve perspectival contents. But now, as we are in the middle of a defense of perspectival contents, can we not help ourselves to such here? Can't rule following itself be grounded in primitive, perspectival contents?

We have been swimming in deep waters for a while in this chapter, but the waters are about to get even deeper. In the Introduction and Chapter 1 we explored a number of areas in which perspectival properties were called upon—the theory of human action and emotion, perception, and normative action. But now I want to suggest that even the question of the computational state we are in rests upon a perspectival fact. Or, to put it another way, computational states of physical systems are perspectival states!

In the next chapter I will go into some detail about the perspectival nature of computational states (and information states) but before we do that there is a puzzle that we want to unravel, and it relates to premise P_3 in Soames's reconstruction of the rule-following argument. The puzzle is this: How could an agent possibly have a priori knowledge of their computational states?

To animate this puzzle, let's return to the case of Huck Finn and the person who senses an oncoming violation of a Ross Constraint. In such cases, the agents in question aren't even aware that they are acting on the rule of respect for persons or the complex noun phrase constraint. So how could they have a priori knowledge of these rules?

Following considerations raised in Chapter 3, it would seem to be the case (on my view) that we all can be reliable theorists of systems of unknown origin. If we think of programs as being ways for programmers to understand and control the actions of the systems they design, we cede authority to the programmer in part because she knows what the system is designed to do and because she is responsible for the ability of others to understand and control the system. But in the case of individuals, who have no known programmers, all of us are potential theorists of the design of the system.

So what happens when we attribute a design or a program to an individual, who rejects it, or claims to be unaware of it? Doesn't the agent we are reporting on get to call the shots on how her mental life is described? And if not wouldn't this entail that she no longer has a priori access to her mental life? And wouldn't this undermine any attempt to reject premise P_3 of the skeptical argument?

The answer to this series of questions tracks controversies surrounding the alleged incompatibility of external content and first person/a priori knowledge of our mental states. A very brief review of that literature may be in order. In that literature (surveyed in Ludlow and Martin (1998)), we are asked to consider cases in which an agent is unwittingly shifted between Earth and Putnam and Burge's Twin Earth. Our unsuspecting agent is later informed of switches having taken place. Does the agent know, for example, whether she was having water thoughts or twin-water thoughts? Presumably not, but she nevertheless still has access to her thoughts, albeit not under all descriptions. She knew she was having *that* thought, which, as it turns out, was a water thought, not a twin-water thought.

How then does this relate to the question of unconscious rule following? The idea is that just as in the case of externalist content, one has access to the content, but not under a robust description of that content; here too one does have conscious access to the rule, but not access under a robust description of that rule. So, for example, Huck has access to the rule only under the description of "this nagging sense that this isn't the thing to do." The agent who sees the impending Ross Constraint violation does not recognize the rule under the descriptions 'Ross Constraint', or 'Complex Noun Phrase Constraint', or 'Subjacency', but only under the description "this sense that this isn't the thing to say." To put it another way, there is a rule N, which the agents have a priori access to, but only under certain (very minimal, indexical) descriptions.

Now it might be objected that rules are a different matter from contents because the structure of a rule is everything, but this objection isn't right. Looking at it from the perspective of cognitive science, the rules that we cognize are objects of empirical investigation. So, just as we can investigate the meaning content of a word like 'water' and come to learn that it consists in part of H_20, we can also empirically investigate the rule represented by and guiding Huck and we can learn that it involves respect for persons (even if Huck denies this).

But you might argue that this is not similar to the case of the computer programmer and the idea that she has a perspectival relation to the program, because she, after all, authored the program and was in a position to tell us exactly what the program was intended to do (even if it fails to do so, she can point to the coding errors or i/o errors that led to the failure).

However, this is a difference in appearance only. In the first place, the programmer can forget what she intended the program to do. Maybe she intended to build an adder but now believes she only wanted to build a quadder. So we can push back and ask what the programmer originally intended to build. But even here, the programmer can change her mind (or forget the goal) in the process of building the program.

So the question becomes, just how much access to the underlying rule N does an agent have, and does this access involve a kind of perspectival knowledge? I would say that the agent has quite a bit of access to the rule—not in the formal description of the rule, but in her grasp of the counterfactual possibilities for the application of the rule. We can ask Huck under what conditions he might turn in Jim. He might not be completely reliable on this score, but that isn't necessary. All we really need is for Huck to have some appreciation for the contours of the conditions under which he would or would not turn in Jim.

In the linguistic case, considering such counterfactual possibilities is the route that linguists take in reconstructing the rules being attributed to an agent. Indeed Ross's (1967) dissertation was an extended exercise in considering permutations of the complex noun phrase constraint and the conditions under which he, at least, would avoid apparent violations of that constraint. Agents have some a priori access to the linguistic rules that are normatively guiding for them—first in a kind of direct access to the rule itself, and second in a grasp of the possible conditions under which "that rule" would be in force (for example, would it make the example better or worse to leave off the resumptive pronoun?).

The agent has the capacity to know, with some reliability, the conditions under which she would act so as to be in compliance with N (not necessarily described in that way). The agent may not have a complete grasp of N, but this does not matter. The agent doesn't have a complete grasp of the future, nor of things spatially before her, nor of the modal space she inhabits. It stands to reason that she likewise would not have a complete grasp of the normative space she inhabits.

As we can see, this doesn't even rely on some subdoxastic or unconscious notion of intentions. The agent intends to act in compliance with the rule, but does not describe the intention this way. The agent rather describes it as an effort to avoid a feeling of discomfit.

This line of argumentation has acquired a long and deep nested structure, so let me walk us back out slowly. First, I see no reason to think that agents do not have a priori access to the rules they are acting upon, even if that a priori knowledge is partial, and on the level of the knowledge that Huck has when he says, "it just didn't feel right." This is enough to defeat premise P_3 of the rule-following argument.

Second, quite apart from the issue of a priori knowledge, there is the question of whether there are nonintentional facts that might ground the fact that an agent is following rule N. Again, if we separate the epistemological question from the metaphysical question, we have precious little reason to doubt that nonintentional facts ground the fact that our agent is following N.

Third, the agent is not merely acting consistently with the rule N and does not merely have a disposition to act in compliance with N, but is legitimately *guided* by the rule. Following Railton, we can say that the rule plays a regulative role in the agent's behavior.

Fourth, these unconscious rules can be seen to be perspectival properties; the rule N, however described by Huck, is understood by Huck as being a rule for him.

Low-level conclusion: There is no reason to doubt that there is unconscious normative guidance involving rules that are metaphysically grounded, but to which agents have some degree of first person/a priori access. In this access, although partial, the agent has a perspectival relation to those rules. The agent has only partial knowledge of such rules.

Next level up: In deploying the Kaplanian account of demonstratives to a particular use of a demonstrative (e.g. an expression like 'I'), an agent deploys the theory as a rule for the interpretation of a particular utterance. In this respect, Kaplan's account of the character of 'I' acts as our rule N, which is represented by the agent and plays a regulative role in the agent's use of demonstratives.

In this, there are two aspects of perspectival content being deployed. First, there is the role of N itself (here representing the character of 'I'), which is a perspectival content for that agent (it is a rule for her). Second, in applying the rule, perspectival contents are also deployed: the rule N applies to *this utterance* and *this context*, for example. In short, the application of the theory is replete with perspectival content. Perhaps more than we recognized at the outset.

A lot of this argumentative structure leans on the perspectival nature of computation, however, and that is a topic that is subtle enough that it would serve us well to slow down and go over it in more detail. We will do this in the next chapter, where we will see that not only is computation perspectival in nature, but that the theory of information is as well.

5

Computation, Information, and Interperspectival Content

5.1 Computational States and Interperspectival Content

Kripke and Wittgenstein are not the only ones to stake out a skeptical claim about the nature of physical computers and other machines. Notoriously, Searle (1980, 1990) and Putnam (1988) argued that any physical system can instantiate any finite state computer program. Notoriously, Searle claimed that even a wall can instantiate a computer program like Wordstar. I can explain Searle's idea using a table, rather than a wall.

Let's imagine a simple rock lying on a wooden table. The idea is that this system can be used to perform computations of arbitrary complexity. Everything turns on how we think about the inputs and outputs to this computational system. Suppose that the input consists of my pushing the rock with my finger using a certain force and the output consists of the final position of the rock on the table. Then the syntactic states of the machine (here taken as the system including that table and my finger) and the force applied (to the rock) and the surface friction and irregularities of the rock and its final resting place on the table constitute the inputs and outputs. Hypothetically, there could be creatures for whom inputting by the appropriate finger movements and "reading" the final resting positions of the rock on the table would be simple. But it isn't simple for us. The problem is that we don't know how to properly encode the input, and we don't know how to read the output. It is not a computational system *for us*.

The example I just gave is not an instantiation of a Turing machine, but is rather a much more simple "finite state" machine. But we can jazz up our wooden table computer if we wish. We could have multiple programs based on multiple trajectories of the rock over surfaces of the table, and perhaps given some very fine carpentry tools, we could "program" our machine with slight changes in the surface of the table. We could even store programs by etching information into the side or a particular region of the table, which, let's say, could be extended indefinitely with additional wooden "leaves."

All of this having been said, Searle is probably wrong in saying that a table, as it is, instantiates *any* computer program. Or in any case, his account is overlooking a critical element in the nature of computation. The problem with the word-processing table is that it is not a computer *for us*, and it does not instantiate computer programs *for us*.

For us, doing computations with the table would be like trying to use a mechanical slide rule without any markings on the device. Someone who had memorized the positions of the markings on a slide rule and could mentally project them on the blank slide rule could perhaps do the calculations. To us observers, the person would just be moving a piece of wood. We could not know how to encode inputs or decode outputs. Perhaps, in the fullness of time, we would figure out the trick, but until we did it would not be a slide rule *for us*.

I submit that the "for us" part is critical, because whether or not something is a computer and if so, what it is computing depends upon us. In part, this is because whether something is information depends upon whether it is information for us (we will take this up in Section 5.2).

This would also be the case for natural systems, like DNA encoding of information in biology. The question is, who gets to call the shots on what information is being communicated in a biological system, and the answer is that *we* do. If it is information at all, it is information *for us*.

This might seem surprising because you might suppose that there are natural ways of reading the coding sequences and thereby understanding what their products will be. But the coding regions on a DNA molecule are not necessarily local. Spilianakis et al. (2005) showed that the control regions do not have to be close to the coding sequence on the linear molecule or even on the same chromosome (the coding sequences only come into close proximity in the nucleus). Kapranove et al. (2005) have shown that in some cases proteins can even be composed of exons from different chromosomes.

But here is the critical point. As Gerstein et al. (2007) argued, the definition of a gene is thus "a union of genomic sequences encoding a coherent set of potentially overlapping functional products." That is, the definition effectively categorizes genes by functional products, whether they be proteins or RNA, rather than specific DNA loci. And those functional properties, even when embedded in a complete theory of the organism or biology, or, for that matter, the ecology of the organism as well, depend upon our interests as theorists.[1]

Here we are running up against two claims that Chomsky has made about computation and natural systems. On Chomsky's view the skeptical arguments from Kripke, Wittgenstein, and others are in fact successful against computers. But, again on Chomsky's view, they are successful against computers because computers are artifacts and not natural systems. The skeptical arguments do not apply to natural systems like human biology and (crucially for Chomsky) the language faculty.

Chomsky's second idea is that while there are natural computational systems (DNA, the language faculty, etc.), those computational systems are nonintentional and aperspectival.

I've already argued in the previous chapter that the Kripke/Wittgenstein skepticism applies to natural systems as well as artifactual systems. Here, I want to focus on Chomsky's claim that the computations of cognitive science (and other natural systems) are nonintentional and aperspectival. I submit he is mistaken on this point.

I'll be drawing on an interpretation of Chomsky due to Collins (2007), and some background will be helpful here. Collins has suggested that a great deal of Chomsky interpretation has missed the mark here, and that much of Chomsky's philosophical writing can only be understood in the context of a nonintentional approach to the mechanisms of the language faculty. For example, Collins believes that many of us have missed the core point of Chomsky's (1959) review of Skinner's *Verbal Behavior*. On Collins' view, Chomsky was trying to show that Skinner was surreptitiously appealing to intentional facts, and he thus did not have a truly scientific theory of mind.

This might come as a surprise, because we often think of Skinner offering a mechanistic account of behavior and we think of Chomsky as

---

[1] This isn't to say that there would be no such properties had we not existed. The modal profile of the properties is fine.

providing an intentional alternative, but if Collins is right, Chomsky is actually trying to show that Skinner's behaviorism is inherently (if not obviously) leaning on the notion of intentions, and is thus unscientific. For example, at one point in his review, Chomsky draws on a claim by Skinner that "if we are shown a prized work of art and exclaim Beautiful!, the speed and energy of the response will not be lost on the owner." Chomsky is having none of this, noting "It does not appear totally obvious that in this case the way to impress the owner is to shriek Beautiful in a loud, high-pitched voice, repeatedly, and with no delay (high response strength). It may be equally effective to look at the picture silently (long delay) and then to murmur Beautiful in a soft, low-pitched voice (by definition, very low response strength)." Chomsky is often taken as making the case for the importance of intentions here, but if you read on you understand that to the contrary, Chomsky thinks Skinner's terminology is just an intentionality wolf in behaviorist clothing.

It is not unfair, I believe, to conclude from Skinner's discussion of response strength, the basic datum in functional analysis, that his extrapolation of the notion of probability can best be interpreted as, in effect, nothing more than a decision to use the word probability, with its favorable connotations of objectivity, as a cover term to paraphrase such low-status words as interest, intention, belief, and the like.

This anti-intentionalist conclusion is also consistent with *much* of what Chomsky has written. Consider, for example, the following.[2]

More generally, intentional phenomena relate to people and what they do as viewed from the standpoint of human interests and unreflective thought, and thus will not (so viewed) fall within naturalistic theory, which seeks to set such factors aside. Like falling bodies, or the heavens, or liquids, a "particular intentional phenomenon" may be associated with some amorphous region in a highly intricate and shifting space of human interests and concerns. But these are not appropriate concepts for naturalistic inquiry. . . . If "cognitive science" is taken to be concerned with intentional attribution, it may turn out to be an interesting pursuit (as literature is), but is not likely to provide explanatory theory or to be integrated into the natural sciences.   (2000: 22–3)

If this is the correct interpretation of Chomsky, then Chomsky is in effect making the claim for cognitive science that others have made for the

---

[2] I am grateful to Rey (2003) for identifying these passages.

basic sciences: perspectival properties have no place in a properly scientific theory of the world. In doing so, however, Chomsky has painted himself into a philosophical corner. There are two reasons for this.

First, from the very early days of generative linguistics, Chomsky has drawn a distinction between linguistic competence and linguistic performance, and throughout this period Chomsky has admitted linguistic judgments as probes into the nature of this competence (for example the judgment that 'colorless green ideas sleep furiously' is acceptable). But how are we to make sense of this distinction if linguistic competence does not involve some form of individual norms? In Ludlow (2011) I developed this normative take on linguistic competence, and made the case that it is at a minimum coherent. But what is the alternative?

One alternative is to hold that the distinction between competence and performance leans on a notion of normal vs. malfunctioning system. So, for example, a wire breaks, and our adder becomes a quadder—the system has malfunctioned.

But we have already seen from Kripke and Wittgenstein that this distinction is problematic, and (as I noted) Chomsky concedes that the distinction is problematic for an object like a computer, which is an artifact and the product of human intentions for Chomsky. But, Chomsky maintains, the same does not hold for natural (e.g. biological) systems in which there is an independent fact about whether the system is malfunctioning or not.

Computer models are often invoked to show that we have robust, hard-headed instances of the kind: psychology then studies software problems. That is a dubious move. Artifacts pose all kinds of questions that do not arise in the case of natural objects. Whether some object is a key or a table or a computer depends upon designer's intent, standard use, mode of interpretation, and so on. The same considerations arise when we ask whether the device is malfunctioning, following a rule, etc. There is no natural kind of normal case . . . Such questions do not arise in the study of organic molecules, the wings of chickens, the language faculty, or other natural objects.   (2000: 105)

The problem here, as we have already seen, is that natural system or no, Kripkean skepticism can apply to natural systems as well—including DNA. Yes, Chomsky is right that DNA encodes genetic information that will cause chickens to grow wings, but it is only *information* by virtue of the fact that we can recognize wings as a salient output. An alien scientist that has no concept of wings might come up with an entirely different story about the information states encoded in the chicken's DNA.[3] If the states identified by the creature are in principle opaque to us, then we can at best say that the creature is doing something analogous to what we do when we describe a natural information-processing system. We are better off saying the creature is engaged in some activity that will forever remain mysterious to us.

But this leads us to the second problem. Whether the system is natural or artifactual, if you describe it computationally you ipso facto describe it in a way that is inherently perspectival. To put it another way, Chomsky wants to describe the grammar as a "computational" system, but how could intentionality possibly be removed from such descriptions? Even the mathematical description of computation given in Turing's (1936) seminal paper is intentional throughout. There are read/write heads that read a square to see if there is a check in the square being read. Based on its state table and based on what it currently reads, the head may move to its right or to its left. It may write a check or erase a check. These are, of course, intentional actions.

These days we think of something being "computational" as a way of saying it is mechanical, and we complain that applying the concept of computation to intentional systems like the human mind/brain is a bad idea, but of course the talk of 'computers' was originally a metaphor, drawing on the persons who carried out computations. Computers were people. The theory of computation was conceived in intentionality, and it may well be that there is no way to exorcise intentionality from the theory of computation. And this is to say that there is no way to exorcise perspectival properties from the theory.

Chomsky could back away from thinking of the theory of grammar as involving computations understood literally—and could say the talk of computation is metaphorical, but metaphorical for what? If Chomsky currently thinks of recursion as being the defining feature of the human language faculty (Universal Grammar) how is that to be understood if it is not to be understood computationally?

---

[3] Here we are being generous in saying the alien is attributing *information* states to the creature. It may be that information is an inherently human-centric concept, no matter how closely the conceptual makeup of the creature overlaps with ours. As a reader points out, we might also want to be stingy about attributing a truth predicate to the creature, unless we want to relativize the truth predicate here. I personally would choose being stingy.

Whatever difficulties Chomsky may have landed himself in vis-à-vis the theory of grammar, you might think that a relatively simpler task, like deploying Kaplan's theory of indexicals to individual utterances of those indexicals, could be handled in a straightforwardly nonintentional, non-normative, noncomputational way. We are simply built to deploy the characters as we do. So, for example, you don't think, "here is the theory of meaning, I must deploy it." You just deploy it without aid of any perspectival properties.

To explain this idea, let's imagine a creature that is exceedingly simple, and only has a couple of behaviors: It can hide from predators, it can feed, and it can signal to others of its kind that they are under threat from predators.

Suppose the creature is wired up in the following way: Certain perceptual input is intuitively local, but the creature does not represent it as "local." Let's say that the local input goes straight into a folder marked "X" (not marked "me," just "X"). The X folder is then connected to a behavioral system. Certain perceptual input in folder X leads the creature to hide. Certain perceptual input leads the creature to feed. Other distal input involving other creatures of its kind goes into other folders. Information in those folders will trigger other behaviors: warnings, invitations to feed, etc.

Now, you might be inclined to say "exactly, we have explained the creature's behavior without any recourse to perspectival contents." But have we?

We can label the critical folder "X", or not label it at all, but clearly that is the folder in which the creature encodes its first person knowledge. If, for example, "predator" is recorded in the folder that effectively means that a predator is in the creature's proximity and it must act so as to save itself.

Now you might reply that there is nothing in the creature's representational system that commits us to this, but the point was not for the creature to represent this information using expressions like the English word 'I'. In fact, as I stated earlier, following the Larson and Ludlow strategy for knowledge attribution (Section 3.4), a speaker and hearer may truthfully describe the mental life of this creature by saying things like "It knows itself to be in danger; it will try to hide now." This description quite successfully satisfies the goals we have in ascribing beliefs to the creature and, as I said, the description is true.[4]

You might object at this point that the description is not true at all. There is no special first person pronoun, or even any predicates being deployed by the creature. It simply perceived a stimulus, and it hid. However, the *best* description is the one that best describes the behavior of the creature relative to our interests. Perhaps we are indifferent to the creature and its life and whether or not it will survive. In that case any description will do. But suppose we have designed the creature specifically to survive. In that case, it is natural to think of its "program" as encoding perspectival contents. It doesn't just record nearby phenomena in an arbitrary folder. That folder is important because it represents things in the creature's egocentric proximity. That is, it represents its perspectival position. It is for this reason that the information in that folder is critically connected to its own behaviors (hide/feed).

If we have designed the creature ourselves with the interest of it surviving, then the more robust description also tracks our understanding of when the creature is malfunctioning. We know it is malfunctioning when it is not representing its situation correctly—when it does not represent itself as being in immediate danger (and hence does not try to hide) and does not represent itself as having feeding opportunities (and hence does not try to feed).

This is even more the case when the system is of unknown origin. Then, given that we have little idea of the low-level execution of its program, our best and perhaps only level of understanding for the creature and whether it is malfunctioning is whether it is correctly representing its immediate dangers and opportunities. That is, whether it correctly represents its perspectival position.

It serves no purpose to say that folder can be dispensed with. Talk of the folder is a metaphor. The point is that the information is carried by the system and the system can act on it. There is no way to escape reliance on perspectival content.

---

[4] It is important to understand that we are not merely talking about an "intentional stance" in the sense of Dennet (1987). These attributions are true attributions of intentional mental states. More strongly, we have no aperspectival way to accomplish these attributions.

5.2 Information and Interperspectival Content

The claims made in the previous section (and at the end of the previous chapter) may strike us as surprising. Computational states depend upon perspectival states? But in a way, this should not strike us as surprising at all. Not only is the language of the theory of computation (beginning with Turing 1936) replete with perspectival content, but so too is the language of information processing, beginning with Shannon (1948), and Shannon and Weaver (1949).

The underlying picture of Shannon's theory, which has become integral to all contemporary work on information transmission and information processing, is that there is a message, an information source, a transmitter, a signal, some noise, and a receiver.

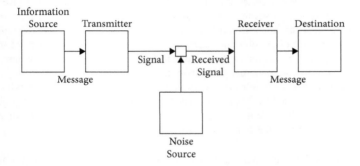

We often think of information as being an objective, aperspectival feature of the world, but this just isn't so. In the first place, the information carried by a signal (or indeed in the entropy of a physical system) depends upon the observer. Let's see why this is so.

The first critical point, one made in Shannon's original paper, is the idea that information transmitted is a function of a set of possible messages. Galistel and King (2009) illustrate this idea with the example of the midnight ride of Paul Revere. According to the historically inaccurate poem by Henry Wadsworth Longfellow, Paul Revere's associate, in the Old North Church, was to hang one light if the British invaded by land, and two if they invaded by sea.[5] Accordingly, for Paul, those lights

---

[5] The poem is historically inaccurate in many ways, but key among them is that the signals were not *for* Paul Revere; he actually ordered the signals to be sent.

(the *signal*, in Shannon's terminology) carried a message. For an observer who did not know that it was a code, they would just be lights. But in addition, the information carried by those lights is also a function of the prior knowledge that Paul had. If he was already certain that the British would come by land, then one light does not carry any new information. The amount of information transmitted in the message is a function of it reducing uncertainty. If the message is not reducing uncertainty it is not communicating information.

Now we can already begin to see that the theory of information is not the objective enterprise that we typically imagine it to be. Here it is worth quoting Galistel and King at length.

Shannon defined the amount of information *communicated* to be the difference between the receiver's uncertainty before the communication and the receiver's uncertainty after it. Thus the amount of information that Paul got when he saw the lights depends not only on his knowing beforehand the two possibilities (knowing the set of possible messages) but also on his prior assessment of the probability of each possibility. This is an absolutely critical point about communicated information – and the subjectivity that it implies is deeply unsettling. By subjectivity, we mean that the information communicated by a signal depends on the receiver's (the subject's) prior knowledge of the possibilities and their probabilities. Thus, the amount of information actually communicated is not an objective property of the signal from which the subject obtained it!

Galistel and King are talking about the "subjectivity" of the message, but there is something else they could say. The information communicated is not merely subjective (not merely relative to a recipient), it is also perspectival! Paul Revere must not only see the lights and know the code, but in many circumstances he must understand that they are a message *for him* (not just for Paul Revere, but for himself). If he thinks the messages are for another person, the lights may not communicate the message.

Here is a case where there is no information for Paul: Suppose we convince him that his light hanger has been kidnapped and that the lights are being place by a British sympathizer. He may then infer that the lights are a signal for the British, or that they are designed to deceive him. In either case, there is little information being communicated. We have effectively corrupted the ability of the signal to transmit information, by convincing Paul that the signal is not *for him* (thanks to our deception, the set of possible messages has expanded greatly, and the signal no longer reduces the probability of certain messages).

You might think that this is merely a case of convincing Paul that the signal is not for Paul Revere, and hence perspectival content does not enter into the picture. But with a few tweaks to the example we can show that this is not the case. Let's suppose that Paul suffers a head injury and does not know he is Paul Revere. He thinks he is someone else—Nathan Hale, let's say. But suppose that he still remembers the code and still believes it is his responsibility (not Paul Revere's) to make the midnight ride. When we convince him that the associate has been kidnapped, we effectively wipe out the information being transmitted. He no longer believes it is a signal *for him*.

Here is a more complicated example: Let's suppose Paul still believes that he is Nathan Hale, but this time let's suppose he has been to the briefings, and although he knows the code he believes that the signal is for Paul Revere and not for himself. When we convince him that the associate in the Old North Church has been kidnapped (and possibly replaced by a British agent) he believes that the signal is carrying misinformation for Paul Revere. He imagines that Paul Revere, observing the two lights, is receiving the false message that the British are coming by sea. He may think the associate in the Old North Church is attempting to mislead Paul Revere.

We don't need Paul Revere to construct these examples. Sometimes the information communicated is aperspectival—for example, it might be information for Peter Ludlow (for example when I wait for help in a large bureaucratic office)—and sometimes the information transmitted is perspectival—it is information *for me*. While I am in the waiting area of a bureaucratic office, someone may call my name. That is aperspectival information. When I go up to the clerk, the clerk may then address me directly, now providing perspectival information. If, while waiting, I forget that I am Peter Ludlow, but imagine I am Hume, I will not get up when my name is called. I do not know that the information is for me. But suppose that I lose track of my identity just as I arrive at the clerk. She tells me to go to window seven. I go to window seven, because I correctly take the information to be information *for me*.

Third parties can recognize this perspectival information as well. Returning to the case of Paul Revere, let's imagine a scenario in which a third party attempts to intercept the information. Let's call this person Eve (for eavesdropper). Eve may have learned Paul Revere's code from a spy or she may have deduced it from previous colonial military actions (she has observed that every time the British invade by sea the colonials hang two lights from a high place). Eve can learn quite a bit about the information flow between Paul Revere and his associate. She may even come to realize that some of the information being transmitted is perspectival. For example, she may realize that the information being transmitted includes instructions for Paul himself. She may even thwart Paul's ride by inducing in Paul the belief that he is Nathan Hale. In this case Paul does not receive the information that he himself is to make the ride. In this case Eve intercepts the perspectival content of the message but the intended recipient, Paul, does not.

What are we to say of information-processing systems in nature? Is the information transmitted by DNA and RNA aperspectival? Following my remarks in the previous section, I believe that the answer must be "no." Although Mother Nature is not directly sending messages to us, our scientific method, by which we come to identify the properties of nature, involves a series of questions and answers. Experimental results are answers to *our* questions. If the question is asked in the right way, it will be asked so that *we* can interpret the answers.

In Chapter 8 we will see that this is true even for concepts like entropy. The Second Law of Thermodynamics is one of the deepest and most fundamental laws we have, but parallel to the reasons that information is sensitive to knowledge so too the entropy of an isolated system is a function of the observer and her knowledge of it. This is a point that string theory pioneer Leonard Susskind has made in his lecture notes on Statistical Mechanics.[6] One way we can take this is as saying that given two observers, A and B, if A observes more about the system due to diligence or experimentation, then A's computed value of entropy will be lower than B's since there are fewer microstates consistent with A's more detailed observations of the system.

This would also be a consequence of the gain or loss of perspectival knowledge. Suppose that A is the god on the tallest mountain and that A has first person knowledge—it knows that it itself is the god on the tallest mountain. Let's suppose that B is the god on the coldest mountain and that it itself has no nonperspectival knowledge. Weirdly, then, the entropy computed by A will be lower than the entropy computed by B, because there are fewer microstates consistent with A's knowledge of its world.

The moral is that we get to call the shots on what information is being transmitted between systems in nature. This is analogous to our interpretation and reports on the beliefs and desires of other persons. The relevant information is information that is accessible to us as observers and is a function of our explanation and understanding of the behaviors of informational systems in nature. In short, all information flow, whether natural or the product of human intentions,[7] ultimately bottoms out in perspectival contents.

---

[7] Assuming that such a distinction actually holds up. I suspect that it does not.

6

A-Series/B-Series Compatibilism

In the preceding chapters I made the case that perspectival contents are indispensible for accounts of human action, emotion, perception, normative behavior, computation, and information, and that they cannot be eliminated or replaced by aperspectival contents. Suppose that this part is correct. What else follows? One idea that has been widely held (and previously held by me) is the idea that tensism is not compatible with the B-series conception of time. Philosophers have not universally held this idea, but it has certainly been widely held since McTaggart's 1908 paper. However, as I stated in the Introduction, I now believe that reconciliation is possible; you can be a tenser and still retain the B-series.[1]

In particular, I will argue that if we adopt proposals about the dynamic lexicon from Ludlow (2014) then we have the necessary ingredients to be compatibilists about tensism and the B-series. And as a bonus we will also see that we have the ingredients to construct a robust story about the flow of time—something that detensers and presentist tensers cannot do.

6.1 McTaggart's Objection

In a famous argument that drove much of the twentieth-century research on time, McTaggart offered a two-pronged argument for the unreality or implausibility of time. The general idea of the argument was to show the incoherence ("unreality" of time in McTaggart's language) by showing that it led to contradiction. The idea was to show first that the A-theory

---

[1] Recall that this is weaker than saying you can still be a B-*theorist*. I am only talking about a series of events, ordered by tenseless relations. A B-*theorist* will hold that tenses cannot be grafted onto the B-series.

conception of time was not reducible to the B-theory conception (in effect, that temporal language could not be detensed), and second that the A-theory is incoherent. Philosophers in the century thence have agreed that McTaggart had this half wrong—they just disagreed about which half he got wrong. A-theorists (tensers) think he was wrong about the incoherence of the A-theory; B-theorists (detensers) think he was wrong about A-series being ineliminable ("more fundamental"). For now, we need only concern ourselves with the alleged incoherence of the A-series.

We begin with the assumption that objects (including propositions and events) cannot have incompatible properties. For example, no event could be entirely in the future and entirely in the past. But, according to McTaggart, that is precisely what the A-series is committed to. Take the event of your reading this book, and let's label that event E. According to McTaggart, we are now committed to the following:

(30)   future(E) & present(E) & past(E)

But wait! The A-theorist now wants to object that this is obviously false—that E's being past present and future don't all hold now, but at different times; in effect we are really only committed to (31).

(31)   E is future/past/present at different times.

Here McTaggart objects that proposition (31) sneaks in an impermissible B-theory notion of "different times."

At this point the A-theorist might decide to avoid talk of "times" (which does look like a bit of B-theoretic vocabulary) and opt for a formulation that is more A-theoretic in tone. So the correct reformulation of (31) might be as follows.

(32)   future(E) has been true & past(E) will be true & present(E) is true

But McTaggart won't buy this, claiming that it constitutes more A-theoretic subterfuge. (32) is using talk of times in disguise.

From McTaggart (1911 par. 331) But what is meant by "has been" and "will be"? And what is meant by "is," when, as here, it is used with a temporal meaning, and not simply for predication? When we say that X has been Y, we are asserting X to be Y at a moment of past time. When we say that X will be Y, we are asserting X to be Y at a moment of future time. When we say that X is Y (in the temporal sense of "is"), we are asserting X to be Y at a moment of present time.

What should the A-theorist say in response to this? Well, Prior contended that it wasn't the A-theorist that is caught in the regress, but the B-theorist, who at every level must attempt to translate a perfectly acceptable A-theoretic formulation into something that traffics in B-series vocabulary:

We are presented, to begin with (in step 1), with at statement which is plainly wrong (that every event *is* past, present, and future). This is corrected to something which is plainly right (that every event either *is* future and *will be* present and past, or *has been* future and *is* present and *will be* past, or *has been* future and present and *is* past). This is then expanded (in step 2) to something which, in the meaning intended, is wrong. It is then corrected to something a little more complicated which is right. This is then expanded (in step 3) to something which is wrong, and we are told that if we correct this in the obvious way, we shall have to expand it into something which is again wrong, and if we are not happy to stop there, or at any similar point, we shall have to go on *ad infinitum*. Even if we are somehow compelled to move forward in this way, we only get contradictions half the time, and it is not obvious why we should get these rather than their running mates as the correct stopping-points.

In Ludlow (1999) I suggested that the McTaggart objection is really the problem of temporal anaphora. That is, it is a problem of how we are to refer to events taking place at different times. If we have some consistent A-series account of temporal anaphora then the McTaggart objection doesn't really get rolling—we can say we are entitled to opt for (31) as a solution.

For example, we could say that E was future during a certain time period, present during a subsequent time period, and past during a following time period. In the Appendix, I'll take up the question of whether this can be carried out with A-series resources only (avoiding untensed temporal positions), but if we can help ourselves to a combi-nation of both tense and the B-series, the McTaggart objection doesn't even get rolling. Why? Because the B-series resources can be used to anchor the temporal reference and temporal anaphora. Thus there would be nothing wrong with formulation (31), assuming we reject McTaggart's idea that the A-series vocabulary is more basic than the B-series vocabulary. And as we will see in the Appendix, a good case can be made that tensed and untensed resources (A-series and B-series resources) are not interreducible. They are equally fundamental.

Still, we are not out of the woods yet, for there is an ancient philo-sophical problem that generates an additional problem for the B-series tenser—the problem of the moving now.

6.2 The Problem of the Moving Now

The problem of the moving now is one of the most ancient in philosophy, and is often traced to Aristotle in his *Physics*.[2] Here is how the puzzle gets started. Let's imagine a standard representation of four-dimensional spacetime with upwards-facing light cones representing the future and downward-facing light cones representing the past. Let's suppose that I am positioned at T0, where the cones meet. I take it that a standard doctrine of the B-theory is that all the information necessary to represent time (and change) can be encoded in this picture.

But now let's suppose that I, a tenser, say that the events in my upward-facing light cone *will* be the case (or are future) and those in my downward-looking light cone *were* the case, and those that obtain at the point where the cones touch *are* present (now). Yet surely, next week some of the events happening now will be in my past, and some of the events that will happen will be happening or will have happened by next week. So, one might worry, one gets movement along the B-series timeline after all. It is as though *now* is sliding upward and the past is growing as the downward cone grows, and the future is shrinking as the upward cone shrinks. So change is taking place. And that appears to violate the basic idea of compatibilism, which is that movement can be encoded in fixed B-series positions with perspectival contents "painted" over those positions. If those painted-on contents must move in any sense at all, that movement presumably takes place in time, and so our account was not complete after all.

To put it another way, if some event is present now, but will be past at a later time, how is the past not growing and the future not shrinking, and how is *now*—that is, the content expressed by 'now'—not moving along a B-series timeline?

I want to emphasize that the problem does not depend on using 'now'. We can generate the same problem with any tensed expressions alone. The events that will happen are shrinking and the set of events that have happened is growing. That is change. But if change is taking place, haven't we given up our compatibilist B-series-plus-tense account of time? Wasn't change supposed to be reflected in some combination of the perspectival contents and the B-series positions?

[2] See, for example, Sorabji (1983).

If we agree that the idea of a moving *now* or the growing block or the shrinking block is quite incoherent we face a dilemma. We were supposedly offering up an analysis of time, but it seems we are forced into talking about elements of our analysis undergoing movement, and movement is supposed to take place in time.

Some have suggested that we could introduce a notion of second-order time or an alternative conception of time through which this movement takes place. Let's consider the possibility for a bit. The idea would be that the indexical property expressed by 'now' *does* move, not in time, but in *second-order time*. So we get this: there is a second-order event of it being now-at-t1, and it is now-at-t1 before it is now-at-t2. The second-order time can then be treated as a detensed second-order spacetime.

The problem is that any reason we had for introducing tense at the first-order level is an equally good reason for introducing tense at the second-order level. So, for example, consider (33).

(33)   I'm glad it's now-at-t2 *now* and not yesterday (said after a visit to the dentist at t1).

Or suppose there is a meeting scheduled for when it is now-at-t2. I realize it is t2 and utter (34) and get up and run to my meeting.

(34)   Oh no, it's now-at-t2 *now*!

Just to make things a bit more complicated we can even introduce cross-level utterances as in (6).

(35)   I'm glad my root canal was now-at-t1 and not now.

Even if introducing a notion of second-order time could solve the technical problem, I don't really understand what it means for *now* to be indexed to a time in this way. It seems that indexing it to a time neutralizes the perspectival content expressed by the operator.

We could think of this puzzle as being the cost of not heeding McTaggart's (1908, 1927) paradox. If you try to combine the B-series (the linear ordering of events) with the A-series (the tensed properties), the story blows up.

As I noted earlier, since McTaggart, philosophers have for the most part broken into one of two camps, being either A-theorists or B-theorists. Each position avoids paradox by carving off the other half, but the resulting story of the flow of time seems impoverished in both cases—not surprisingly if the flow of time, as I suggested, critically requires both components.

For example, B-theorists, who argue that tense is not actually a property of the physical world, hold that there really is no genuine change; we can at best characterize the notion of change in the following way:

(36)   x changes iff x has property P at time t1 and x does not have P at time t2, where t2 is later than t1.

And A-theorists and tensers like Prior also have what we might consider a throttled-back notion of change. Prior (1968) argued that for something to change is just for it to fit this schema.

(37)   It was the case that p, and is not now the case that p.

Prior believed, as have many tensers, that to be coherent a tenser has to be a presentist, for any other story is going to commit one to the absurdity of a temporal operator moving along the B-series.

I think that it is easy to get tripped up while thinking about the flow of time, but I also think that it is possible to endorse both of these positions and not get tripped up.

So what causes us to get tripped up? As I have already suggested, I think the core problem arises when we think that tenses themselves undergo change or in some sense move within a four-dimensional spacetime representation (or, if you prefer, along a B-series timeline). Is there a way to avoid this? I think there is and I think the answer lies in how tense works in the dynamic lexicon.

6.3 An Interlude on the Dynamic Lexicon

In Chapter 3, building off of Larson and Ludlow (1993) and Ludlow (2014), I made the case for an approach to word meaning in which we think of the lexicon as being highly dynamic. Word meanings change radically over the course of a conversation. In some cases, as I argued, word meanings are litigated—for example, we litigate what the meaning of 'planet' or 'person' or 'terrorist' is to be. But in other cases, word meanings are automatically recalibrated.

For example, in Chapter 3 I made the case that many indexical expressions automatically undergo meaning shift as time passes—not in the sense that the referential contents of the expressions shift, but in the sense that contents of the expressions are recalibrated as well. That is to say, the sense content of an expression like 'today' shifts every day.

To refresh our memories on why this should be, let's return to the following passage from Frege (1956).

> If someone wants to say the same today as he expressed yesterday using the word 'today', he must replace this word by 'yesterday'. Although the thought is the same, the verbal expression must be different so that the sense, which would otherwise be affected by the differing times of utterance, is readjusted.

As we noted in Chapter 3, Perry (1977) argued that Frege's view got him into philosophical troubles. In particular, Perry's worry was that if the sense of a sentence is composed from the senses of the words it contains, then a sentence containing 'today' and a sentence containing 'yesterday' will have to have different senses and hence express different thoughts. But you can't keep the distinct senses of 'yesterday' and 'today' while at the same time preserving the possibility that 'yesterday was fine' expresses the thought that 'today is fine' expressed the day before. To put it another way, it seems that the senses of 'yesterday' and 'today' must be distinct in some cases, but the same for others.

Pivoting from talk about senses to talk about perspectival contents (not much of a pivot), the answer offered by the dynamic lexicon is that the perspectival content expressed by 'today' and the perspectival content expressed by 'yesterday' do in fact shift over time. Each day, these expressions are infused with a new perspectival content reflecting the new temporal perspectival position. The result is that the perspectival content that is expressed by an utterance of 'today' today is the same sense that is expressed by an utterance of 'yesterday' tomorrow.

As we also saw in Chapter 3, if we want to express the same perspectival content in different ways, then what we need to do is develop a theory that affords perspective-sensitive axioms. For example, here is how we might handle the example introduced by Frege.

(38)   if yesterday s left a message m, having the form 'today is a fine day', then for s, m, 'today is a fine day' was true iff it was a fine day yesterday.

To be clear, the idea is not that a semantic theory would consist of theorems of this form, but it would consist of a theory of the capacities that allow us to build theorems like this on the fly. In effect, a theorem like (38) is part of a "passing theory" in the sense of Davidson (1986) or a "microlanguage" in the sense of Ludlow (2014). Semantic theory would be concerned with how we construct such passing theories. In talking about the theory of cognitive tracking abilities in Chapter 3 we have already touched on basic elements of such a passing theory. For example, one principle that sometimes guides us in constructing theorems like (38) is what Branquinho (2006) has called the "natural realignment claim," drawing on the idea that we can naturally realign our means of expressing our earlier thoughts so that we can continue to express those thoughts from new perspectival positions. But our abilities to realign also enable us to track belief contents when things misfire badly, as they appear to do in the Rip van Winkle case.

6.4 How A-Series/B-Series Compatibilism Works

We can now extend this dynamic lexicon idea to expressions like 'now' and the tense system more generally. The perspectival content expressed by an utterance of 'now' right now is not the same as the perspectival content expressed by an utterance of 'now' at a later time. There are, if you like, multiple words spelled n-o-w, but each one not only picks out a different time, but has a different meaning by virtue of expressing a different perspectival content.

On this theory, then, it is a kind of equivocation to think that there is a moving now. There are many expressions of the form 'now' and they are all picking out different perspectival contents.

This helps explain why our explanations for actions must be "recloaked" when we use them at different times and places and for different persons. When I realize it is three o'clock I can offer an explanation of my action thus: "I just realized I have a meeting now." But you recast the explanation as "You realized just then that you had a meeting then." I say the explanations are "recloaked" because they are the same explanations, appealing to the same interperspectival contents from different perspectival positions. And this is possible because expressions like 'now' express different perspectival contents at different times of use. To re-express the content you have to deploy different expressions.

The same will hold for the case of tense. The past does not grow and the future does not shrink. Each subsequent use of a tensed expression expresses a slightly different perspectival content, which is related to the new perspectival position from which it is uttered. If I say 'I will be at the party' several times throughout the day, each utterance of 'will be' is expressing a new perspectival content corresponding to my new perspectival position. It is not that the future is shrinking; it is just that each subsequent utterance of 'will be' expresses a new temporal perspectival content, and each subsequent perspectival content, so expressed, has fewer events in its range.

Dean Zimmerman (1998a: 212) has expressed strong reservations about the possibility of combining tense with the B-series in this way. In his view, it locks us into an implausible view about the nature of past and future events and objects.

But the combination of rejecting presentism while taking tense seriously is an unstable one. For the primary motivation for treating the fundamental truth-bearers as mutable and true now is the desire to do justice to the feeling that what's in the past is over and done with, and that what's in the future only matters because it will eventually be present. This is the source of the importance Prior attaches to the exclamation "Thank goodness that's over!" If yesterday's headache still exists, and remains as painful as ever, why should I be relieved now?

Quentin Smith (1993) anticipates this worry, and I believe effectively neutralizes it. The problem with Zimmerman's worry is that the event that we characterize as "yesterday's headache" is not "as painful as ever." It isn't painful. It *was* painful. Now, in the worst case we might have to say that the headache is (tenselessly) painful. But so what? It isn't painful now. The headache happened. It isn't happening.

Tenseless contents are inert with respect to our actions and emotions (that's why we needed the tensed contents to begin with!). Furthermore, it is not even clear we need to say that the headache is (tenselessly is) painful. All we really need to say is that it exists (tenselessly). I take it that this is the point made in Williamson (1999: 195), when he says "A past table is not a table that no longer exists; it is no longer a table." I would argue that we refer to the bare particular with its perspectival properties (e.g. it *was a table*). If it also has tenseless properties, I believe these are harmless.

Zimmerman has a response to this line of argument:

Although this view makes sense of our relief when pain is past, I find it unappealing in the extreme. The past and future events and objects it posits are too ghostly to be real. A painful headache cannot exist without being painful; a tanker explosion cannot exist without being violent and loud; Plato cannot exist while having neither body nor soul. What's left of these past and future things and events is too thin: yesterday's headache is still an event, but it isn't painful or throbbing or much of anything else; Plato is still a substance, I suppose, but he doesn't talk or think or walk or sleep or have any spatial location. Neither Plato nor headache has any of the ordinary intrinsic properties it displayed while present. Smith's efforts to preserve the intuition behind "Thank goodness that's over!" while rejecting presentism are, I judge, unsuccessful. Past and future things become nearly-bare particulars, unreal echoes of their once or future selves. The serious tenser is much better off without them.   (1998a: 212)

I don't think Zimmerman's response to Smith is persuasive. Even if it is correct that when we refer to past things we are referring to things that have no detensed properties besides existence (tenseless existence), it does not follow that those events and things are "unreal echoes" of their once or future selves, for they continue to have features that are described with perspectival contents (perspectival properties, if you prefer). It is still true that that headache I refer to *was horrendous*. It is still true that Plato *was a great philosopher*. The tanker explosion is (tenselessly is), but it needn't be (tensed be), loud and violent now. It is enough that it *was* loud and violent. Plenty of perspectival contents hold true of these objects, and those perspectival contents play a role in explaining our past, present, and future behaviors: I didn't come to work because my headache *was terrible*, I am currently relieved that it *has ceased to be*, and I will stay hydrated so that it or something like it *will not happen* again.[3]

6.5 Compatibilism and the Flow of Time

One of the most gripping intuitions that people have about time is that it in some sense "flows." This sense of flow has been articulated in a number of ways, ranging from us moving into the future or the future rushing towards us, and there has been no shortage of metaphors and

---

[3] Zimmerman has another concern, which is related to the problem of temporary intrinsics. Since it is tied up with his defense of presentism I'll set that concern aside for now.

descriptions to characterize this sense of passage. In a classic essay, Williams (1951: 461) catalogued some of the metaphors as follows.

Time flows or flies or marches, years roll, hours pass. More explicitly we may speak as if the perceiving mind were stationary while time flows by like a river, with the flotsam of events upon it; or as if presentness were a fixed pointer under which the tape of happenings slides; or as if the time sequence were a moving picture film, unwinding from the dark reel of the future, and rewound into the dark can of the past. Sometimes, again, we speak as if the time sequence were a stationary plain or ocean on which we voyage, or in a variegated river gorge down which we drift; or, in Broad's analogy, as if it were a row of house fronts along which the spotlight of the present plays. "The essence of nowness," Santayana says, "runs like fire along the fuse of time."

Despite the many forms of the metaphor and its widespread use, it has been argued that there is a deep conceptual problem in any assumption that time "passes" or "flows." The issue is that despite the natural appeal of metaphors that lean on the idea of "movement," movement itself takes place in time. So, whether one regards time as consisting in movement of an individual along a timeline, or one thinks of the future approaching the individual and moving past like a river, the idea expressed by the metaphor is supposed to be incoherent.

But is the idea expressed by this metaphor really incoherent? I believe that the metaphor can be unpacked as representing three features of temporal experience, and while these features together appear to lead to paradox, I will argue that correctly handled they do not.

One of the interesting features of the catalogue of metaphors provided by Williams is that there is a structural similarity running through most of them. There is an idea of an in-progress event indexed against some fixed linear ordering of events. So, for example, the fixed ordering might be the "tape of happenings," or the sequence of cells in a "moving picture film," or the coordinates of a "stationary plain" or a "river gorge" or a "row of houses." I think even the "fuse of time" and the river with the "flotsam of events" on it serves this role as well.

For the purposes of the metaphor it doesn't matter if the indexed sequence flows past us or we flow past it—the point is that this seems to be a critical element of the metaphor. And indeed, having some indexed reference frame does seem to be critical to our experience of time. Consider a case where you are in an airplane at night. It is sometimes hard to experience this as a kind of directed movement. Unless we are aware of some external index (e.g. in-flight maps or mental maps) against which we move there really is no experience of directed movement.

The second component of the metaphor is what I will call *tense*—understood (as it has been throughout this book) as expressing first person perspectival content that is not reducible to a linear ordering of events. So, for example, if I say an event is future, it is not merely later than the time of my utterance, it is future with respect to my perspectival position.[4]

This component, as we noted in Chapter 1, is motivated by concerns that Prior (1959) articulated in his "Thank Goodness" argument. To refresh our memories, the idea is that while nonperspectival properties *might* be serviceable enough for most scientific explanation, if we are interested in explaining human action and human emotion we need to reference perspectival properties. So, for example, to explain why I get up and run to the meeting when I realize the meeting starts *now*, it is not enough to say I realize the meeting starts at a certain B-series temporal index. I need to know my perspectival position relative to that index. Similarly when I express relief that my root canal is over with, it is not enough to say that I am relieved that my root canal is earlier than some B-series index. I need to know my temporal egocentric position with respect to that index.[5]

My view, developed in Ludlow (2015), is that the flow of time requires both of these elements. We need a linear ordering of events (or a four-dimensional plotting of events) to serve as an index and we need a perspectival notion of tense so that some of the plotted events are in our future (with respect to our perspectival position) and some are in our past.

In addition to this we also need an additional irreducible aspectual property—progressive—meaning that the overarching event we are participating in is in progress. So, for example, if we are floating down a river, that event is *in progress*. When I say that this progressive element is

---

[4] If you are concerned about relativistic effects you can relativize this to an inertial frame if you wish. We will get to this in Chapter 8.

[5] The "new B-theory" might spot me this but argue that the relevant perspectival properties can be cashed out in terms of our psychology—we need not take them as being properties of the physical world (see Mellor 1998 for an example). If one is an anti-Cartesian about psychology (as I am) it is difficult to see how this view makes sense. As I argued in Section 4.2, if there are no tensed physical states it is difficult to see how there can be tensed psychological states.

irreducible I mean that, contra Sider (2001), it cannot be reduced to something like an at-at theory; that is, it cannot be reduced to saying something like x is in state 1 at time t1 and in state 2 at time t2. Being *in progress* is a primitive property, as I proposed in Ludlow (1999).

Here is how I imagine the three elements combine in cashing out the metaphor of temporal flow, drawing on the metaphor of my drifting along a riverbank. First, there is an index of objects and points of reference along the shore. Second, there is the fact that some of the indexed points are in my past and some are in my future. This is the tensed component of my experience. Finally, there is the fact that this is *in progress*. I am not frozen on the river with some of the indexed points forever in my future and others forever in my past. Some events, like my floating downriver, *are happening*. Other events are just *beginning* to happen.

The metaphor can be applied to temporal experience in the following way. When I experience the flow of time there is an indexed ordering of events—let's say organized by the earlier-than/later-than relation. So, there are events like my fifth birthday, which precede events like my graduating high school, which in turn precede events like my death. Second, I am temporally embedded in this linear sequence so that some of those events are future with respect to my perspectival position and others are past. Finally, there is a spanning event that is in progress. For example, my aging is such a spanning event. Many other events in my life are likewise happening or beginning to happen.

Notice that in cashing out this metaphor I have not relied on a traditional notion of actual movement, except insofar as I said that there is a progressive property that holds. To be sure my death will happen, and it is in some sense in the process of coming about, but you should not think of this as me actually sliding across the indexed timeline. That is unnecessary and only leads to conceptual confusions.

Given A-series/B-series compatibilism, we have the resources to make sense of all the basic components expressed by the metaphor of temporal passage without needing temporal operators, or really anything, to move along the B-series or upwards in a spacetime diagram. (Let's stick with talk of a B-series timeline to keep things simple.)

The B-series serves as our index. Meanwhile we are perspectivally anchored in the B-series and can express claims about the future and the past by using tenses and expressions like the linguistic form 'now' to express perspectival contents—contents the expression of which are sensitive to our perspectival positions. Finally, we can express the fact that there are overarching events that are in progress—relying on progressive aspect to express this additional content. Tomorrow, we will express new perspectival contents using the words (or, if you prefer, the forms) 'now' and 'today'. The contents that they express today do not "move along" the B-series, and similarly the past does not grow and the future does not shrink. Tense and the B-series are entirely compatible, and both play a fundamental role in—indeed are critical to—the flow of time.

Ultimately the idea that there must be movement across the B-series index is an abuse of the metaphors collected by Williams. All of those metaphors involved movement, but what I am saying is that the movement taking place in those examples *consists in* the three elements I introduced. There is no movement *in addition to* those elements.[6]

---

[6] Williams, for his part, thought that the movement could be cashed out solely in terms of the B-theoretic relations. That seems exceptionally optimistic to me.

7

Some Additional
Metaphysical Questions

I've been making the case that perspectival content is necessary for the explanation of much of human activity, and that the best approach to tense is to think in terms of interperspectival contents. We've already covered a number of metaphysical worries about tense and perspectival contents (McTaggart's argument, for example) but there are two additional worries that need to be addressed. The first has to do with the problem of truth-makers. The second has to do with the kinds of contents that are metaphysically admissible. One metaphysical issue that I won't take up in this chapter (but will in the Appendix) is the question of whether tensism commits us to presentism, and if so, whether that is a problem.

7.1 The Truth-Maker Problem

Some philosophers contend that for propositions to be true, there must be "truth-makers" by virtue of which they are true. These truth-makers might be facts or states of affairs or some such thing. As a first pass, following work by Martin (1996), and Mulligan et al. (1984), one might characterize the requirement as follows, from Sider (1991: 36).

The vague assumption that truths must be 'grounded' can be made precise in a couple of ways. One is the truth-maker principle: for every truth, T, there exists an entity—a 'truth-maker'—whose existence suffices for the truth of T. These truth-makers are often called states of affairs or facts, and are thought of as concrete constituents of the world in the tradition of Russell (1910–11) and Wittgenstein (1961).

Sider (2001: 36) then suggests that this formulation of the truth-maker principle will not do as it stands, for it does not handily ground the truth of negative existentials ('No unicorns exist') and presumably also at least some general claims that are grounded by arbitrarily large regions of the world. If this is a concern, Sider suggests we follow proposals by John Bigelow (1988: 130–3) and David Lewis (1992: 215–19) and formulate the grounding principle as the claim that *truth is supervenient on being*:

> [W]hat is true supervenes on what objects exist, what properties those objects have, and what relations they stand in. This principle does not require the existence of a fact that there are no unicorns; it merely requires that since 'there are no unicorns' is true in the actual world, it must also be true in any world in which the same objects exist, those objects instantiate the same properties, and those objects stand in the same relations as they do in the actual world.
> (1991: 36)

What is the motivation for this? Sider puts it this way:

> Either way the grounding principle is cashed out, the point is to rule out dubious ontologies that posit 'ungrounded' truths, for example 'brute counterfactuals' with no basis in the way things actually are. The thought is that it is illegitimate to postulate truths that 'float free' of the world.   (1991: 36)

One might ask what is wrong with brute counterfactuals. To be sure, if something (say a vase) is fragile, we wouldn't find it satisfactory to say that it is fragile because if it were dropped it would break. A more helpful explanation would be that the vase has certain underlying physical properties. But cases like this don't undermine the need for brute counterfactual properties in general—say at the micro level. The question is, what is driving the objection to brute counterfactuals and (in our case) perspectival contents?

Let's move this discussion from talk of brute counterfactuals to perspectival contents just so we can stay on point with the concerns of this book. The truth-maker challenge would be that perspectival facts "float free" of the world while at-at facts don't. Well, why? You can't just stipulate that only at-at facts are descriptive of the world, because that is the point at issue. And, for that matter, why can't there be freely floating at-at facts? The problem is that the expression 'freely floating' is nothing if not metaphorical and it is not at all clear how the metaphor is supposed to be cashed out.

One way to take the metaphor would be the idea that something would float free of the world if it was inert with respect to causal relations and explanations. In other words, it contributes nothing in the broader scheme of things.

I assume this is Sider's point about "what objects exist, what properties those objects have, and *what relations they stand in*" (my emphasis). Inert facts or situations would be situations that are isolated, that don't connect with the web of things nor with actions we engage in; they are not related in meaningful ways to other salient events. But surely perspectival facts are densely interconnected with other perspectival facts and if you are a four-dimensional tenser, with nonperspectival facts as well. Indeed, if I am right, it is the tenseless facts that are more or less inert—they play little role in the explanation of much of human life.

Perspectival contents (and perspectival properties, if you like properties) don't "float free" of the world in this sense, because, as we've seen in this book, perspectival contents play critical roles in our causal explanations of actions, emotions, perception, and even the normative action of digital computers. Without such resources we have no explanations for a large class of events that we not only *need* to explain, but are *highly successful* at explaining (meaning we can explain things like when we get up and go to meetings).

But maybe the concern about free-floating facts has nothing to do with whether the facts are inert and more to do with whether the facts are properly anchored in some other sense—like they aren't anchored in things, irrespective of inertness. But it is hard to see how this strategy can be executed without question begging. If a perspectivalist believes in facts then she will believe in perspectival facts, and she will believe they are no less real or important than at-at facts. Why would perspectival facts be unanchored? Now of course it is possible to argue that they can't be anchored in physics, and this is a serious question that we will take up in the next chapter, but apart from such concerns it is hard to see how an argument against such properties gets rolling.

There is another question that the perspectivalist might ask as well. Why do nonperspectival facts get a free pass? Why wouldn't they be unanchored? If we go with the inertness account of "floating free," we could make the case that the at-at accounts are problematic. We need the perspectival accounts not just for explaining human actions, emotions, and normative judgments, but also for our explanations of computation, information flow, and biology. What, exactly, are those at-at facts even good for?

Now obviously there is a lot more going on in the world than facts about human life (we are, let's face it, an infinitesimally small part of what is happening in the Universe), but on the other hand, if our theories of computation and information (and information-theoretic sciences) rely on perspectival contents, we are hardly talking about a narrow spectrum of the Universe. Furthermore, as we will also see in Chapter 8, perspectival contents run through our explanations of base-level physical properties of the Universe as well—even the non-information-theoretic properties.

But perhaps there is something else missing. Maybe a certain *kind* of fact is called for and perspectival facts are just not the right kind. Some philosophers have argued that perspectival contents (and others) violate the principle of Humean supervenience. The question is, why do they think this is a problem, and are they right?

7.2 Humean Supervenience

In the previous section I argued that sentences with perspectival predicates (or utterances of such sentences) have perfectly reasonable truth-makers—truth conditions deploying perspectival contents. I argued that there was no obvious sense in which such contents "float free" of the world or are inert or in some sense alien. However, one might wish to push harder on this point and insist that perspectival contents fail another desideratum—what David Lewis called "Humean supervenience." Here is Lewis' pithy version of the idea.

It is the doctrine that all there is to the world is a vast mosaic of local matters of particular fact, just one little thing and then another.   (Lewis 1986: ix)

If this is Humean supervenience, so far it doesn't sound too objectionable. It doesn't yet seem inconsistent with the account of perspectival contents I offered. Past tense statements or claims could supervene on states of affairs consisting of individuals, perspectival positions, and interperspectival contents—again, if you prefer properties, you could talk about perspectival properties.

However, one might object that things like interperspectival contents and perspectival positions are not local matters of fact. In my view, of course, they are nothing if not local matters of fact. I even earlier characterized perspectival facts in terms of local theories. So what, exactly, is the problem? Perhaps we could get some insight into the problem by considering some other kinds of content that are supposed to run afoul of Humean supervenience.

For example, position in space and time is supposed to be OK (again, assuming some form of location in a Minkowski spacetime diagram). What are properties that are not supposed to be OK? Well, typically it is claimed the Humean supervenience is violated by properties like intrinsic velocity—velocity is thus not an intrinsic property, it is rather a property that reduces to something like being at location l1 at time t1 and at location l2 at t2. Similarly, properties like angular momentum (for example, in a spinning ball or spinning disk) are not OK. Instead the spinning ball/disk are at various states at various times. For example, a "spinning" ball would be grounded in a series of snapshots of the ball in slightly different positions.

In general the demands for OK properties all extrude from a position that I will call the "frame-by-frame" view of fundamental reality—that the fundamental facts just pertain to things being in certain configurations at certain times. If you looked at the frames in a movie, for example, each frame would just provide a snapshot of things in a certain configuration. There is nothing moving or accelerating in the individual frame of the movie. What motion comes to is the change in position from frame to frame.

A classic example of this position is Quine's (1960) take on objects. Objects are built up out of time-slices or stages of those objects. As Quine famously said in reference to Heraclitus, you can step in the same river twice, but you can't step in the same river *stage* twice.

Of course the point on which this needs to be engaged is the question of why on Earth anyone would endorse this frame-by-frame approach to metaphysics. What is the case for it?

There has been plenty of discussion of spinning disks, for example, and it has been observed (correctly, in my view) that in a very boring world with just a uniform spinning disk (or spinning ball), the frame-by-frame object stage analysis will not be equipped to characterize what is happening unless we allow the frames to encode information like inertial velocity.[1] (Imagine a movie of this spinning disk—if the camera is stationary, every frame of the movie will be the same.)[2]

---

[1] My introduction to the problem was through a bootleg videotape of Saul Kripke lecturing on the topic at UC Davis in the 1970s. A recent discussion with a good literature review can be found in Zimmerman (1998b). See also Lewis (1999).

[2] It has also been objected that Humean supervenience does not hold up well in physics—in particular with Bell's Theorem (Maudlin 2007: Ch. 2).

But another way to come at the problem is to ask why the frame-by-frame story cannot avail itself of perspectival contents. First, there is no reason that the frames can't encode perspectival positions. Let's return to the video game metaphor. When we think of frame-by-frame records of something (say a 2D movie) we are apt not to capture any perspectival positions except for the third person position of the camera in that record. But it is also possible to do a video capture of a first person shooter's gameplay in which the player's perspectival position is captured frame-by-frame.

But if perspectival position can be captured in a frame-by-frame way, then we have the resources to build the interperspectival contents, which, as we saw in Chapter 3, can be thought of as predictive theories of the agents in those different perspectival positions, with the theory expressed in different ways from the different perspectival positions based upon a theory of cognitive dynamics. If the perspectival positions can be encoded into a frame, then it should be possible to encode the rest of the theory as well, for example by bundling frames from multiple perspectival positions into a single holographic frame that would represent the interperspectival content. Alternatively, if you think of 3D video games, you can imagine a 3D state capture; each frame of the capture would allow one to move about and see the world from various perspectival positions. Nor do we need holograms and video games to illustrate this idea. 3D computer modeling of architectural plans does the same—allowing the user to assume multiple perspectival positions. Both the movie film and 3D video game captures are metaphors, to be sure. My point here is that we should not restrict our metaphors to those involving Jurassic technologies.

If there are lingering worries about perspectivalism and Humean supervenience, I believe that it can be helpful to get a handle on what motivated the principle of Humean supervenience for Lewis in the first place; I believe we are not at cross-purposes here fundamentally. Weatherson (2016) argued that Lewis' motivation was to use Humean supervenience as a kind of recipe for the reduction of nomic, intentional, and normative concepts to the physical. On Weatherson's take, Lewis's idea was that if you could have a reduction to these basic OK properties, then you would have a guaranteed reduction to the basic physical level. Lewis's project was not to eliminate the nomic, intentional, and normative but to find ways to secure it in the natural order. If those concepts are reducible to the simple resources afforded by the Human Mosaic, then surely they have a place in the natural/physical order.

What Lewis's defence of Humean supervenience gives us is a recipe for locating the nomic, intentional and normative properties in a physical world. And it is a recipe that uses remarkably few ingredients; just intrinsic properties of point-sized objects, and spatio-temporal relations. It is likely that ideal physics will have more in it than that. For instance, it might have entanglement relations, as are needed to explain Bell's inequality. But it is unlikely to have less. And the more there is in fundamental physics, the *easier* it is to solve the location problem, because the would-be locator has more resources to work with.

Weatherson draws our attention to the following passage from Lewis to support the idea that Lewis is not really concerned with Humean super-venience in and of itself, so much as having a strategy to streamline the establishment of the supervenience relation between the nomic and the intentional to the physical.

Really, what I uphold is not so much the truth of Humean supervenience as the *tenability* of it. If physics itself were to teach me that it is false, I wouldn't grieve... What I want to fight are *philosophical* arguments against Humean supervenience. When philosophers claim that one or another common-place feature of the world cannot supervene on the arrangement of qualities, I make it my business to resist. Being a commonsensical fellow (except where unactualized possible worlds are concerned) I will seldom deny that the features in question exist. I grant their existence, and do my best to show how they can, after all, supervene on the arrangement of qualities.   (1986: xi)

In spirit, at least, I am in accord with Lewis here. I too believe that commonplace features of the world do supervene on the arrangement of qualities. It is my view, however, that the basic-level features of the world, whether they are properties or qualities, include perspectival positions and interperspectival contents. They are not outside the natural order, but very much part of it. As we will see in Chapter 8, they must be.

8

Interperspectival Content and Physical Theory

In this book I've made the case that linguistic tense and other perspectival language (indexical language, if you prefer) are used to express interperspectival contents and that such contents are needed to explain and understand a number of phenomena, ranging from human action and emotion, to perception, consciousness, normative behavior (understood broadly enough to include the behavior of computers), etc. I've also argued that the fact that physics may not need perspectival contents does not undermine the case for such contents. Still, some philosophers believe that perspectival approaches to time and tense are refuted by recent work in physics. What are we to say about these claims?

One of the core objections to perspectival contents has to do with the Special Theory of Relativity. In this chapter I'm going to argue that that objection falters if we can help ourselves to the idea that different inertial frames give rise to different perspectival positions, and these in turn give rise to different ways of expressing interperspectival contents. But this will lead in turn to the question of why tenseless accounts of reality should get off without scrutiny—why are they considered unproblematic for physical theory?

In the first place, B-series temporal order must be relative to an inertial frame too, so the temporal ordering of events will depend upon the inertial frame. But we can also ask whether the core B-theoretic relations (earlier-than/later than) are natural primitives for physical theory. For example, we can ask whether the earlier-than/later-than relation isn't just a relational tense. McTaggart held some form of this view. As he saw it, 'A is earlier than B' just reduces to 'when A is present B is future'. Or, if we are talking about past events, 'when A was present B was future'.

My own attempts to give an account of temporal anaphora using temporal connectives (see Appendix) can also be understood as treating the 'before/after' relation as a kind of primitive binary tense, as in 'A was true before B was true'. You could certainly think of '. . . was true before . . . was true' as a single relational tense. And even if it isn't a relational tense, what kind of primitive is it? Why is it any more acceptable than accepting perspectival positions and interperspectival contents?

Some detensers (notably Reichenbach) have worried about the status of the 'earlier-than/later-than' relation and have attempted to ground it in physical theory. I'll review that discussion to highlight that this is in fact a problem for the detenser.

Ultimately, though, we will see that even basic science has need of perspectival contents. First, it needs them for the understanding of the practice of science—both in the context of discovery and the context of application. But we will also see that the context of discovery—the experimental context—cannot be separated so neatly from the physical theory itself. We will see that physical theory too has need of perspectival contents.

8.1 The Alleged Relativistic Problem for the Tenser

The theory of relativity is supposed to present problems for the tenser (perspectivalist), but what is this problem? In the Special Theory of Relativity there is no absolute notion of simultaneity. For someone moving past us—let's say at 0.9 speed of light—what counts as simultaneous will be quite different for them than for us. Or, to put it another way, what is happening "now" is quite different for them than it is for us. Consider someone who is spatially separated from us—let's say that they are several light years away, and also moving at 0.9 speed of light relative to us. In this case what we assert to be happening now may be in the past from their perspective. In effect what is "happening now" depends upon one's inertial frame.

So far what I have said is perplexing, but it isn't yet an objection to the perspectivalist. The objection requires an additional premise to the effect that we don't get to be chauvinistic about what is happening now—we have no ground to say that our inertial frame is special. And this premise seems fair enough—there may be other scientists and other philosophers in other frames of reference and they may rightly ask why we puny Earth-bound beings get to call the shots on what is happening now—especially when it is clear to them that what we insist is "happening now" is, from their points of view, in the past or in the future. The conclusion we are driven to is that because no one's notion of past, present, and future is privileged, modesty forces us to admit that all are equally real.

That's the concern in a nutshell. Can it be answered? To get a handle on the problem I'll begin with a discussion of what the detenser will say about all of this and then I will take a look at the best responses for the perspectivalist.

8.1.1 What the a perspectival account looks like

From time to time we have talked about the detensed, B-series picture of time in terms of a timeline with events stacked up along that timeline—frozen in place, as it were—ordered by an earlier-than/later-than relation. The Special Theory of Relativity raises questions about this picture, given that, as noted in the previous section, whether an event is earlier than another depends upon one's inertial frame.

One way to approach this problem would be to have many B-series timelines—one for each inertial frame—but this doesn't help us to understand the relation between the different inertial frames. The solution that was hit on in physics was to follow Minkowski (1915) and deploy spacetime diagrams. To understand how a Minkowski spacetime diagram can preserve a static picture of time within the relativistic framework, we can illustrate with a particular example.

In the following diagram we represent the temporal dimension on the vertical t axis and the three spatial dimensions on the horizontal d axis. The unannotated 45-degree diagonal lines indicate the light cones for event A, represented by the dot at their intersection. If A were a light signal (a flash, for example) the distance traveled by that signal would define the outer edge of the forward (upward) light cone. The backwards (downward) light cone would represent the outer limit of earlier signals that might have arrived at A. Let's say there is an observer o, where the ct line represents the temporal history of o through spacetime. ct' indicates the history of another observer o' moving past o at a relative speed of 0.5 c (where c, of course, is the speed of light). B is an independent event. We can think of the line d as representing "now" for observer o, and d' as representing "now" for observer o'. We can already see that event B is in "the future" for observer o and "in the past" for observer o'. We can also see that A occurs "before" B for observer o, but A occurs "after" B for observer o'.

The scare quotes are being used here to indicate that we are using expressions like 'now' and 'future' in a way that is metaphorical. We might just as well speak of the events directly in terms of their relation to the d lines (above or below or on the line). Even the expressions 'before' and 'after' come to relative north/south positions within the diagram.

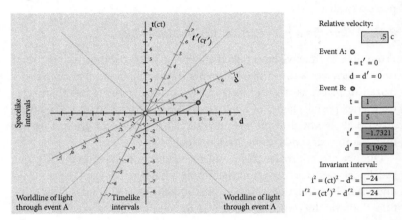

We can identify the precise spacetime location of B for both observers in the following way. For each observer, to fix the time for event B, draw a line through B, parallel to their "d line" (line d for o and d' for o'). The point at which that line intersects their respective "t line" (t for o and t' for o') fixes the time of event B for each observer. In the inertial frame for o, this is pretty simple because d is horizontal. That line intersects d at time 1 (one unit in the future). For observer o' we follow the same procedure, now drawing a line through B parallel to d'. In this instance the line intersects t' at −1.7321 (−1.7321 units "in the past").[1]

---

[1] I made this diagram with the Interactive Minkowski Diagram program of Kristian Evenson at http://www.trell.org/div/minkowski.html (last accessed January 6, 2018). The calculations are based on the inverse Lorentz transformations.

We proceed similarly for spatial position (distance from A). In this case we draw a line through B parallel to the t axes, yielding d = 5 for observer o, and d' = 5.1962 for observer o'.

What this affords us is a way of graphically representing the relative spacetime locations of events A and B for observers in multiple inertial frames. And we do it not with a bundle of different timelines, but we have a theory that connects those different timelines, or actually we have several candidate theories connecting the timelines. The Minkowski diagram doesn't care if we use Lorentz transformations or the Theory of Relativity. The point is that the relative positions of the events in each inertial frame are static.

8.1.2 What the perspectival account looks like

For the B-series *tenser* matters are not so different. As I argued in Ludlow (2016), one merely needs to annotate the Minkowski diagram with expressions of perspectival contents. So, for example, for observer o events expressed as *happening now* would consist of events located along d, events that o says *will happen* would be those events "north" of d, and events that o says *have happened* would be those events located "south" of d. For the observer in inertial frame ct', the story would be analogous, with d' substituted for d.

Now, some caution is necessary here. Not every way of executing this strategy works. For example, I don't think it works to take notions of future and past to be relative to an inertial frame, and think of tense as involving an index to a frame. In Section 3.1 we saw concerns about that view—concerns raised by Williamson (1999) and Hawthorne (2015).

The way Hawthorne expressed the worry is by suggesting that if you are thinking in terms of propositions indexed to times, you don't really have a handle on change. And the thinking is that if a (tensed) proposition is true at some time t1 and false at t2, well then it looks like you don't have a genuine notion of change happening.

But the approach to perspectival contents that I have been developing does not work this way. There is not a single word 'now' which gets indexed to times and inertial frames, but there are many words having the form 'now' that are found in numerous microlanguages. Let's say that someone in another inertial frame is speaking another microlanguage. Then the best way to think about annotated Minkowski diagrams is that they are translation manuals for the expression of interperspectival contents across inertial frames.

So, for example, suppose that we are observer o and that observer o′ is moving past us at 0.5 C velocity, and there is an event B, consistent with the Minkowski diagram above. Then we want to say that when observer o′ in inertial frame ct′ utters the words 'that event was −1.7321 in the past', o′ is saying that the event is happening now!

You might object that this sounds like the proposal I called Chauvinism. Should we not charitably translate o′ as saying that the event was −1.7321 in the past for o′? But I think the tenser will want to resist the locution "in the past for o′," for that locution is trading on a specialized tenseless notion of "past"—it is merely talking about a B-series position with respect to o′. It is invoking a time-indexed predicate analogous to true-in-a-world and true-at-a-time; in this case it is true-in-a-frame and it is just as problematic as the other cases of indexed perspectival contents.

The best strategy is to say that o′ *uttered* something of the *form* 'B happened at −1.7321 in the past'. If o wants to express the tensed proposition that o′ expressed using a genuine tensed predicate, o must translate the utterance by o′ of 'x happened 1.7321 in the past' as 'x is happening now'. Full stop. In effect, the Minkowski diagram gives us the realignment strategy necessary to express the perspectival contents expressed in other inertial frames.

Now, someone might object, saying "Look, you can see that these events are south of the line d′ and of course south of line d is past for us, so isn't south of d′ past for those in inertial frame ct′?" But the tenser is under no compunction to accept this. First, the tenser will reject a tensed understanding of 'past for us' and 'present for them'—she will reject the frame-indexed language. The tenser need only say that events south of line d are past, and that contents expressed by o′ must be realigned as the diagram indicates. She will simply say that she is giving the best translation of what the speaker in ct′ is saying. There need be no suggestion that o′ is wrong about anything. o′ is entitled to translate the contents of what we say as prescribed by the diagram and her descriptions of the events A and B will be true in her mouth. We are not being Semantic Chauvinists after all!

This approach has a lot going for it, I believe. For one, as noted, it is the natural extension of the approach we took to perspectival contents.

The same expression type, produced at different times and places (and now inertial frames), expresses different perspectival contents. Often, the same perspectival content is expressed in different ways in different perspectival positions. The approach preserves all the advantages of perspectivalism while seamlessly integrating perspectivalism with the Special Theory of Relativity.[2]

8.2 On the Alleged Innocence of the Earlier-Than/Later-Than Relation

Much of the principal argumentation against perspectivalism, and in particular presentism, has been the assertion that it does not dovetail well with base-level physical theory. In the previous section I raised some doubts about whether this is in fact true—at least as regards relativistic issues. In this section I want to raise the question of why B-theoretic properties have escaped similar scrutiny. As we will see, closer scrutiny suggests that B-theoretic properties really should not be given a pass.

As I noted earlier in this chapter, McTaggart thought that these relations reduced to the tenses PAST, PRES, and FUT. And indeed, if you look at the etymology of these expressions, they clearly have histories as perspectival predicates. 'Before' and 'after' are from spatial perspectival properties (fore and aft).

Of course the case could be made that all the perspectival content has subsequently been bleached from the meaning of these terms, but has it? We can certainly visualize events laid out on a "timeline," but what does that sequence of referenced events on that line actually represent? One possibility is that they simply represent the aperspectival temporal positions of various events and individuals. But why can we not say that they represent the positions of events with respect to the perspectival positions of hypothetical observers embedded in the timeline?

That is, pick any point on the line and consider an observer in that position. Place the future events to the right of the observer and the past events to the left. Or, for that matter, imagine an observer embedded in

---

[2] However, if we want to defend *presentism* (a view according to which there are no future or past events), things get more interesting. Clearly, in this case, one has to rethink what the Minkowski spacetime diagram is representing. I'll take up presentism in the Appendix.

the timeline with a direction of intention towards the future. In that case we can define 'later than' as being in the direction of attention.

This is not farfetched. Take any historical timeline and think about how we might go about discussing it. We point to an event—say the description of a battle—and the language may go like this. "At this point General Smith believed that his enemy was going to attack."

Now to be honest I don't expect anyone to be persuaded by this line of argumentation, but I do think it does place some burden on the detenser to explain exactly what the nature of the earlier-than/later-than relation is. If it doesn't supervene on perspectival contents then what kinds of contents does it supervene on?

Interestingly, Reichenbach (1956) saw the urgency of this question, and devoted a great deal of energy to the project of giving a reduction of the before/after relation into nontemporal features of the physical world. Whether reducibility is a sign of metaphysical respectability is perhaps a point for debate, but a more pressing concern is whether such reductions really can be carried out.

In what follows I'm not going to break any new ground, but just give a partial review of work done by van Fraassen (1970), Reichenbach (1956), Price (1996), Horwich (1987), and others. Not only will my survey be derivative, but it will also be incomplete. The topic still deserves a book in itself—indeed several more books—and I can't do it justice in one section of a chapter here. My hope, however, is to develop the problem enough so that the nature of the problem will become clear.

Fundamentally, any reduction of the earlier-than/later-than relation must answer two questions.

(i) What non-temporal properties of physical theory can account for temporal *order*?

(ii) What non-temporal properties of physical theory can account for temporal *direction*?

Consider first, for example, the problem of accounting for temporal order. Is it possible to show that the earlier-than/later-than relation can be reduced to some physical property that does not involve perspectival properties? A fair bit of work has actually been done in this vein, and one strategy has been to show that one can reduce temporal order to causal order (or something akin to causal order). Very crudely, one could say something like the following:

(39)   E is before E′ iff E causes E′

Of course one needs to say more than this, as there will be a number of causally non-related events that succeed each other temporally, but this is certainly a start. The problem is that at some point we shall want an analysis of causality, and it will be important to demonstrate that our analysis of causality does not already contain some notion of temporal order.

Recall Hume's critique of causality—that one does not perceive a necessary connection holding between two events E and E′ (say E is the moving of the cue, and E′ is the moving of the cue ball). What one sees, according to Hume, is the motion of the cue, followed by the motion of the cue ball. All that causality can really amount to for the thoroughgoing empiricist is the following:

(i)   constant conjunction in past experience
(ii) contiguity in space and time
(iii) temporal succession

So, when we say that E caused E′, at best we are saying that we are used to seeing events of the same type as E connected with events of the same type as E′; E and E′ occurred at roughly the same place and time; and E occurred before E′.

Obviously, if this is what causality comes to then the causal theory of time collapses in a hurry. We may have successfully reduced temporal order to causal order, but causal order turns out to incorporate the notion of temporal order. Worse than that, it incorporates the notion of temporal *succession*, which assumes temporal direction.

It might be thought that the introduction of spacetime will allow a reduction of temporal order to something physical, but without the appeal to causality. This idea turns out to be incorrect, however. Reichenbach (1958) observed that the theory of relativity, and in particular Einstein's definition of simultaneity, presupposes a definition of causality. For example, in the way Einstein defines simultaneity, it is crucial that there be a light signal which caused a certain effect in an apparatus. Strictly speaking, the signal need not even have been a light signal, but simply a signal that had a certain causal effect. (Recall as well that physicists informally characterize the forward light cone as all those events that could be affected by the emission of a signal, and the backward light cone as all those events that could have affected the event of emission.)

For his part, Reichenbach held that it would be necessary to come up with a theory of causal order that did not presuppose a notion of temporal order. His proposal, which has come to be known as the "mark method," can be sketched as follows.

If E1 is the cause of E2, then a small variation (a mark) in events like E1 is associated with small variations in events like E2, whereas small variations in events like E2 are not associated with variations in events like E1.

To illustrate, suppose that E1 is the event of throwing a stone across a river. Suppose that E2 is the event of the stone landing on the other side. The idea is that a mark placed on the stone in E1 is correlated with a mark on the stone in E2, but not vice-versa. So, for example, I might write something on the rock before I throw it, and that mark will most likely be on the rock when it lands on the other side. But if I pick up the rock after it has traveled across the river and mark it then, I do not thereby change the rock at E1.

The exposition I just gave was of course thick with temporal language ("I pick up the rock *after* it . . . "), and it is really no good to say it can be given the usual B-theoretic gloss, because this temporal language is popping up in what was supposed to be our reduction of the basic B-theoretic relation into physical theory. But can the temporal language be avoided here? There is a serious question as to whether one can give an account of the mark method that is free from appeal to temporal concepts.

Mehlberg (1962) and Grünbaum (1963) subsequently observed that there is in fact tacit use of temporal concepts in the mark method. For example, it must be stipulated that the marking process is irreversible. Certain variations on the rock may well come undone in flight. For example, if I mark the rock with a piece of chalk, then the chalk may rub off in flight. Clearly, Reichenbach must exclude cases like these as illegitimate examples of marking—presumably on the grounds that such chalk markings are not irreversible. But what exactly is an irreversible process? Suppose we adopted the following definition.

A marking process is *irreversible* when the mark cannot be removed without destroying the object or returning it to the state that it had previous to the marking.

The troublesome part of this definition is clearly the reference to the "previous" state of the stone.

Temporal concepts do not intrude immediately in this proposal, but as we have seen they nonetheless do intrude. Graphically, the steps are as follows:

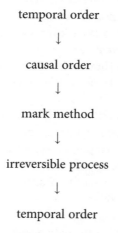

temporal order

↓

causal order

↓

mark method

↓

irreversible process

↓

temporal order

It appears that Reichenbach's theory of causation (as well as subsequent related attempts) must smuggle temporal order into their definitions of causal order.

This is of course no argument that theories of causal order *must* presuppose a notion of temporal order. In a bit, we will discuss recent work in causality—particularly work that ties the notion of causation to explanation or, alternatively, causal dependence—that may well successfully exorcise temporal order. But once we have secured a theory of causation that does not presuppose temporal order, very serious questions arise. In particular, it appears that such theories are not useful if the goal is reducing temporal concepts to causal concepts.

Recall that the central idea behind causal theories of time is that it may be possible to give the following sort of reduction for temporal order.

(40)   E occurs before E' iff either E causes E' or some other event E* contemporaneous with E causes E'

Notice that this sort of reduction would be blocked immediately if backwards causation were possible. For example, if I were able to do something today (E′) that would affect the outcome of some past event E (for example, by sending a cyborg back in a time machine) then we would have the embarrassing consequence that E is before E′, but E′ causes E. And this would appear to undermine the causal theory of time just considered. But is backwards causation possible? That may depend upon our definition of causation, and in particular on whether the definition includes the notion of temporal order.

One knee-jerk reaction to backwards causation is simply to say that it is conceptually incoherent, or that it is impossible by definition. For example, if we adopted Hume's definition of causality, then by definition a cause must precede its effect. But crucially we have already rejected definitions like Hume's because they pack in the concept of temporal order. Such definitions will not be afforded to us if our goal is to reduce temporal order to something non-temporal.

One might say that temporal relations are determined by the *dominant* direction of causal arrows, but as we will see in a bit, this may not work when we think in terms of statistical mechanics or if we find ourselves in a region of the Universe where causal arrows run in a different direction than the rest of the Universe.

Humean causality is not the only possibility. A number of contemporary accounts of causation have tied the notion of causality to that of explanation. One famous early statement of this position comes from Hanson (1958: 54).

There are as many causes of x as there are explanations of x. Consider how the cause of death might be set out by the physician as 'multiple haemorrhage', by the barrister as 'negligence on the part of the driver', by a carriage-builder as 'a defect in the brakeblock construction', by a civic planner as 'the presence of tall shrubbery at that turning'.

Van Fraassen (1980: 125) interprets Hanson's example as showing that "the salient feature picked out as 'the cause' in that complex process, is salient to a person because of his orientation, his interests, and various other peculiarities in the way he approaches or comes to know the problem—contextual factors."

Very crudely, then, if we give up Humean causation we might adopt a notion of causality along the following lines:

(41)   E causes E′ iff the presence of E explains (relative to our interests) E′

A couple of points are worth noting here. First, we are now very close to smuggling perspectival relations back into the definition. If we need to lean on explanation, a good case can be made that what counts as an explanation depends not only upon our interests, but also (or perhaps therefore) on our perspectival positions. Here we have come full circle to my example of the impending meeting with the boss. The only content that explains why I got up and went to the meeting is content that contains a perspectival property—my grasping that the meeting was at that very time (a thought that I then expressed using the word 'now'). The detenser's story cannot bottom out with a notion of explanation, for a case has been made that we need perspectival content to account for much of the explanation at issue.

If you think about it, perhaps perspectival properties already intruded with any account of the mark method. The worry is that the strategy behind the mark method relies upon the encoding of certain information on the rock. But in this sense, the rock that is either marked or unmarked is very much like the simple switch machine I envisioned in Section 4.4. Is the mark on the rock correctly encoding the necessary information? Well, to know that it would seem we have to consult the designers of this system. And now we are knee deep in perspectival contents just as we were with questions about whether a system is a correctly functioning adder or a malfunctioning quadder. In this case we want to know whether the system is a correctly functioning marked rock, or a malfunctioning system (due to the mark rubbing off or some such thing).

It may well be that perspectival content gets pulled into any strategy we employ. Suppose, for example, we tried to ground things in a Lewis (1972) counterfactual account of causation. That account in turn relies on a notion of causal dependency. But is that temporally asymmetric? Lewis thought it was only contingently asymmetric. It certainly doesn't rule out backwards causation. You might be inclined to think that we could go with the direction of most causal dependencies, but as we will see, this is not obviously a successful strategy.

The problem is this: Once we unhook causation or explanation or causal dependency (or whatever) from temporal direction, how do we establish without mere stipulation that causation or explanation or causal dependency (or whatever) has forward-looking direction? Once we abandon the stipulation that causation and explanation have temporal order packed into them, it is open season for backwards causation. There is nothing incoherent about it.

Dummett (1964), for example, has suggested that one can imagine cases where individuals hold coherent (if possibly false) beliefs that entail that an effect precedes its cause. Dummett's thought experiment involves an exotic culture where a tribal chief dances while the tribe's hunters are away on a hunt. The chief believes that the dancing will cause the hunt to be successful. Crucially, the chief dances until the return of the hunters (presumably after sundown) even though it is clear that the hunters broke off their hunt some time ago. If we point this out to the chief, he or she will insist that when the dance was terminated early in previous years the hunt was a failure. In short, the chief believes in backwards causation.

Shortly, I will get to the question of whether this belief is coherent. For now it is important to note that one needn't invent exotic (to us) cultures to find examples of belief in backwards causation. As Dummett noted, cases like this are actually quite common with prayer. For example, one might pray all day that a friend has a successful operation even if it is clear that the operation ended in the morning. Or, hearing of a fire or disaster in a friend's neighborhood, one might pray that the friend was not harmed. The question is whether the beliefs that give rise to such behavior are *coherent*. One objection to backwards causation which Horwich (1987) calls *bilking* is designed to show that they are not.

The bilking argument, which Horwich attributes to Tolman (1917), involves setting up an experiment in which we:

(i)   wait for the alleged effect E;

then:

(ii)   try to prevent the alleged cause E' from happening.

For example, in the case of the dancing chief, we might wait for the hunters to have a successful hunt, and then proceed ahead (perhaps by helicopter) to prevent the chief from dancing.

If we do this, then one of two results will obtain. Either E will often occur without E', or we will be unable to prevent E'. If E occurs regularly without E', then the hypothesis that E' was the cause of E is discredited. If we cannot prevent E' after E has taken place, then what we have is evidence that E is causing E' and not the other way around (e.g. it would appear that the good hunt causes the dancing). Either way, the thesis that there is backwards causation looks untenable.

But Horwich argues that the bilking argument is defective. Let's consider each of the two possible results. First, let's suppose that we successfully run the bilking experiment—that we observe E, and then prevent E' from taking place. So, for example, we observe a successful hunt, call our cohorts in the village, and have them tie up the chief to prevent further dancing. Does this really show that E is not regularly caused by E'? At most it shows that E' does not cause E when we are bilking. One might object that it is suspicious that backwards causation is unnecessary only when bilking. Isn't this a rather embarrassing coincidence? Perhaps not to the chief. Perhaps the deity chooses not to show its hand directly, and thus does not let the bilking experiment reveal its hand (leaps of faith or nothing, reasons the chief).

Alternatively, let's suppose that after we observe E taking place, we continually fail in our efforts to prevent E'. So, for example, suppose all of our attempts to get to the chief fail (perhaps our radios break, or our helicopter crashes). Perhaps repeated attempts to run the bilking experiment meet with this end. Does it really follow that E must be causing E'? Horwich suggests not.

The fact that E is necessary for E' is compatible with the view that E' causes E, at least on the non-Humean view of causation which the advocate of backwards causation will adopt. If it is objected that forward-oriented causation is to be preferred, then we can respond that this is simply begging the crucial question. Recall we began this discussion by calling into question the Humean definition of causality.

There is, however, surely something unexpected in these continual failures to carry out the bilking experiment. Why should bilking fail every time we attempt it? Horwich is inclined to argue that these would simply be inexplicable coincidences. Alternatively, we can once again imagine coherent, if supernatural, explanations. Perhaps the deities will thwart any attempts to test the effectiveness of petitioning them. This explanation would certainly fit the facts as well as anything.

Let's be clear about what the import of this discussion of backwards causation has been. If one adopts a causal theory of temporal order, then one must abandon theories of causality like Hume's in which temporal order is part of the definition. But once such definitions are abandoned it appears that backwards causation cannot be dismissed as incoherent. But if backwards causation is to be admitted, then the attempt to reduce temporal order to causal order will fail. We are left, then, without a physical property to which temporal order can be reduced. Perhaps we can reduce earlier-than and later-than to some other physical property.

Are there alternative physical reductions of temporal order? van Fraassen (1970) and Mehlberg (1935) have drawn attention to a proposal due to the French philosopher Georges Lechalas. Lechalas' (1896) proposal was that one might be able to reduce temporal concepts to the concepts of classical physics. The key to Lechalas' proposal was the idea (propounded by Laplace 1798) that each state of a mechanical system is determined or caused by other states of that system, and that this determination is described by the laws of mechanics. In short, the idea would be that temporal order might be reduced to the notion of causal order determined by classical physics.

Central to the idea of classical mechanics is the notion that macroscopic bodies consist of collections of particles, and that these particles are in turn governed by Newton's laws of motion:

(I) The Law of Inertia
A body continues in a state of rest or uniform motion along a straight line, unless it is subject to a force.

(II) Force = Mass X Acceleration
If a force acts on a body, then the body has an acceleration in the direction of that force, and the magnitude of the acceleration is directly proportional to the force, and inversely proportional to the mass of the body.

(III) For Every Action, There Is an Equal and Opposite Reaction
The forces exerted by two bodies on each other are equal in magnitude and opposite in direction, along the line joining their positions.

Following Laplace, Lechalas' general thesis was that given the state of every particle (or small region of the continuum) at t, and given these laws, all subsequent states are determined. Lechalas observed that given such a physical theory, the notion of temporal order might be reduced to the order of events entailed by the theory.

The first problem is that a given description of the state of a particle will have to include not just its position and mass, but also its velocity. But since velocity is defined in classical mechanics as distance/time, it appears that temporal concepts have once again been smuggled in—not in a definition of causality, as before, but in the state description of a particle. Lechalas might try to take velocity as a primitive, but as we saw in Section 7.2, this would flout Humean supervenience, and if we can make an exception for intrinsic velocities, why could we not also make an exception for perspectival contents like those expressed with the use of tensed language?

The second problem has to do with the appeal to the notion of the state of every particle at t. If temporal concepts are to be exorcised, then this formulation is not benign. What is needed is a definition of simultaneity that does not appeal to temporal concepts.

Lechalas apparently saw this difficulty and proposed the following.

Take particles X and Y. We can find the state of X that is simultaneous with the state E of particle Y in the following way.

Find the force with which X attracts Y at E. The simultaneous state of X is one in which Y attracts X with equal and opposite force.

Even ignoring the relativistic concerns, there are a couple of difficulties with this proposal. First, it may well be that two bodies can attract each other with the same force at different times. For example, consider the case of the earth orbiting the sun (or some idealized version of the same phenomenon). At least once a year they will attract each other with the same force.

Even if concerns about the reduction of simultaneity can be answered, other difficulties remain. For example, there is some question as to whether the laws of mechanics rule out all but one ordering of states. According to van Fraassen (1970), it is certainly conceivable that given knowledge of the disposition of every particle in the universe at a particular time t, there would be a number of possible alternative dispositions for every particle at some time t', later than t.

Most importantly, Newton's laws are time reversible. So, even if Lechalas' strategy could be successfully exploited to achieve a temporal order, it certainly would not yield a reduction of temporal direction. That requires other moves.

So far we have only been discussing physical ways of cashing out the order of events, but that is at best only half the problem. Now we need to ask: what nontemporal physical properties can account for the *direction* of time? One commonly pursued solution to the problem of the direction of time is to appeal to the Second Law of Thermodynamics. One might exploit the law of entropy in giving a physical basis to the direction of time, thus:

The Law of Entropy
If S1 and S2 are states of system X, and S2 is of higher entropy than S1, then S2 is later than S1.

Entropy, crudely, is the general propensity for systems to become less organized through time. For example, it seems to be the case that the Law of Entropy governs the state of order in my office. Over time, it becomes messier rather than more organized. Another standardly given example is the fact that cream does not separate out from coffee. Rather, when one puts cream in coffee it gradually mixes with the coffee.

The problem with this strategy, however, is that if we define time as the direction of greater entropy, then what becomes of the Second Law of Thermodynamics? It then appears to say nothing more than that "if S1 and S2 are states of system X, and S2 is of higher entropy than S1, then S2 is of higher entropy than S1." But the Second Law does not appear to be so vacuous. It appears to have clear empirical content.

Even if we wanted to hold that time is the direction of greater entropy, matters are complicated by the fact that since the reduction of thermodynamics to statistical mechanics, the Second Law has been stated probabilistically.

Law of Entropy revised
A change occurring in an isolated system will probably lead to a state of greater or equal entropy.

But Boltzmann observed that there would be no physical counterpart for the relations before and after in the universe as a whole, since the universe as a whole is most probably in a state of thermal equilibrium.

However, there are local disturbances in which portions of the universe are in a state of disequilibrium. For these localities, before and after might be reducible to the notions of increasing entropy.

Then in the universe, which is in thermal equilibrium throughout and therefore dead, there will occur here and there relatively small regions of the same size as our galaxy (we call them single worlds) which, during the relatively short time of eons, fluctuate noticeably from thermal equilibrium . . . For the universe, the two direction of time are indistinguishable, just as in space there is no up and down. However, just as at a particular place on the earth's surface we call "down" the direction toward the center of the earth, so will a living being in a particular time interval of such a single world distinguish the direction of time toward the less probable stated from the opposite direction (the former toward the past, the latter toward the future).   (Boltzmann 1964: 446-7)

It has thus been proposed that the direction of entropy might be defined for "branch systems." Suppose that a system is isolated from its environment. Then the following holds.

(i) If the branch system is in equilibrium initially, it is usually still in equilibrium when its isolation ceases.

(ii) If the branch system is not in equilibrium initially, its entropy increases most often during its isolation.

Suppose that we thought of the visible Universe as a branch system. We might conclude that the visible Universe is not in a state of thermal equilibrium and that therefore the entropy of the visible Universe is most likely increasing. So, we might conclude, the future is the direction of increased entropy in the visible Universe.

There is a problem, however. There are branch systems in which entropy is decreasing. Consider such a region and consider the denizens of such a region. They may have hit upon a Second Law theory of temporal direction, and may well have attempted a reduction of temporal direction to entropy. We might laugh at their situation; for what they thought was future would actually be the past. But before we become too amused we should consider matters from their perspective. They will doubtless think that we are the ones who have things backwards! Who's right? According to Mellor (1981), it is a matter of "majority vote" in our region of space.

This is a possible response for certain purposes, but if we are interested in cashing out a concept related to that of temporal direction it seems that we have jumped the rails. If newly discovered vastly larger regions of the Universe have reverse entropy from our region, are we really prepared to say that we have had the future and past reversed?—that our childhoods lie in the future and our deaths lie in the past? Is this an acceptable position?

There is one final, very important, point that needs to be made about Boltzmann's notion of entropy—one that I alluded to in Section 5.2. On Boltzmann's theory, entropy is clearly perspectival. This is a point that is noted by Galistel and King (2009: 1877), in comparing Boltzmann's work on entropy with Shannon's.

Shannon called his measure of uncertainty entropy because his formula is the same as the formula that Boltzmann developed when he laid the foundations for statistical mechanics in the nineteenth century. Boltzmann's definition relied on statistical considerations concerning the degree of uncertainty that the observer has about the state of a physical system. Making the observer's uncertainty a fundamental aspect of the physical analysis has become a foundational principle in quantum physics, but it was extremely controversial at the time.   (1877)

So just as we saw in Chapter 5 that the notion of information leans heavily on perspectival contents, so too does the notion of entropy in nineteenth-century statistical thermodynamics.

If entropy will not help us in an attempted reduction of temporal order, will anything else? Are there any physical laws or processes that are temporally asymmetric? This is certainly an empirical question (the question is open at the subatomic level—or at least has been during the process of writing this book), but current evidence suggests that there may be no such processes. If there *is* a time asymmetric process in nature, however, it doesn't settle the issue of which is future and which is past, and finally, if we attempt to reduce our understanding of the direction of time to such processes, we thereby undermine the integrity of the claim that the process is time asymmetric. Hence the aperspectivalist can claim no advantage on this score.

8.3 The Need for Interperspectival Content in Scientific Practice

At points previously in this book I've suggested that much of the practice of science relies upon the extensive use of indexicals and other ways of expressing perspectival contents. In the experimental setting, perspectival contents are used to talk about individual experimental apparatus and particular objects of investigation (including specific samples), methods tried and modified by the experimenter, when and where experiments are to take place, and who will be doing the work or assisting in the work. In this vein we are fortunate that the open source movement in scientific publishing has extended to the online publication of lab notes. There are many such examples one can find online, but to illustrate I've chosen two "notebook" entries from the biologist Rachel Jane Harding on her site labscribbles.com (reprinted with permission) (http://labscribbles.com/

2016/03/15/domain-mapping-of-full-length-huntingtin-by-limited-proteolysis-with-chymotrypsin (last accessed August 27, 2018).

Domain mapping of full-length huntingtin by limited proteolysis with chymotrypsin
Posted on March 15, 2016 Author racheljaneharding1
Comment

I am continuing to try and understand the domain architecture of the huntingtin protein. In a bid to validate my previous limited proteolysis/mass spectrometry experiment, I wanted to see if I could get similar proteolytically stable fragments by digesting my remaining aliquot (courtesy of the generous Stefan Kochanek and Bin Huang) of full-length huntingtin protein with a different enzyme, chymotrypsin, instead of trypsin. Using an orthogonal enzyme with a different cleavage specificity is a good way to validate the regions of protein which are truly accessible to proteolytic enzymes which therefore likely represent less structured regions of the huntingtin protein and are possibly linker regions between the more structured domains of the protein.

In an eager attempt to see what, if any, fragments are proteolytically stable, I stained the gel for too short a period of time, so it is back in the silver-coomassie stain overnight. However, some bands are visible (wahey!) around 100 kDa and 120 kDa so I am very hopeful as to what I will see tomorrow! You can read all about the details and see a picture of the gel on Zenodo [https://zenodo.org/record/47678]. More on this in the morning.

Obviously the use of the first person pronoun jumps out here. She is, after all, giving us a report from *her* lab. And her report is also temporally perspectival. She previously didn't stain her sample enough previously, so now she is going to stain it again. The sample is properly identified perspectivally—it is *her* sample. She doesn't need to tell us its spacetime coordinates. Some of the bands of stained gel *from her sample* were visible to her, etc.

The following lab notes were posted two months later.

http://labscribbles.com/2016/05/29/test-expression   (last   accessed August 27, 2018).

Test Expression of Huntingtin Domain Constructs in Insect Cell Culture

Posted on May 29, 2016 Author racheljaneharding1

I am back from vacation and other distractions and now have some new and exciting data to share with everyone.

Following on the previous limited proteolysis experiment where I chopped up the protein into proteolyticaly stable nuggets which allowed me to work out the potential domain boundaries of the huntingtin protein, I designed constructs which would allow me to make these regions of the huntingtin protein in insect cells. Insect cells were chosen as the expression system of choice as this system generally performs well when trying to make more complicated human proteins.

Most of this lab work was not done by myself but by some seriously talented members of the SGC Toronto biotechnology group—Peter Loppnau (cloner extraordinaire), Ashley Hutchinson (talented insect cell production and test expression scientist) and Alma Seitova (expert in eukaryotic expression systems). Thanks to all of them for their help with this work.

On to the results! As per usual, all of the data I have is uploaded to Zenodo [https://zenodo.org/record/53738] so feel free to browse through and let me know what you think. This is also very preliminary—we will be following this work up with some validation steps shortly.

Most of the designed constructs do not express although there are some clear positive results which is great! Having chatted to other scientist completing similar experiments, this does seem in line with their own experiences. I am now aiming to scale up production of these hits to see whether I can make and purify meaningful quantities of the protein for other experiments AND whether the protein generated is of sufficient quality i.e. is it folded and functional?

All of the constructs are designed with the predicted secondary structure in mind and it does seem that including additional helices or short runs of amino acids either end of a predicted domain boundary does make a huge difference as to whether soluble expression of the protein is achievable in insect cell culture. This suggests that perhaps some of the weaker hits could be optimised further with subtle changes to the N and C-terminal boundaries so I will need to get my thinking cap on to see if I can design something better.

More data to follow soon!

In this case we see further discussion of the sample from the original experiment, and changes and modifications to that particular sample. Harding was not talking about the sample in the abstract or from a third person perspective, but clearly had a first person perspectival relation with the sample. It is not incidental or unimportant that she describes the sample in this way. If she did not do so we would have little reason to trust her on the nature of the sample, how it was modified, or for that matter on the achieved experimental results. If she did not have a first person perspectival relationship to the testing equipment we would feel the same way—similarly if she did not have a first person perspectival relation with the resulting bands of stained gel. Like the importance of chain of custody, so too in the experimental setting the experimenter needs to be perspectivally related to the laboratory equipment, the sample material, and the medium in which the result is reflected.

You might think that we could bleach Harding's lab notes from all of the perspectival content. We could replace the 'I's and 'my's with 'Dr. Harding's, we could replace the 'now' with the date, etc. Obviously, this will lead to some pretty wooden lab notes, but we could live with that. The problem is that this bleaching method can lead to the loss of the ability to express important content.

Let's set aside the easy John Perry cases here. Let's suppose that Harding knows who she is and doesn't have any other philosophical problems (burning pants, etc.). So we aren't going to worry about cases where she becomes angry because someone named Rachel Harding is taking credit for her work, nor about cases where (having lost track of the date) she complains that she did the work years before Rachel Harding did. Let's also forget about her concern over why the SGC Toronto biotechnology group is assisting her arch nemesis, Rachel Harding.

Setting all this aside it still seems to me that there is impending content loss, and that it shows up in the epistemic strength of her lab notes. Saying that she herself was there when it happened seems like a stronger epistemic claim than saying that Dr. Harding was at location l at time t. By situating herself in the experimental process she is strengthening her epistemic claim and authority concerning the ongoing experiments.

This certainly applies to the remarks on the intentions and plans of the experimenter as well. Reading about the plans of some Dr. Harding is one thing; reading a first person report of plans is quite another. Now of course she could always take credit for writing the notes herself at a later time (saying something like "I wrote those then"), but in doing so she infuses the perspectival content at that later time. She is effectively inviting us to swap in 'I's for the 'Dr. Harding's at a later time.

I believe that the use of first person expression in the lab notes also underwrites normative claims here. By describing the experiments in a first person vocabulary, she is expressing personal responsibility for the work. It probably also makes her expression of thanks to others a bit more sincere as well. When she says "more data to follow soon!" that is a kind of promise, which, as we saw earlier, has a normative perspectival element to it as well.

Insofar as epistemic position, responsibility, sincere gratitude, and keeping promises are important to scientific practice, they are important elements of those lab notes as well. Bleaching the notes of their expressions of perspectival content likewise bleaches them of their epistemic and normative contents. The expression of perspectival content is not window dressing in those notes—it is the key to understanding the value of those notes.

8.4 The Need for Interperspectival Content in Scientific Theory

In the previous subsection I made the case that the practice of science is replete with perspectival content. However, so far I've been giving the detenser the benefit of the doubt that scientific *theories* themselves are free from perspectival properties—that they offer us the view from nowhere. But is this actually correct? Work in quantum physics casts some doubt upon this idea.

The issue raised by quantum physics can be illustrated by way of the so-called double slit experiment. As many readers will know, firing a random pattern of electrons towards a plate with two slits in it yields a wave interference pattern. This wave pattern occurs even when the particles pass through one at a time. But if one sets up a detector to see which slit the particle is passing through, the wave function collapses. One does not get a wave interference pattern but rather simply two slit patterns, as though individual electrons were passing through the slits.

There are numerous interpretations of this experimental result, ranging from the Copenhagen interpretation of Bohr (1934, 1961) and Heisenberg (1930) to the Many Worlds interpretation of Everett (1957) and the Relational Interpretation of Rovelli (1996). The competing accounts of the phenomenon do not concern us here. What does concern us is that in some way or other, all accounts must integrate the role of observation into the theory.

The point, in a nutshell, is that the context of observation (which is perspectival, if anything is) has itself become an important—indeed critical—component in the fabric of scientific theories. Abner Shimony (1993: 4) puts the situation like this:

The replacement of classical physics by quantum theory was, of course, the result of puzzling sets of physical phenomena, and not of philosophical reconsideration. Nevertheless, there are several philosophically significant respects in which quantum physics differs from classical physics, the most important being that the concept of an "observation" plays a central role in the quantum physical picture of the world. The relation of elements to the physical theory to experience no longer seems to be extraneous to physics, but seems to be an intrinsic part of physical theory itself.

Famously, von Neumann's (1955) interpretation of quantum physics was that a change of state is only complete when "the result of the observation is registered in the observer's consciousness" (Shimony's gloss). And, as we have seen, consciousness presupposes the deployment of perspectival properties.

Niels Bohr didn't press for the need for consciousness in the theory, but did hold that "the change of state is the consequence of the fundamental assumption that the description of any physical phenomenon requires reference to the experimental arrangement" (Shimony 1993: 3).

Notice that while previously we saw that Rachel Harding's lab notes made frequent references to her experimental apparatus, those references presumably do not make it into the ultimate description of the genetic material she is working with. However, at the quantum level this is no longer the case. The experimental apparatus and its locus of attention is a factor in the character of reality itself. This is sometimes taken as being a weird consequence of quantum physics, but perhaps it should not be surprising.

In Shimony's view there had always been an uneasy tension in classical physics between the theory itself being mechanistic and the experiential aspects of science. The assumption was always that the theory itself could be completely mechanistic, but the discovery and verification of the theory (and application of it) was not.

Classical physical theory was consistently "mechanical" in the sense that the fundamental physical entities were considered devoid of sensuous qualities; and it was "empirical" in the sense that most of the classical masters recognized that the truth of physical theory is tested by its predictions regarding the observable behavior of things. However the apparent discrepancy between the "mechanical" and the "empirical" aspects of classical physics did not seem to impede the development of the science. It was possible to relate fundamental physical concepts to common characteristics of the objects encountered in daily life and in the laboratory, and these common characteristics could somehow be recognized by an observer.   (1993: 4)

Here I believe that Shimony is talking about the kind of experiences reported by Harding in her lab notes. For it is in the laboratory, of course, where the theory intersects with our lived world. But Shimony goes on to observe that this question—how exactly do we accomplish this?—remained unexamined and obscure.

(This was already understood, in a matter-of-fact way, by Galileo and Newton, who were, after all, experimenters as well as theoreticians.) Thus, a relation between the physical Weltbild and experience could be established, even though the process whereby the observer performed his act of recognition was very obscure. Indeed, classical physics was indifferent to attempts to explain this relation ontologically – e.g., by means of a causal connection between mental and physical events. The network of more or less tacit rules for applying theoretical physics to ordinary objects and of normal procedures for dealing with the common characteristics of these objects allowed classical physics to by-pass the fundamental ontological problem.   (1993: 4)

Shimony, I believe, is thinking of this problem in terms of a mind–body dualism. I'm not sure that the mind/body distinction is coherent, but I do believe that a coherent distinction can be drawn between perspectival and aperspectival contents and whatever role consciousness plays in the experimental context and in the application of scientific theories to the lived world, perspectival contents are a key part of that role.

With quantum physics we get to a point where the clean distinction between aperspectival theories and perspectival experimental setting collapses, for now we have to confront the possibility that the theory must incorporate observations or other perspectival contents as part of the theory itself (not just as a ladder we scale to get to the theory). In other words, the neat philosophical firewall between observation and theory breaks down. It is no longer clear that mature physical theory can avoid the deployment of perspectival contents.

Of course, philosophers have a long history of extruding philosophical conclusions from minimal knowledge of quantum physics, but my point is not tied to any particular story that physicists have offered about quantum physics. My point is rather that, right or wrong, if those stories, offered by physicists, are coherent, then we need to make room for perspectival contents in the theories offered in physics. On the flip side, it would seem to follow that true aperspectivalists are committed to dismissing large regions of contemporary quantum physics, simply because of the perspectival content being drawn on at the most fundamental level. Whether the stories being proposed by Bohr, Heisenberg, Rovelli, Everett, Shimony, etc. are wrong is one thing; my point is that philosophers should not rule them out as incoherent because of their philosophical aversion to perspectival contents.

9

Conclusion

We have covered a lot of ground in this book, but it is my hope that three central ideas have been clear throughout.

First, interperspectival contents, like those expressed using tense, are indispensible. We need them to explain the motivations for our actions and the reasons for our emotions. We also need them to explain important features of our perceptual and other conscious experiences. We need them to make sense of normativity understood very broadly, ranging from our moral behavior, to our linguistic behavior, all the way to the behavior of the computational systems which we build, and perhaps computational systems of unknown origin. More generally, we need them to make sense of the basic ideas of the theory of information.

Second, the great rift that has been with us since McTaggart (1908)—the A-series/B-series divide—can be reconciled. There is no paradox inherent in combining tense and the B-series—to the contrary, both resources may be necessary to have a coherent story about the flow of time.

Third, interperspectival contents are ineliminable. They cannot be reduced to more (seemingly) friendly aperspectival properties. There is no metaphysical reduction, and, as we have seen, there is no way to eliminate them from scientific practice. Even at the biological and physical level they are critical to the experimental setting, to the application of theory, and ultimately, our description and understanding of reality itself.

Beyond these three ideas, there is another question: What is the scope and range of interperspectival contents in our world? In this work, we have examined three "core" examples of interperspectival content—temporal, spatial, and personal. Are there others?

Informally, we talk about diverse perspectival positions that we may find ourselves in—positions sometimes characterized in terms of gender, or class, or race, or ability. Often, we despair of being able to communicate across these divides, and to be sure we can never fully know what it is like to be in someone else's perspectival position. But our study of temporal, spatial, and personal perspectival contents suggests that we should not be too hasty in despairing of the possibility of communication across these divides. It is at least possible that these additional perspectival positions will afford interperspectival contents of their own—contents that do not exhaust what it is like to be in someone else's shoes, but nonetheless make it possible for them to share their thoughts and attitudes with us, should we choose to listen.

Appendix: Presentism

In the main body of this book I argued that tense (and interperspectival contents more generally) is indispensable and ineliminable, and I also argued that A-series/B-series compatibilism is a coherent and attractive doctrine for a number of reasons. But nothing in that said that we *had* to endorse B-series resources. So far, we have only looked at arguments for the need for inter-perspectival contents. Could we dismiss the B-series and go down the route typically taken by tensers—being presentists?

In my view this is very much an open question. On the one hand there are deep concerns about the very coherence of presentism. More pressingly, I believe that cross-temporal reference and temporal anaphora present thorny difficulties for any defense of presentism. In this Appendix, I explore those worries.

A1 Is Presentism Either Trivial or False?

Presentists say that only present things exist. That leads to the following question: Is the predicate 'exists' tensed, or not? If 'exists' is tensed it is presumably present tensed, and then the claim that only present things exist comes to the claim that only present things *presently* exist (and who would argue with *that*?). Alternatively, the presentist might reformulate the claim as "everything that did exist, exists, or will exist presently exists." But prima facie this seems absurd, since, for example, the first baby born in the year 500 existed but does not presently exist. So it looks like presentism is either trivial or false.

Thomas Crisp (2004a,b) claims that we can defuse this argument by showing that it is unsound. His line of argumentation is helpful because I think it helps us burrow our way to the deep problem underlying this question, so I will follow his argumentative structure for the most part. Crisp begins by distinguishing the following three possible versions of presentism:

(Pr_a) Only present things exist now (i.e. presently exist).
(Pr_b) Only present things existed, exist, or will exist.
(Pr_c) Only present things (tenselessly) exist.

The anti-presentist argument claims first that (Pr_c) collapses into (Pr_b),[1] so we can just concentrate on (Pr_b) and (Pr_a). But (Pr_b) is manifestly false and (Pr_a) is

---

[1] If you think this step looks suspicious, you're right; I'll come back to it later.

trivially true. Accordingly, the formalized argument against the coherence of presentism goes as follows.

(P1)   Presentism is either (Pr_a), (Pr_b), or (Pr_c).

(P2) (Pr_a) is trivially true.

(P3) (Pr_b) and (Prc) are trivially false (or rather, (Pr_c) collapses into (Pr_b) and (Pr_b) is trivially false).

(C)   Presentism is either a trivial truism or a manifest falsehood.

That's the argument. What is the presentist to say?

Crisp claims that the answer to this argument is to stand our ground on (Pr_b) and hold that it is not trivially false. Crisp's strategy involves seeing that (Pr_b) can be formulated either as (Pr_b') or (Pr_b'').

(Pr_b') For every x, if x existed, exists, or will exist, then x is a present thing.

(Pr_b'') For every x, x is a present thing.

How does this help with the case of the first baby born in the year 500 (which, recall, existed but is not present)? Well, for the presentist, the domain of quantification does not include the first baby born in the year 500, so, for example, (Pr_b'') makes no claim about the first baby born in the year 500 presently existing. On the other hand, we can still make sense of the past tense claim that the first baby born in the year 500 existed if we leave 'for some x, x is the first baby born in the year 500' safely embedded within the scope of the past tense operator, as follows.

(RE1)   WAS(for some x, x is the first baby born in the year 500)

The idea is that (Pr_b'') and (RE1) can be happily conjoined, allowing us to say both that the first baby born in the year 500 existed and that everything exists presently. The analysis in (RE1) is not unique to Crisp's proposal. This idea has been a standard move for presentists since Prior (1967, 1968), and there are a number of familiar complications that we are putting on the back burner here.[2]

---

[2] One problem with this is that (running into the teeth of Kripke (1980)) we apparently need a descriptive theory of names for this to work. If names are referring expressions, then of course no embedding is going to help keep their referents out of the domain of discourse. So, for example, Prior (1967, 1968) argued that since Queen Anne was deceased, a description would have to go in for her name in a sentence like 'Queen Anne existed'. Presumably one will want to say that 'The Roman Empire' is (or stands proxy for) a description of some form—likewise for 'The Holy Roman Empire'.

Another stock worry that we will address later in this chapter has to do with cross-temporal relations. For example, suppose I wanted to utter something like the following.

(i)   I resemble Fitz Hugh Ludlow.

In the discussion to follow, I'll also set aside these issues and take up the more narrow issue of whether the strategy is workable for all presentists and explore some of the complications that arise in formulating the definition of presentism.

A1.1 Why Crisp's solution is no help to the Very Serious Tenser

Consider the following doctrine, which is inspired by Zimmerman (2005).

(**Very Serious Tensism**): Every natural language predication is inherently tensed. There are no untensed predications—in particular no time-indexed verbs/predications—in natural language, hence none can be employed in the metalanguage of the semantics for natural language.[3]

By saying that there are no time-indexed verbs or predicates, I mean that no natural language predicates are of the form 'Pred(x,t)', which would mean something like x is (timelessly) Pred-at-t.

The problem is that Crisp's solution to the triviality objection offers little comfort for the Very Serious Tenser. To help the Very Serious Tenser, Crisp needs to find a form of quantification that doesn't involve predication. Why?

Since Fitz Hugh (author of *The Hasheesh Eater*) is long departed from this planet (in several senses, but here I merely mean that he is dead), we have a difficulty with the resemblance relation. We need the name 'Fitz Hugh Ludlow' to remain within the scope of a past tense operator. The problem is that we have a present tense resemblance relation, which means that its argument positions are not in the scope of past tense.

Finally, what do we say about sentences that require span operators (consider Lewis' example, 'There have been many queens named Anne' as well as considerations raised in Zimmerman (1998a,b), or, for that matter, objects that can go in and out of existence (like committees and nations)?

(ii)   Something existed, does not exist now, but will exist again.

This seems to be blocked on Crisp's story, since it involves quantification into the scope of the past and future tense operators. In effect:

(iii)   ($\exists$x) PAST(exists(x)) & ~exists(x) & FUT(exists(x))

We will take up these questions in Section A2.

[3] There are a number of details I'm skipping over here. For example, a Very Serious Tenser would presumably hold that a verb with past tense morphology, like 'walked', is going to include a past tense morpheme ('-ed') and an inherently present-tensed verb ('walk'). Both morpheme and stem would carry tense. As I argue in Section A2, this leads to puzzles in its own right. Another possibility, employing an event-style analysis, would have 'John walked' come to something like this: 'there is an e, e is a walking and John is the agent of e' was true. This sort of analysis, which was discussed in Ludlow (1999: section 8.2), might then take the gerundive tense (as in 'walking') as being a basic inherent tense. Notice also that there are a lot of occurrences of 'is' in this analysis, and the Very Serious Tenser is presumably going to take all of them as being tensed as well.

Because if we say something like 'for every x, such that x is . . .', we have that auxiliary 'is' involved, and according to Very Serious Tensism that 'is' must be tensed. Crisp thinks that he can meet this challenge—easily, in fact—by giving the account of presentism in (Pr_b'') above, or in its alternative formulation (Pr_b'). In Crisp's words, "(Pr_b') involves an *unrestricted* quantifier, one that ranges over *everything*. The presentist who construes her thesis thus proposes of each thing x in our most inclusive domain of quantification that if x existed, exists now, or will exist then x is a present thing." (Pr_b'') is supposed to have similar virtues.

Now, the appeal to an unrestricted quantifier that ranges over absolutely everything is controversial, and there has subsequently been a great deal of work on the topic, some of it anthologized in Rayo and Uzquiano (2007). In that volume, for example, Charles Parsons (2007) expresses concerns about logical problems related to Russell's paradox. Gabriel Uzquiano (2007) notes that there are problems when we have theories with conflicting vocabularies and ontological commitments (which theory does 'absolutely everything' actually quantify over?). Michael Glanzberg (2007) argues that on pain of generating semantic and set-theoretic paradoxes, quantifiers need to be understood as restricted, or at least the domains must be restricted in important ways.

My concern, which I developed in Ludlow (2004), is somewhat related to Glanzberg's point, although the motivation is different. My point is that quite independently of any concerns about paradox, natural language simply does not have unrestricted quantification. My basic worry boils down to this: What are we to make of the predicates 'thing' and 'in our most inclusive domain of quantification'? They are surely predicates and by Very Serious Tensism they are therefore tensed.[4] Accordingly, his claim comes to "each present thing presently in our domain of quantification is a present thing." The triviality objection is reborn.

I don't think that any amount of playing around with talk of "domain of quantification" is going to be at all helpful here for the simple reason that one is going to have to say something about what makes it into the domain of quantification, and no matter how general one makes the characterization of membership it is still going to involve a tensed predicate. Indeed, even if one dispenses with any meaningful characterization of the domain and tries to give a trivial account like 'x is in the domain iff it is in the domain', there is still the relational predicate 'is in', which is tensed.

One might object that one *can* say tensed things about what goes into the domain that wouldn't render presentism trivial. For example, one could make the

---

[4] If you think it sounds strange to talk about nominal predicates like 'thing' as being tensed, hang on. In a bit I'll show that even if they aren't strictly speaking tensed, this problem will re-emerge when we attempt to give a semantics for these constructions.

following speech: "Absolutely *everything* goes in the domain. Even among present things, there are to be no restrictions: big things, small things, short things, tall things—all of them go in. And future objects go in too, if they exist. For example, anything that *will be big*, anything that *will be small*, anything that *will be short*, and anything that *will be tall* goes into the domain. Likewise, anything that *was* a dinosaur goes in." Can't the presentist thus say some significant things about the domain using tensed language without making it trivial that only presently existing things are in the domain?[5]

Unfortunately, this strategy doesn't help. Crisp's idea is that you can avoid worries about 'everything' if you appeal to an independent notion of widest possible domain of quantification that is somehow more basic than the quantified expression with its restriction. The suggestion of saying *"everything* goes in the domain" inverts matters by relying on a more primitive notion of quantification to explain what goes in the domain. That's fine, but then it renders the talk of the domain superfluous. In effect, it amounts to the next strategy I will take up—taking the quantifier 'everything' to be primitive.

So, *could* one avoid these difficulties by just introducing unrestricted quantification directly and taking it to be primitive?—i.e. not defined in terms of domains of quantification? This strategy is more promising, but ultimately I think that it also fails. The problem is this: if unrestricted quantification is primitive, then one must give unrestricted quantifiers a disquotational semantics. The reasoning here is that a semantical primitive just is a term or expression that is given "as is" in the metalanguage without any further reduction. The new problem is the one I mentioned earlier: There are no unrestricted quantifiers in natural language, so you can't give unrestricted quantifiers a disquotational semantics.

Now you might say, "who cares about the semantics of natural language, I'll provide a regimented metalanguage that departs from natural language in that it *has* unrestricted quantification." That's a possible reply, but this metalanguage is going to stand in need of interpretation, and this interpretation must (ultimately) take place in a language that we understand—i.e. a natural language.

That probably went by pretty fast; so let me try to spell it out a bit more carefully. I'll begin with the following doctrines:

(SA) Semantic Accountability: Inherent semantic properties of natural languages cannot be regimented away by introducing metalanguages that lack those properties (ultimately those introduced metalanguages will need to be interpreted in a natural language metalanguage).

---

[5] This hypothetical objection is in fact not hypothetical at all, and has been put to me by Ted Sider in more or less precisely those words.

(PUPU) Phonologically Unrealized Predicates are Ubiquitous.

(SAQ) Seriousness about Quantification: Inherent properties of natural language quantifiers cannot be regimented away in the metalanguage. (For example, if all natural language quantification is restricted—possibly by a phonologically unrealized predicate—natural language quantification cannot be regimented into unrestricted quantification.)

(NLQR) Natural Language Quantification is Restricted.

If one is serious about semantics one has to recognize that there are a number of predicates in natural language that are phonologically unrealized—i.e. not visible on the printed page and not pronounced. So, for example, there is no visible difference between present tense 'hit' and past tense 'hit', but by hypothesis there is a phonologically unrealized past tense morpheme attached to the latter verb. (PUPU) is the thesis that such phonologically unrealized predicates are ubiquitous in natural language—and they had better be if one is a Very Serious Tenser, given that many natural languages don't have overt tense. Accordingly, if you endorse Very Serious Tensism you appear to be committed to (PUPU).

Now, if you are committed to Semantic Accountability then you must also endorse Seriousness about Quantification (it is actually something of a corollary of Semantic Accountability). This means that there are no properties of natural language quantification that you can regiment away without having some really good alternative story. Unfortunately, all natural language quantification is restricted (NLQR), so the introduction of unrestricted quantification into the metalanguage would require regimenting the metalanguage. So you're stuck.

Here is a rough formalization of the argument.

(P1)   Semantic Accountability is true.

(P2)   Semantic Accountability entails Seriousness about Quantification.

(P3)   Seriousness about Quantification entails that if all natural language quantification is restricted then all metalinguistic quantification is (ultimately) restricted.

(P4)   All natural language quantification is restricted (possibly by phonologically unrealized predicates).

(P5)   If unrestricted quantification is a primitive then some metalinguistic quantification must (ultimately) be unrestricted.

(C)   Unrestricted quantification can't be a primitive.

Of course this just takes us to a conclusion about quantification in natural language. One might wonder why we can't use a formal language in the metalanguage—one in which quantification is not restricted. The problem, again, is that if we are delivering a theory of meaning, the metalanguage needs to be one that we understand, which is to say one for which an interpretation can be given. This brings us back to semantic accountability. All the interpretations on offer involve the use of natural language quantifiers in the metalanguage—quantifiers that are restricted. Model theoretic semantics are of course possible, but even here the description of the model will involve natural language quantifiers (see the discussion of generalized quantifiers below). Furthermore, we want our semantics to deliver more than just entailment relations; we shall want an absolute semantics if we are interested in delivering the meanings of object language sentences. Just as tense cannot be escaped, I believe that natural language quantification cannot be escaped.

If this is right, then there's not much hope for the primitive-quantifier strategy, but a lot turns on premise (P4).[6] Is it really the case that there is no unrestricted quantification in natural language? First, let's get clear on what we mean by restricted quantification (Crisp uses the terminology differently,[7] so we have to be careful here). By a restricted quantifier, I mean a quantifier expression that comes with a (possibly phonologically unrealized) predicate restriction. So, for example, in 'All men are mortal', 'men' is the restriction on the quantifier (or *determiner*) 'all'. Now it is standard practice in formal logic to dispense with these restrictions (or at least *appear* to dispense with these restrictions) in cases like '$(\exists x)F(x)$' and '$(\forall x)G(x)$'. Natural language is not so accommodating, as examples (42) and (42) show.

(42)   *Every is mortal.

(43)   *No exists.

Even where we seem to get by without an explicit restriction, as in 'all is lost', it is pretty clear that we understand an implicit predicate as in (44).

(44)   All (hope) is lost.

Now one might object that we do give the semantics for '$(\exists x)F(x)$' and '$(\forall x)G(x)$' and when we do so we use unrestricted quantification in the metalanguage. But do we? Notice that our informal gloss on these is something like 'there is an x, such that x is F' and 'for all x, x is G'. I'm not going to raise a fuss about the verb 'is' in 'there is an x'—we can avoid that by employing a locution like 'for some x'.

---

[6] I don't mean that the other premises cannot be challenged. They do seem to be premises that most philosophers of language, having reflected a bit, would find uncontroversial. (P4) is the premise that might spark controversy since it is, after all, an empirical claim.

[7] When Crisp speaks of 'restricted quantification' he means that the domain of quantification is restricted. It's clear enough what he means, but the usage is nonstandard so I'm not going to follow it here.

The real problem is that the philosopher's syntax is fractured if taken at face value. The first occurrence of 'x' is standing in for a predicate and the second is standing in for a grammatical object (grammatical argument). To see this consider (Pr_b'') with linguistic category labels substituted for the variable positions. We get something like (45), where 'N' stands for *Noun* (a predicate) and 'NP' stands for *Noun Phrase* (an argument), the index 'i' indicates the relevant binding relationship, and the star (*) indicates that the linguistic structure is somehow ill-formed.[8]

(45)   *For [every N_i], NP_i is a present thing.

Is (45) really ill-formed? Yes, as it is similar in form to (46).

(46)   *For [every boy_i], he_i is a present thing.

Both represent examples of catastrophic type-mismatch—identifying predicate positions with argument positions.

Now of course we can understand utterances of (46) but presumably only by instituting some tacit repairs. The thought is that if we are confronted by utterances of (46) we recognize that they are ill-formed and make some minimal modification to their structure in order to process them. In this case, we might try something along the lines of (46r), where the repair is accomplished by shifting the index from the noun to the NP.

(46r) $[_{NP}$ every boy$]_i$ $[_S he_i$ is present$]$

In this case we can give a standard generalized quantifier semantics for 'every boy' (more on this in a bit). We can repair (45) as well, this time by introducing a phonologically unrealized predicate N to serve as the restriction on the quantifier, which in turn allows us to shift the index to the NP 'every N' (the 'e' is what linguists call a trace (of movement of the NP) and it is interpreted as a bound variable):

(45r) $[_{NP}$ every N$]_i$ $[_S e_i$ is present$]$

The problem is that any repair that is going to make (45) well formed is going to involve the introduction of a phonologically unrealized predicate. Since, by Very Serious Tensism, any such predicate must be tensed (whatever the abstract noun N is—'exists', 'is self-identical'—it must be tensed), the triviality argument rears its head once again.

---

[8] We can think of a noun phrase (NP) like 'every boy' as being composed of a noun (N)—in this case 'boy', and a determiner—in this case 'every'. The noun by itself is ordinarily taken to be a predicate. The noun phrase is not a predicate but is an argument that is capable of saturating some predicate (as in 'every boy is mortal') or perhaps a quantificational element that binds into an argument position (that is, it might bind a pronoun as in 'every boy is such that he is mortal'). Some noun phrases will evince more complexity (e.g. 'every tall boy with red hair') and others will—on the surface at least—appear to have less complexity (e.g. the pronoun 'he' or the demonstrative 'that').

One might object here that just because N is tensed it doesn't follow that it must be *present* tensed, and hence the mere introduction of a tensed predicate N will not be enough to make the triviality argument work. One might insist that N could be past tensed and that this would allow us to dodge the triviality objection.[9] For example, one might hold that it is not at all trivial to say "every former dinosaur is present"—a non-presentist would reject that 'former dinosaur' is past-tensed, so tensed.[10] Applying this argument to (45r) the idea would be that an utterance of (45r) comes to the claim that every former-N, present-N, and future-N is present and that this is hardly something that is trivially true— any non-presentist would reject it.

Matters are a little complicated here. In the first place, it seems doubtful that 'former dinosaur' is past tensed. It is arguable that 'former dinosaur' is a present tensed predicate that is true of absolutely nothing. Being a former dinosaur is like being a former Beatle or a former Syracuse professor. It is in fact a property that one has in the present. 'Former dinosaur/Beatle/Syracuse professor' is *presently* true of those individuals that were dinosaurs or Beatles or Syracuse professors but are no longer. 'Former N' is a present tense predicate, whatever the N. Indeed, even if we had past tense morphology (i.e. elements like '-ed') on our nouns it is not clear that PAST-Syracuse-prof wouldn't just mean that you are *currently* a former Syracuse professor.

In languages that *have* overt temporal morphology on their nouns, matters play out in basically this way. According to Burton (1997), with a fair bit of cross-linguistic consistency (e.g. in the Coast Salish languages Squamish and Halkomelem and the Ojibwe language), these morphemes tend not to work like the verbal tenses—rather, they are understood as devices marking death, destruction, and loss. For example, 'my pencil-PAST' means my currently broken (or lost) pencil; 'the dog-PAST' means the dead (or lost) dog.[11]

---

[9] This suggestion needs to be dressed up a little bit. One idea would be that not only is there a phonologically unrealized noun, but a noun with tense built into it:

(45r')   [$_{NP}$ every TNS-N]$_i$ [$_S$ e$_i$ is present]

[10] This objection is due to Ted Sider (pc).

[11] Here Crisp (2004b) raises an objection. He asks us to consider (i).

(i)   Past football games were televised.

We aren't talking about present football games that have retired in some sense. Thus, claims Crisp, 'Past' in (i) is doing something that looks very much like tense on a noun.

One response is that 'Past' here is actually providing tense for all of (i). It works like the expression 'quick cup of coffee'. When I say "Let's have a quick cup of coffee," we aren't talking about a special kind of coffee; we are saying that our coffee drinking will be expedited. So maybe we should think of the tense, if it is a tense, as being applicable to the whole business.

(ii)   PAST[football games were televised]

If it is really the case that nouns cannot have future or past tense, then one might be tempted to say that they aren't tensed at all. That is, one might try to hold that the restricting noun in (45r) is untensed. In effect, this strategy gives up Very Serious Tensism but hangs on to a nearby doctrine that we could call *Very Serious Tensism-VO* (VO because it only applies to verbs only).

The problem here is that the inner event (the event of being televised) needn't be past tensed, as we see in (iii).

(iii)   Past football games are frequently rebroadcast on ESPN Classic.

Notice, however, that this still presents a problem for Crisp, for now the problem of cross-temporal relations rears its ugly head:

(iv)   Past football games are rebroadcast on ESPN classic but *they* don't exist.

One might wonder if the games themselves are rebroadcast. Perhaps what get broadcast are *recordings* of the games? This doesn't seem right given the possibility of cases like the following.

(v)   Past football games are rebroadcast on ESPN unless their recordings have been lost.

I do think there is something going on here that undercuts Crisp's position, however. Acrisio Pires (pc) has suggested that these allegedly tensed nouns only really work with "eventie" nouns. So, for example, we have the following contrast.

(vi)   #Past dogs are being televised tonight.
(vii)   Past dog shows are being televised tonight.

I think this alleged noun-attached tense also tends to like nouns that are names for occupations. Thus the following contrast. Let's use 'former' to be vivid.

(viii)   #Former books are boring.
(ix)   Former bookbinders are boring.

It isn't just that bookbinders can undergo change and books cannot. Consider (x).

(x)   #Former caterpillars are beautiful.

This is still off, even though we can think of butterflies as being former caterpillars.

ex' is a bit different than 'past' and 'former', and it introduces some strange properties of its own.

It clearly likes certain nouns that aren't obviously eventive ('wife', 'husband', etc.) but not all nouns. For the most part, 'ex' too prefers eventive nouns. Thus we have the following contrast.

(xi)   #Ex dogs are fun.
(xii)   Ex dog trainers are fun.

What is weird, though, is that if there is an intervening adjective, like 'fun', the judgments flip.

(xii)   #Ex fun dog trainers are annoying.

This is true with husband and wife as well.

(xiii)   #Ex fun husbands are annoying.

So this suggests that the ex is not really latching onto the noun phrase, so much as whatever it is adjacent to. If this is right, then if we introduced an eventive adjective the judgments would flip back again. And behold.

(**Very Serious Tensism-VO**) Every natural language *verb* is inherently tensed. There are no untensed verbs—in particular no time-indexed verbs—in natural language, hence none can be employed in the metalanguage of the semantics for natural language. There may, however, be predicates (nouns, for example) that are untensed.

The verb/noun distinction is unstable (or nonexistent) in some languages, but let's set this complication aside for the time being and see if this relaxation of Very Serious Tensism buys us anything.

Unfortunately, it won't buy us much—not if we want a compositional semantics (i.e. a theory of meaning) to be possible. To see this, we need to consider a simple semantic theory for (45r) employing generalized quantifier (GQ) theory. The basic idea behind GQ theory is that determiners like 'every' and 'some' denote relations between sets of objects. So, for example, consider the sentence (46r) again. In this case 'boy' denotes the set of all boys and 'is present' denotes the set of all things that are present (for the sake of simplicity I'm just considering an extensional fragment of English, and am overlooking issues about co-extensive predicates). Using "[[ϕ]]" to speak of the meaning or denotation of an expression ϕ, we have the following.

(47) [['boy']] = {x: x is a boy}

(48) [['is present']] = {x: x is present}

The determiner 'every' denotes a relation holding between sets of objects (in this case):

(49) [['every']] = {<X,Y>: |X-Y| = 0}

(xiv) Ex take-no-prisoners dog trainers are annoying.

(xv) Ex hardworking husbands are annoying.

This is not the time or the place to work out the fine details of what is going on in these constructions, but a crude generalization may be in order. When an expression like 'ex' or 'past' or 'former' attaches to a standard noun, if the result is grammatical it has a meaning on the order of something that is presently no longer a thing of that type (ex-husband). The exception is when these elements attach to a noun phrase that has an internal event structure, in which case tense or something very much like tense is operating on the internal predicate (presiding, or training, or working hard or being a football game).

If this is right, then developing an idea from Larson (1998) we can make explicit this internal event structure. So, for example, the noun 'president' might have a semantics in which there is an event structure consisting of an event of presiding and an expression of agency.

But this only gets Crisp halfway there, for it only allows us to formulate presentism for events and event-based nouns. It still does not allow us an account of 'everything exists now'.

Skipping some details, our little semantics tells us that 'every boy is present' is true just in case the following holds:

(50) $|\{x: x \text{ is a boy}\} - \{x: x \text{ is present}\}| = 0$

That is, take the set of all boys, and remove all of those that are also in the set of everything that is present. If the result is a set with cardinality 0 (i.e. if the result is the empty set), then what you said is true (and vice versa).

This is a very simple semantics, but we can already see that the move to Very Serious Tensism-VO has bought us nothing. The first problem comes in with the axiom for 'boy', where the set membership is identified via the metalinguistic locution 'is a boy'—notice that the pesky verb 'is' has returned. Even if we try to finesse this away somehow, there is the 'is' of identity (disguised as '=') in the same rule (47), and an 'is' of predication (cardinality of X-Y *is* zero) in the rule for 'every' (49). Finally, there is the metalinguistic expression '*is* the denotation of' which is used in the interpretation of (47)–(49). The point is that the semantics is overrun with explicit and implicit occurrences of the auxiliary 'is' and even by Very Serious Tensism-VO, these are supposed to be tensed.

Any compositional semantic theory is going to run into this eventually. For example, in giving a truth-conditional semantics (in the spirit of Davidson 1967a,b) for (46r), the semantics for the restricting noun 'thing' is going to require an axiom like "x is a semantic value of the noun 'thing' iff x *is* a thing" or perhaps "'thing' *is* true of x." Notice again that pesky 'is'. In addition, the sentence-level theorem will be something of the form "is true iff there *is* an x, such that x *is* a semantic value of 'boy' and x *is* a semantic value of 'is present'." Want to introduce properties? Then you get "x *is* the semantic value of the noun 'thing' iff x *is* the property of being a thing." A sentence-level theorem will be something like "is true iff there *is* an x that *has* the property denoted by 'boy' and *has* the property denoted by 'present'." Even if you try and avoid the auxiliary 'is' (and 'has') and do some Heideggerian language stylings, saying that "x things," you have converted 'thing' into a verb, which is supposed to be tensed according to Very Serious Tensism-VO.

The dialectic here is starting to get a bit subtle, so let's pause and reflect on where we've been and where we are going. The initial concern was whether tensism could even be stated in a way that didn't reduce it to triviality. One initial thought was that the problem stems from having to tense the predicate on the restriction of the quantifier, which in turn leads to triviality (all present things are present). The strategy was to try and get rid of the restriction (which, I argued, does not work) or moving the tense off the restriction (which, I argued, doesn't work either). The problem is that the tense will return when we try to give the semantics for the restriction, for in doing so we are using verbs (taking 'is' to be a verb) and thus they must be tensed.

At this point it looks like the only move available is to give up on the idea of Very Serious Tensism, under either formulation, and allow at least limited use of a tenseless predicate 'be'. That is: Allow the possibility of an untensed vocabulary in addition to tensed vocabulary.

This would be consistent with my views about tense and perspectival contents in this book; I never said that *all* predicates are tensed, merely that tensed predicates are ubiquitous, important to the explanation and understanding of a number of phenomena, and ineliminable. It doesn't follow that there can't be a tenseless 'is', and in point of fact, allowing both tensed and untensed vocabulary was critical to my A-series/B-series compatibility thesis in Chapter 6. Let's call a view that incorporates both ineliminable tensed predicates and tenseless predicates *Somewhat Serious Tensism* (still serious because tense is important and ineliminable, but less serious than other options because we allow untensed (aperspectival) language). Where does this get us?

A1.2 Somewhat Serious Tensism

Let's suppose that we can allow both tenseless verbs and tensed verbs, and suppose further that the tensed verbs are not reducible to the detensed verbs and vice versa. So, for example, 'x will exist' is not reducible to 'x tenselessly exists at t, where t is later than the time of utterance' and vice versa, and 'x tenselessly exists' does not reduce to 'x existed, exists, or will exist' and vice versa. We've already given a name to this doctrine:

> **Somewhat Serious Tensism**:   There are genuine tensed predicates and genuine tenseless predicates in natural language and they are not interreducible.

If, for some reason, the tensed predicates were reducible to the detensed predicates (or vice versa) then we would either have Very Serious Tensism or Serious Detensism (i.e. a completely detensed metalanguage), and then all is lost for the presentist.[12]

Does Somewhat Serious Tensism help? Ultimately I think that it does help, but notice first that in the short run it undermines the argumentative structure of Crisp's defense of presentism. The first problem is that if we adopt Somewhat

---

[12] All is lost, because if the tensed predicates are reducible to detensed predicates presentism doesn't get off the ground, and if the detensed predicates collapse into the tensed predicates, then we are back to Very Serious Tensism, which cannot escape the triviality objection.

Serious Tensism then the various versions of Pr_b offered above are no longer equivalent. Let's review those formulations.

(Pr_b')   For every x, if x existed, exists, or will exist, then x is a present thing.

(Pr_b'')   For every x, x is a present thing.

If one were a detenser or a Very Serious Tenser then these formulations are arguably equivalent, but that doesn't seem to be the case if Somewhat Serious Tensism is true. This is so for it is *logically* possible that there be things that exist (tenselessly), but of which no tensed existence predicates are true. It follows that these formulations of (Pr_b) are not equivalent.

If this is not obvious, perhaps some additional explanation will help. If Somewhat Serious Tensism is true, then we need to introduce two sets of tenses—genuine tenses ($PAST_t$, $PRES_t$, and FUT_t), and detensed "tenses" ($PAST_d$, $PRES_d$, and FUT_d) which are not genuine tenses at all but state-relative B-theory positions—for example, stating that some event is $PAST_d$ if it (tenselessly) holds earlier than the time of utterance. We would then want to provide two different versions of (Pr_b') to avoid conflating these predicates:

(Pr_b'-t)   For every x, if x existed$_t$, exists$_t$, or will exist$_t$, then x is a present$_t$ thing.

(Pr_b''-t)   For every x, x is a present$_t$ thing.

(Pr_b'-d)   For every x, if x existed$_d$, exists$_d$, or will exist$_d$, then x is a present$_d$ thing.

(Pr_b''-d)   For every x, x is a present$_d$ thing.

Whether we are using the tensed (-t) formulations or the detensed (-d) formulations, it is logically possible that there are things that are (for example) $PAST_t$ but not $PAST_d$ and vice versa. In such cases, the universal quantifiers in (Pr_b''-t) and (Pr_b''-d) will range over *both* kinds of objects, and this is why they will diverge in truth value from (Pr_b'-t) and (Pr_b'-d) respectively. To illustrate, suppose that everything that existed$_t$, exists$_t$, or will exist$_t$ is indeed a present$_t$ thing, but suppose also that there is an object (or proposition) that did$_t$ not exist$_t$, does$_t$ not exist$_t$, and will$_t$ not exist$_t$, but which does$_d$ exist$_d$. In such a case (Pr_b'-t) is true but (Pr_b''-t) is false.

The key point now, however, is that given Somewhat Serious Tensism, formulations of presentism are possible which mix the tensed and untensed contents. Thus, for example, we have the following:

(Pr_m)   Only present$_t$ things existed$_d$, exist$_d$, or will exist$_d$

This is far from trivial, and it seems to be a coherent presentist position. It might be what Crisp had in mind by (Pr_c), repeated below, but if so then on Somewhat Serious Tensism, Crisp would be mistaken to insist that (Pr_c) collapses into (Pr_b). Crisp's claims about the relationship between (Pr_c) and (Pr_b) come unglued once we adopt Somewhat Serious Tensism.

(Pr$_b$)   Only present things existed, exist, or will exist.

(Pr$_c$)   Only present things (tenselessly) exist.

So let's consider (Pr$_m$) on its merits. This is a claim that any B-theorist or four-dimensionalist is going to be happy to reject, but it is not manifestly false—or at least no more obviously false than is presentism in general. Arguably then, Crisp has dismissed the most promising formulation of presentism. In sum, I think that a plausible definition of presentism can be offered, but only if one is careful to distinguish tensed from untensed predicates.

I recognize that the argumentative structure above is a bit dense, so perhaps a recap is once again in order. We began with the question of whether tensism was either trivial or false. Crisp argued that it is not trivial because we can help ourselves to unrestricted quantification to express the presentist's thesis. But I argued that if we hold Very Serious Tensism, Crisp's move won't work, because the talk of domains introduces predication, which is tensed. Sider (pc) suggested a way out of this—namely that we can use primitive unrestricted quantification, but I argued that this won't work because natural language quantification is restricted by a noun, which must be tensed. To this Sider (again p.c.) suggested that the noun wouldn't have to be present tensed, but I argued that if those nouns are tensed they are present tensed. What if they aren't tensed at all? Well, in that case the (present) tense rears its head when we do the semantics for the quantifiers—in our metalanguage we used tensed verbs (copulas) to express the semantics for generalized quantifiers or truth-conditional semantics or, really, any semantics at all. I concluded that the only way to really resolve the problem is to bite the bullet and admit tenseless predicates in addition to the tensed predicates.

Another way to put my conclusion is that our only way to avoid having either a vacuous or false formulation of presentism is to allow some degree of A-series/B-series reconciliation—specifically we must allow the *intelligibility* of tenseless B-series predicates. The presentist doesn't need to admit the existence (tenseless) of past and future objects and events. However, as we will see in the next section, avoiding commitment to them is easier said than done.

A2 Presentism and the Problem of Temporal Anaphora

The problem of temporal reference and anaphora is this: Presentists hold that there are no future or past events,[13] even though we routinely use apparent cases of temporal reference and temporal anaphors. So, in the example below from Partee (1973), there is an intuitive sense in which I am not saying that I turned off

[13] See Prior (1967, 1968).

the stove once in the past, but rather am saying that I turned it off during a particular temporal interval.

(52)   I turned off the stove.

We can be neutral about whether this is a case of temporal reference (to the time interval in which I left the house) or a case of temporal anaphora (since, as Partee showed, it bears similarities to the pronominal anaphora system). I will predominantly use the term 'anaphora', because the presentist will ultimately want to avoid talk of reference, which is often taken to entail an ontological commitment to the thing referred to.

Temporal reference/anaphora is found in other environments as well. For example, Reichenbach (1947) showed that some account of temporal anaphora is crucial to providing a semantics of tense for sentences with complex tenses like the past perfect and future perfect. Reichenbach distinguished three events (or event times) S, R, and E, where S is the utterance event, E is the event under discussion, and R is an understood reference event. The complex tenses were then defined in terms of the relative ordering of S, R, and E. The past perfect, for example, would be the case where E is before R, which is before S. The paradigm can be partially fleshed out as follows:

Pluperfect: $<$--E---R---S--$>$
Future perfect: $<$--S---E---R--$>$
Future in Future: $<$--S---R---E--$>$
Future in the Past: $<$--R---S---E--$>$ or $<$--R---E---S--$>$

It has widely been held by semanticists that complex tenses simply cannot be accounted for without Reichenbach's reference event R or some other form of temporal reference.

Additional work by Enç (1986, 1987) has stressed that temporal anaphora can also be argued to hold within noun phrases. So, for example, in (53) one intuitively is not talking about current hostages, but rather those individuals who were hostages during a certain time interval.

(53)   The hostages came to the White House.

The above three arguments do not exhaust the considerations that have been advanced on behalf of temporal reference, and a number of semanticists have developed this general theme, including Hinrichs (1981, 1986), Partee (1984), and Webber (1988). The metaphysical issue, of course, is that if the semantics of natural language is committed to reference to past and future events, then the metaphysics entailed by the semantics of natural language must admit such entities. But then presentism must be false.[14]

---

[14] The case for temporal anaphora has been persuasively made, but sometimes it is oversold. Higginbotham (2009) used the phenomena of sequence of tense (SOT) and dual aspect readings (DAR) to press the case for anaphora-based theories of tense. Here I am not persuaded. First of all, consider the DAR reading of (i).

(i)   Gianni said that Maria is pregnant.

Notice that there is no reading of an utterance of (i) in which Maria's entire pregnancy is future with respect to Gianni's utterance. She must be pregnant at the time of Gianni's utterance (even if Gianni correctly predicts Maria's pregnancy, a subsequent utterance of (i) by speaker S is infelicitous if Maria isn't pregnant at the time of Gianni's utterance). Thus, it looks like the present tense 'is pregnant' has been shifted into the past, and Higginbotham suggests that this is support for the idea that the events are chained in a temporal order on the B-series: Before the utterance of (i) there was an utterance event by Gianni, and at the time of Gianni's utterance event Maria's pregnancy holds (tenselessly).

On the other hand, it also must be conceded that an utterance of (i) asserts that Maria is still pregnant at the time of that utterance. But if this is right, then it isn't entirely clear that the present tense has been shifted into the past. No matter how we cook up the context surrounding the utterance of (i), it doesn't seem the utterance would be felicitous if Gianni uttered it last month seconds before Maria's giving birth. But why isn't it felicitous if the tense has truly been shifted?

An alternative story would be that Gianni and whoever is uttering (i) share a particular specious present (as in 'Hubble said the Universe is expanding'). One way of thinking of this is that the event of her pregnancy is present (in an expanded specious present) even while the event of Gianni's remarking on the pregnancy is in the past relative to our egocentric perspective. This avoids the nesting problem for genuine tenses by opting for a kind of conjunction of tenses, which strikes me as fairly coherent in this instance.

Higginbotham presses back against such a view, arguing of the 'Maria is pregnant' clause that it "cannot match in content any speech of Gianni's in which the (alleged) situation of Maria's [continued?] pregnancy is future to that speech." By this, Higginbotham means that while Gianni may have thought the pregnancy would continue (and perhaps he had to have thought that it would continue for an utterance of (i) to be true) the content expressed by an utterance of 'Maria is pregnant' does not get at that future tensed thought. But surely Gianni could have used the specious present in speaking of Maria's pregnancy (how could he not have?), in which case there is no problem of content mismatch.

I think a better case for anaphoric tense can be found in the SOT cases, which are also discussed by Smith (1975, 1978), Ladusaw (1977), Dowty (1982), Stowell (1995a,b), Enç (1987), Hornstein (1990), Abusch (1997), and Giorgi and Pianesi (1997). Consider the contrast between (ii) and (iii):

(ii)   Gianni said that Maria was ill.
(iii)   Gianni saw a woman who was ill.

There is a reading of (iii), not found in (ii), in which the woman was just recently ill (perhaps well after Gianni saw her). The question is why this reading isn't available with (ii) and it appears that what we have is a case of obligatory SOT—the internal past tense operator in 'Maria was ill' has to be shifted back to the time of Gianni's utterance or before. Dowty (1982) and Ladusaw (1977) thought that this reading could be pragmatically derived, but not persuasively in the view of Higginbotham and others. To see the difficulty

Another construction that seems to rely on temporal anaphora involves what Lewis (2004) called "tensed quantifiers." Tensed quantifiers are idioms of quantification that embed tensed verbs—for example, 'there was', 'there have been', 'there will be', etc.

In simple cases, tensed quantifiers present no problem, but Lewis argues that plural quantification is another matter. Consider the following examples.

(54)   There have been at least two queens named 'Elizabeth'.

(55)   There have been many kings named 'George'.

Focusing on (54), the problem is that the presentist can't simply give the past tense operator (assuming an operator theory of tense here) wide scope over the whole sentence. To see this, consider (54a).

(54a)   PAST[There have been at least two queens named Elizabeth]

It simply isn't true that at some point there were two queens named Elizabeth. You might think that there has to be a brute force translation of this construction that gets the truth conditions right, but Lewis is correct that such a strategy is not promising. Consider (54-bft), for example.

(54-bft)   PAST[($\exists x$) x is a queen named 'Elizabeth'] and PAST[($\exists y$) y is a *another* queen named 'Elizabeth']

As Lewis notes, a presentist can't help herself to this. (If Elizabeth I doesn't exist, what sense does it make to say there is "another" Elizabeth?)

Suppose we tried nesting one tense within the other?[15]

of the pragmatic strategy, consider (ii') where we have loaded the context to favor a forward-looking reading:

(ii')   The amazing fortune-teller Gianni said that Maria was ill.

This still seems to require that Maria's being ill must shift back at least to the time of Gianni's speaking, even though there seem to be enough pragmatic resources to force a reading where Maria's illness occurs well after Gianni spoke. For example, even though it is salient, thanks to Gianni's occupation, that he is frequently in the business of making prognostications, we still don't extract the interpretation that Maria would be ill between the time of Gianni's utterance and the time of utterance of (ii'). Thus, the story I proposed for DAR cases in Ludlow (1999) does not seem to work here. On the other hand, it must be observed that Higginbotham's shifted tense story does not work all that well either. Consider (iv).

(iv)   The amazing fortune-teller Gianni said that Maria will be ill.

Notice that Maria's illness must now be future to the time of utterance of (iv), but on Higginbotham's story it should be possible for the illness to be any time in the future relative to Gianni's utterance.

[15] As I argue in Ludlow (2012), nesting tense operators in this way creates difficulties of its own, but let's play along for now.

(54-bft*)   PAST[($\exists x$) x is a queen named 'Elizabeth' and PAST[($\exists y$) y is a queen named 'Elizabeth' and x=/=y]]

Here the problem is that overlapping queens are possible (consider two kingdoms with overlapping queens named Elizabeth).[16] Perhaps we need a disjunction?

(54-bft**)   PAST[($\exists x$) x is a queen named 'Elizabeth' and PAST[($\exists y$) y is a queen named 'Elizabeth' and x=/=y]] v PAST[($\exists x$) x is a queen named 'Elizabeth' and ($\exists y$) y is a queen named 'Elizabeth' and x=/=y]

We can immediately see that things get messy with examples like 'There have been 17 kings named Charles', or 'There have been more kings named Charles than kings named George', and what about infinite quantities? (Imagine a dynasty that has endured from the beginning of time and consider (55).)

(55)   There have been infinitely many kings named Charles.

Or, if you are looking for a less fantastical example, consider an example with vague or underspecified quantifiers:

(56)   There have been quite a few kings named Charles.

Lewis' conclusion is that the "presentist is accustomed to boast that his metaphysic of time is the view of the common man, uncorrupted by philosophy. The unsuspected complexities that we've just been exploring should therefore come as very bad news."

In a bit we will look at presentist approaches to temporal anaphora, but first I want to consider a nonanaphoric solution that Lewis floats and then shoots down. Suppose you said that a past tense operator should not be thought of as an operator that quantifies over moments of time, but rather as an operator that picks out spans of time. To make this vivid, we can imagine extending the pronunciation of 'has' to indicate we are talking about a span— we say 'haaas'.

(54-pso)   It haaas been that (there are two queens named Elizabeth).

The other part of this is that we don't think of this as an objectual quantification over a span; we think of the operator being . . . sorry . . . span-ish. Just as for a presentist the simple 'has' does not quantify over earlier times, so too here 'haaas' does not quantify over intervals. Lewis's central objection to this strategy is that

---

[16] I suppose one could argue that the nested PAST operators only require that one queen precede the other by the narrowest unit of time possible, but we could imagine a process by which two queens named Elizabeth are installed simultaneously in a single act.

"span operators are so badly behaved that nobody should claim to have a primitive understanding of them."

For example, Lewis contends that they create ambiguities "even when" prefixed to a sentence that is not ambiguous.

(57)   It haaas been that (it is raining and the sun is shining).

As he notes, (57) could mean that there is a past interval with a sun shower or that there is a past interval with at least one rainy interval and one sunny interval.

Lewis also contends that the span operator can be appended to contradictions to make truths.

(58)   It haaas been that (it rains and it doesn't rain).

Further, it will make different truths when prefixed to different contradictions. Sometimes they will make new contradictions.

(59)   It haaas been that it rains nonstop and it doesn't rain.

Lewis concludes, then, that primitive span operators are hyperintensional operators. He also offers the following dilemma for the fan of primitive span operators. Either (a) you discard the two-subinterval disambiguations, in which case you lose your ability to handle example (54), or (b) you discard the throughout-an-interval disambiguation, in which case you still have the problem of embedded contradictions and you lose the original motivating idea.[17]

We have catalogued quite a few objections to presentism that trade on the problem of temporal anaphora, but before we move on there is one additional objection that doesn't involve temporal anaphora, but still involves apparent reference to other times—the problem of cross-temporal relations. Consider example (60), which expresses a resemblance relation between me and the nineteenth-century writer, Fitz Hugh Ludlow.

(60)   P.J. Ludlow resembles F.H. Ludlow.

This time it won't do to throw everything into the scope of a past tense operator, even if we convert both names into descriptions.

(60a)   PAST[the author of *Semantics, Tense, and Time* resembles the author of *The Hasheesh Eater*]

This doesn't say that I resemble the author of *The Hasheesh Eater*, it says that I *resembled* him—past tense. At best, (60a) will be an ok thing to say after I pass away or otherwise cease to resemble Fitz Hugh, or it may be fine if we have a

---

[17]   We will return to the worry about span operators, but for further discussion of Lewis' position and some possible responses, see Brogaard (2007).

particular salient stage of me in mind (for example, when I attended last year's big *Come as Fitz Hugh Ludlow Party*). However, if we think of the past tense operator as ranging over slices of times there is still no time when I resemble Fitz Hugh Ludlow, as there was no time-slice when we both existed.[18] Span operators would be required.

Such are the problems for the presentist posed by temporal anaphora and cross-temporal reference. What are the solutions?

A2.1 Ersatz presentism

By 'ersatz presentism' I speak of a broad class of proposals on which presentists need not speak of future or past objects or events or even times, because substitute stand-in objects can be constructed out of materials that exist in the present.[19]

For example, to deal with future and past times, we might point to a series of numbers, some of them positive and some of them negative, and insist that they represent the future and past time points respectively. Rather than future events and individuals we might try to avail ourselves of descriptions or some other dummy objects constructed out of presently existing materials. So, for example, one might build ersatz objects out of presently existing properties, or one might stipulate arbitrary objects to "stand in" for these objects. For example, I might stipulate that the glass of water next to me is ersatz Fitz Hugh Ludlow.

Obviously more needs to be said here. Whatever object I decide will stand in for Fitz Hugh Ludlow (let's call it 'fitz'), when I say that 'Fitz Hugh Ludlow existed' I am strictly speaking saying that fitz has the property of corresponding to a negative number. And happily, fitz is associated with a negative number (chosen based upon how long ago Fitz Hugh Ludlow lived—so let's say fitz gets a value of -100, or a range from -182 to -138).

The question is, what makes it true that fitz has a value between -182 and -138? Or if it isn't strictly speaking true, what is it that makes it truthy or sort of true? Whether true or sort of true, or even just slightly somewhat hinting at truthiness, these sentences must be doing so by virtue of some facts in the world. By virtue of what is it true (or even truthy) that fitz has a value of -182 to -138? Well, we want to say that it's true because Fitz Hugh Ludlow was born 182 years ago and died roughly 138 years ago (at the time of this writing). But we can't help ourselves to that!—not if it means he lived during that past time interval. For the presentist there is no such past time interval.

We can animate this problem by returning to the present tensed sentence 'I resemble Fitz Hugh Ludlow.' For the ersatz presentist, fitz must stand in for Fitz

---

[18] Thanks to an anonymous reviewer for discussion here.

[19] See, for example, Markosian (2004), Bourne (2006), and Crisp (2007).

Hugh Ludlow, but in what way do I resemble fitz? If fitz is a glass of water next to me it is obviously a problem. But even if fitz is a bundle of presently existing properties it isn't clear that I resemble him. Suppose the bundle consists of properties like being bearded, being glassy-eyed, etc. Whatever the resulting object/bundle is, I don't resemble it, because I don't resemble a bundle of properties. As Oaklander (2010) has argued, problems like this arise for *any* relations between abstract ersatz objects (for example, in what sense does one occur before another?).

Perhaps a better way to put the point is thus: The ersatzer is trying to exploit a representation relation between the ersatz object and the real object. But the representation relation holding between those objects is just as problematic as cross-temporal relations, so it isn't clear what's been gained.[20]

In Section 4.2, I examined the idea that tense might be a narrow psychological property, and we dismissed that idea because psychological states are grounded in states of the external world. The ersatz presentism strategy is another version of this unpromising strategy. What the ersatz presentist seeks is a representation that is to do the work that the past and future objects were supposed to do. But whatever resources the ersatz presentist deploys in an effort to represent past and future events/persons/times, she cannot successfully do this, because you cannot represent properties that have no reflex in the external world.

There is another way to put this point. I can use a series of numbers to represent things. I could represent points along a road, for example. But I can do this because there is a road to represent, and I can establish what numbers in my series correspond to what points on the road. But if there were no road, my series of numbers would not be a representation of the road.[21]

To be sure, we can misrepresent things. I can represent a stick in the water as broken even though it is not, and I can represent a bird in the sky when there is

---

[20]   Thanks to an anonymous reviewer for discussion here.

[21]   As an anonymous reader reminds me, in the front of *The Lord of the Rings*, there is a map of Middle Earth, and of course, there's no Middle Earth to represent. There are a couple of things one can say here. The first is that it isn't actually a map, but a fictional map. That is, the "map" in the front of the book is a part of the fiction. You engage in a pretense that it is a map. Alternatively, one could say that it is a map of a fictional world—it represents Middle Earth as being thus-and-so. But it can do this only because maps *can* represent mountains and rivers and lakes and forests. Critically, maps can do this because there *are* mountains and rivers and lakes and forests. Were there no such things, the "map" of Middle Earth would be pretty useless. Of course this discussion invites the idea that we could go fictionalist about temporal discourse, but as I've discussed elsewhere above, it is one thing to say that our claims about Middle Earth are not true (except in a special sense of "true in the fiction") and quite another to say that all of our claims utilizing temporal reference and anaphora are not true, for this would be to go fictionalist about most of what we say.

no bird but only a drone or perhaps something in my eye. But the possibility of error does not undermine my ability to represent broken sticks and birds, because there *are* broken sticks and there *are* birds and I am designed to (usually) represent them correctly. What I cannot do is represent a class of things (past things or future things) that simply do not exist or are not composed of things that do. There is no way for the representation relation to be established.

All of this having been said, I don't believe the situation is fatal for the presentist. I think the mistake here was the supposition that what is wanted is something to "stand in" for the past and future things (and the relations between them). Something can stand in effectively only if it can represent the thing it is supposed to stand in for. But what if we could find an entirely nonreferential account of temporal anaphors? That is, what if we had an account that didn't need stand-ins because there was no attempt to represent past or future individuals/events/times? How would this be possible? The idea would be to explore the possibility of E-type temporal anaphora.

A2.2 E-type temporal anaphora

In Ludlow (1999) I offered a theory of E-type temporal anaphora on which temporal anaphoric elements are not treated as referring expressions. The basic idea was simple enough: just as E-type nominal anaphors stand proxy for descriptions (not construed as referring expressions, but, following Russell (1905), as quantifier expressions), E-type temporal anaphors might stand proxy for temporal conjunctions. Consider a case like (61), which we discussed earlier.

(61)   I turned off the stove then.

Partee (1973, 1984) seemed to assume that 'then' must *refer* to a moment or period of time. However, this assumption was not necessary. It is alternatively possible that 'then' is standing proxy for a temporal conjunction. For example, 'then' could be standing proxy for 'when I finished cooking', or 'when you recently asked me to'. If we represent this ellipsed clause as '[s ...]', then the logical form of a sentence like (61) might be rendered as follows.

(61')   [s [s PAST [S I turn off the stove]] when [s ...]]

Note the similarity to theories of E-type pronominal anaphora; the key difference is that whereas E-type pronominal anaphors stand proxy for descriptions, temporal anaphors stand proxy for expressions of this form: 'when [s ...]', 'before [s ...]', 'after [s ...]', 'while [s ...]', 'during [s ...]', etc. This is the basic idea, but of course the devil is in the detail, so a brief exposition of the semantic theory is in order.

Let's suppose that our language involves temporal conjunctions; something like the following, where TCP stands for "temporal conjunction phrase" and TP for "tense phrase." Assuming, for expository purposes, a traditional Priorean account of tense we will assume there are tense morphemes that work as operators (so, a tense phrase—TP—will consist of a tense T and a clause S).[22]

TCP → TP1 'when' TP2
TCP → TP1 'before' TP2
TCP → TP1 'after' TP2
TP → TNS S
TNS → PAST, FUT

For the semantics, we begin with the assumption that verbal stems have an intrinsic present tense that cannot be stripped from the verb. So, for example, in the axiom for 'hits' (Val(<x,y>, 'hits' iff x hits y), we need to regard the right-hand side of the axiom as being tensed. If the verb receives a Davidsonian event-style analysis (Davidson 1967b), then the tense still cannot be stripped from the right-hand side of the axiom; it will adhere to the verb 'is' in the axiom, as follows.

(T0)   Val(<x,y,e>, hit) iff there *is* an e, e *is* a hitting, x *is* the agent of e, and y *is* the patient of e

We next introduce a notion of morphological tense, which can handle the basic past and future tense morphemes. We can think of the morphemes as elements that move into prenex position and act like operators, or predicates that take sentence-like objects as their arguments. Accordingly, the syntactic constructions in which we find these morphemes would be as follows, where TP is a tense phrase containing a tense morpheme and a sentential clause,

Morphological Past: $[_{TP} PAST[S]]$
Morphological Future: $[_{TP} FUT[S]]$

The semantics for these morphemes would be as follows, where we rely upon a tensed metalanguage to state the axioms for the past and future tense morphemes.

(T1)   Val(x, PAST) iff x was true
(T2)   Val(x, FUT) iff x will be true
(TP)   Val(true, $[_{TP}$ TNS S]) iff there is an x, s.t.
Val(x, TNS) and x = []S[]

In the axiom TP, we use the closed bracket notation '[]' around 'S' ('[]S[]') to indicate a proposition-like object related to S. We say proposition-like because such objects are not "eternal" like standard propositions; their truth value will

---

[22] Again, the wisdom of operator theories of tense are questioned in Ludlow 2012.

shift over time. In Ludlow (1999) these objects were taken to be "interpreted logical forms" in the sense of Larson and Ludlow (1993).

The next step is the treatment of relative tense. In the Reichenbachian framework, relative tense involves the temporal position of the reference event R. Since appeal to such reference events is not possible for the presentist, another strategy is required. Accordingly, we rely upon the use of implicit temporal conjunctions to do the work that would otherwise be done via temporal reference.

Relative Present:
On Reichenbach analysis: E,R (simultaneous)
Logical form on a presentist analysis: [S] when [. . .]

Relative Past:
on Reichenbach analysis: E—R
Logical form on a presentist analysis: [S] before [. . .]

Relative Future:
on Reichenbach analysis: R—E
Logical form on a presentist analysis: [S] after [. . .]

Crucially, when we provide the semantics for these temporal conjunctions we cannot take 'when' to mean "at the same time," but rather we must take it as a primitive relation holding between proposition-like objects. Likewise for 'before' and 'after'. Accordingly, we have the following axioms for temporal connectives:

(W1)   Val(true, [$_{TCP}$ TP1 'when' TP2]) iff
Val(true, TP1) when Val(true, TP2)

(W2)   Val(true, [$_{TCP}$ TP1 'before' TP2]) iff
Val(true, TP1) before Val(true, TP2)

(W3)   Val(true, [$_{TCP}$ TP1 'after' TP2]) iff
Val(true, TP1) after Val(true, TP2)

Given these axioms and the analysis of relative tense above, we can construct a strategy for giving an account of the complex tenses without appeal to temporal reference. This can be done by positing an implicit temporal conjunction in each sentence containing a complex tense. The resulting logical forms would be as follows:

Pluperfect
On Reichenbach analysis: E—R—S
Logical form on presentist analysis: PAST[S] before PAST[. . .]

Future perfect
On Reichenbach analysis: S—E—R
Logical form on presentist analysis: FUT[S] before FUT[. . .]

Future in the Future
On Reichenbach analysis: S—R—E
Logical form on presentist analysis: FUT[S] after FUT[. . .]

Future in the Past
On Reichenbach analysis: R—E—S
Logical form on presentist analysis: PAST[S] after PAST[. . .]

To illustrate, given the above logical form for a past perfect sentence and a semantics that incorporated a Davidsonian event theory, we would yield the following truth conditions for a sentence like 'I had walked'.

(62)   Val(true, 'I had walked') iff
[][($\exists$e)(walking(e) & agent(I, e) & culminates(e)][] was true before [] . . . [] was true.

What about additional tenses like present perfect? Presumably these involve some aspectual features and we have not had the opportunity to introduce aspect here (notice that perfect aspect has been smuggled into (62)). Until incorporated in a fuller theory involving aspect, we can treat them as morphological tenses as follows.

(63)   Val(x, PRESPERF) iff x has been true

The reader is referred to Ludlow (1999: ch. 8) for the treatment of a number of other constructions, including calendar names, apparent quantification over times ('I've been to New Jersey 18 times'), and so on.

One kind of temporal anaphora that was not treated in Ludlow (1999) is temporal anaphora on temporal intervals. The kinds of cases that I have in mind here include the following, where the italicized 'It' and 'then' appear to be anaphors that refer to temporal intervals (the Middle Ages and George's—and Henry's—youth accordingly).

(64)   a. Abelard lived during the Middle Ages.
       b. *It* was an interesting period.

(65)   a. George made many mistakes in his youth.
       b. Henry made many mistakes *then* too.

What is the presentist to say about temporal intervals? It seems to me that the natural strategy is to bank on the meaning of temporal conjunctions and their ability to temporally situate events with respect to intervals, not just with respect to time points. Accordingly, (64a) might be taken to have the logical form in (64a').

(64a')   PAST[Abelard lives] when PAST[(it is) the Middle Ages] yielding the following truth conditions.

(64a*)   [][Abelard lives][] was true when [][(it is) the Middle Ages][] was true

Or alternatively, if this doesn't have the necessary notion of containment, following a suggestion due to Gil Harman (pc), we might shift the position of 'when' as follows.

(64a**)   when [][Abelard lives][] was true [][(it is) the Middle Ages][] was true

Now, what of the temporal anaphor in (64b)? The suggestion would be that it has the following logical form and truth conditions respectively:

(64b′)   PAST[it is an interesting period] when PAST[(it is) the Middle Ages]
(64b*)   [][it is an interesting period][] was true when [][(it is) the Middle Ages][] was true

Note that the 'it' is pleonastic and not what many have taken to be the temporal anaphor. A similar sort of story could be told for the cases in (65), thus we have the following logical forms and truth conditions.[23]

(65a′)   PAST[George is making many mistakes] when PAST[(it is) his youth]
(65b′)   PAST[Henry is making many mistakes] when PAST[(it is) his youth]
(65a*)   [][George is making many mistakes][] was true when [][(it is) his youth][] was true
(65b*)   [][Henry is making many mistakes][] was true when [][(it is) his youth][] was true

Note also that this story helps to shed light on the possibility of "sloppy identity" here—i.e. the possibility that (65b) can be either about George's youth or Henry's youth. On an analysis in which there is an anaphor referring to some already-identified interval it is difficult to see how this could be explained.

One construction that is discussed in Ludlow (1999), but not in sufficient detail, involves the different senses of 'since'. It would be an interesting project to tease apart the different senses and to show what elements give rise to them, but

---

[23] An anonymous reviewer wonders if there might not be nearby examples in which the 'it' is referential, offering the following: 'It was an interesting period that lasted for three centuries.' Setting aside the issue of whether the pronoun is pleonastic, it seems clear to me that it is not referential. For one thing, if it were referential you would expect it to be stressed: 'IT was an interesting period', but it is unstressed. Indeed it is the sort of construction that admits of the now archaic construction "'twas" (as in 'twas the night before Christmas...'). In this case: ''twas an interesting period'. If we insist that the pronoun refers to some period of time, the presentist can always say that such readings are false.

for our purposes it will be enough to consider three cases, each involving temporal intervals.

case 1: 'continuously since'

(66)   Fred has been lucky since Barney joined the club

In this case we think of (66) as an explicit temporal conjunction, with the conjunction having a meaning that we might gloss as 'ever since'. Accordingly, we can posit the following logical form and truth conditions for the example.

(66')   PRESPERF[Fred is lucky] (ever) since PAST[there is an event of Barney joining the club]

(66*)   [][Fred is lucky][] has been true (ever) since [][there is an event of Barney joining the club][] was true

case 2: 'once or more since'

(67)   Fred has won the raffle since Barney joined the club.

Here 'since' intuitively has the sense of "once or more since." The treatment of this case parallels (67'):

(67')   PRESPERF[Fred wins the raffle] (at least once) since PAST[there is an event of Barney joining the club]

(67*)   [][There is an event of Fred winning the raffle][] has been true (at least once) since [][there is an event of Barney joining the club][] was true

case 3: 'during the interval since'

(68)   Fred has won the raffle three times since Barney joined the club

Once again, after the sense of the temporal conjunction is fixed the analysis proceeds as above:

(68')   PRESPERF[There is an event/situation/case of Fred winning the raffle] (during the interval) since PAST[there is an event of Barney joining the club]

(68*)   [][There is an event/situation/case of Fred winning the raffle][] has been true (during the interval) since [][there is an event of Barney joining the club][] was true

This really only sketches one approach to temporal duration and temporal anaphora that might be pursued within a presentist program. Clearly, handling a full range of linguistic phenomena would involve a much more detailed study.

I hope it is clear that my immediate goal is not to solve the problem, but just to show how daunting it is. And we are just getting started!

A2.3 What about Lewis' objections to span operators?

Here, finally, we come back to Lewis' case of 'two queens have been named Elizabeth'.[24] Let's return to example (57) and recall the concerns that Lewis had with span operators. First, they create ambiguities "even when" prefixed to a sentence that is not ambiguous.

(57)   It haaas been that (it is raining and the sun is shining).

As Lewis observed, this could be true either if there were a past interval with a sun shower or there was a past interval with at least one rainy interval and one sunny interval. Lewis found this to be ill behaved on the part of the operator, but if we choose to insert the E-type temporal anaphors into the construction things don't seem that ill behaved at all. The idea would be that to get the case where there is a sun shower in the interval, the E-type temporal anaphors are the same, as in (57a).

(57a)   It haaas been that (it is raining [when . . .] and the sun is shining [when . . .]).

When there is an interval of rain and a separate interval of sun, then we have two distinct E-type temporal anaphors.

(57b)   It haaas been that (it is raining [when . . .] and the sun is shining [when ___]).

Or alternatively this reading could be glossed as in (57c) with two separate span operators.

(57c)   There haaas been rain [when . . .] and there haaas been sunshine [when ___].

The second concern that Lewis had about span operators is that they could be appended to contradictions to make truths. Recall that his concern was with an example like (58).

(58)   It haaas been that (it rains and it doesn't rain).

---

[24] For a similar-in-spirit but different-in-execution response to Lewis, readers may be interested in Brogaard (2007).

However, if the temporal anaphors are made explicit this worry evaporates. On the assumption that there are two separate temporal anaphors (one for each of the conjoined clauses) then we get (58′).

(58′)   It haaas been that (it rains [when . . .] and it doesn't rain [when ___]).

It is not really making a contradiction true; it is just making manifest the implicit temporal anaphors.

Lewis further worried that the span operator, when prefixed to contradictions, sometimes makes new contradictions. Consider the case where we append the span operator to 'It rains nonstop and it doesn't rain.'

(59)   It haaas been that it rains nonstop and it doesn't rain.

Here we start out with a contradiction and we end up with the possible outcomes that Lewis envisioned. Maybe we get a brand new contradiction, since one possible result is that it rains nonstop for an interval and it doesn't rain in that same interval. Or, maybe we get no contradiction, as when it rains nonstop for one subinterval of the span and doesn't rain during another interval in the span. To get the noncontradictory case we need two distinct E-type temporal anaphors.

(59a)   It haaas been that (it rains nonstop [when . . .] and it doesn't rain [when ___]).

To get the brand new contradiction, we need to lean on the same subinterval.

(59b)   It haaas been that (it rains nonstop [when . . .] and it doesn't rain [when . . .]).

Here is another way to put my point: Lewis's core concern was that the span operators were hyperintensional and hence poorly understood. But the appearance of hyperintensionality derives from an appearance of nonsubstitutability of strong equivalents. But once we have a story that incorporates elliptical clauses, then the argument for hyperintensionality disappears, because things that look the same on surface form aren't really the same after all, and thus there can be a failure of intersubstitutability without the introduction of hyperintensionality.[25]

Now, I recognize that this approach to temporal anaphora has a brute force quality to it, and is not particularly elegant. Moreover, it will run into whatever problems the E-type nominal anaphora encounters. For example, one "corker" for pronominal E-type anaphora that is widely discussed in the linguistics literature is the following.

---

[25] I owe this excellent formulation to an anonymous reviewer.

(69)   If a bishop meets another bishop, he blesses him.

The problem with this example is how to recover the descriptive content of the E-type pronouns 'he' and 'him'. We know that each description involves a bishop, but which bishop? The bishop who met another bishop? But they both met another bishop.

At one point (Ludlow 1994) I experimented with running the discourse anaphora off the thematic roles (thematic roles are predicates like 'agent' and 'patient'). In this case the roles wouldn't be agent and patient, but let's suppose there are distinct roles that we could characterize as theme-1 and theme-2. Then the result would be something like 'the bishop that is theme-1 in the event blesses the bishop that is theme-2 in the event'.

The temporal analogue of this would be (70).

(70)   When a bishop prays before another bishop prays, he keeps praying until the other bishop prays.

The puzzle here is that there is no way to get separate when-clauses because there is no descriptive information that can distinguish the temporal conjunctions. Again, one is tempted to say 'the former' and 'the latter' but which is which?

All of this work and we still haven't dealt with the problem of cross-temporal relations (PJL resembles FHL)! But as we will see, there is something to be said about such relations, and our analysis of them can also inform our understanding of temporal anaphors.

A2.4 Events with tensed thematic roles

Recall the puzzle we faced with cross-temporal relations. The example we fixed on was (60), and we noted that simply replacing the names with descriptions and burying the whole thing in the scope of a tense operator, as in (60a), will not solve the problem.

(60)   P.J. Ludlow resembles F.H. Ludlow.

(60a)   PAST[the author of *Semantics, Tense, and Time* resembles the author of *The Hasheesh Eater*].

As we noted, the problem here is that we don't want the whole thing to be stuffed within the scope of the past tense, as (60) continues to be true, and hopefully will continue to be true.

In the previous section I mentioned the possibility of drawing on thematic roles to account for the content of E-type pronouns. Introducing thematic roles for this or some other reason presents a rather tantalizing possibility. Those thematic roles can be tensed!

To illustrate this idea, let's suppose that in a sentence like (60) the resembler (me) and the resembled (Fitz Hugh) receive different thematic roles. Let's say that theme-1 is the resembled and theme-2 is the resembler. Then we might have an analysis of (60) as in (60b).

(60b)   [There is an event/situation e: resembling (e)] WAS [the x: author of *The Hasheesh Eater*(x)](theme-1 (x, e)) and theme-2 (P.J. Ludlow, e)] when [. . .]

In this case, the scope of the past tense only includes the thematic relation of bearing theme-1 to the event (being the resembled in the resemblance event). Resembling (the relation I bear to the resemblance event) remains present tensed. So, in a nutshell, we have that there is a present event in which I presently resemble something and it was the case that Fitz Hugh Ludlow was the resembled.

This analysis has a quirky ontology. It means that the event of my resembling Fitz Hugh Ludlow started a long time ago—at least 150 years ago, and there was a long gap in the event in which not much happened. From the passing of Fitz Hugh until my arrival there wasn't much going on in this resemblance event, but that is ok.

How far can we take this? Can the strategy allow us to give a presentist-friendly account of B-theoretic relations? Consider (71).

(71)   WWII was earlier than the writing of this book.

(71′)   [There is an event/situation e: temporal-precedence(e)], WAS[theme-1 (WW2, e)] and [the x: x is the writing of this book]theme-2 (x, e)]] when [. . .]

The B-theoretic relation earlier-than gets exploded into an event that is (perhaps) benignly called "temporal precedence," and individuals are related to that event via thematic relations. Some of those thematic relations are past tensed (WWII *was* the theme-1 of the precedence relation).

Still, one might wonder how this avoids ontological commitment to a past event like WWII. Even if it can be characterized by a description, as Kripke showed us we can't do this with every name.

However, there remains an interesting possibility for the treatment of names. Rather than taking them as descriptions in disguise, could we not rely upon the reference relation as having thematic relations as well and extend this analysis to the reference relation itself?

Consider (72).

(72)   'Fitz Hugh Ludlow' refers to Fitz Hugh Ludlow.

If we expand this to reveal the event structure, we would have something akin to (72a) in which the name and the referred-to thing both are assigned thematic relations. Let's say that theme-1 is intuitively the referred-to element and theme-2 is the vehicle-of-referring element.

(72a) [There is an event/situation e: referring(e)], WAS[theme-1 (F.H. Ludlow, e) and theme-2('F.H. Ludlow', e)]

Now, you can rightly ask about the use of names inside the scope of the past tense operator and ask why it is not ontologically committing, but one available response is to say, sure fine, it refers, but let's unpack that reference relation, giving us something like (72a) all over again.[26]

In previous chapters I have been negatively disposed to the idea of running infinite regresses to escape Semantic Accountability. I was not a fan of the idea for indexical content and the self-attribution relation, and I don't see that this new regress is any less problematic. The problem is not that there is a regress in the works, but rather that we are trying to eliminate or hide something (tense or, in this case, reference) by running it up a regress. To put it another way, there is nothing wrong with regresses, but there is something wrong with using regresses to try and banish unwelcome contents.

My goal in this section has not been to make a definitive case either for or against E-type solutions to the problem of temporal anaphora and cross-temporal reference. Rather, it has been to survey some of my earlier work in this area so as to expose the complexity of the task. I remain cautiously pessimistic about the possibility of a solution here.

The question is, is there another way?

A2.5 Eternal objects and weak presentism

Earlier, we briefly touched on Williamson's (1999) story about objects existing, as it were, eternally. Let's take the case of Fitz Hugh Ludlow. We can quantify over Fitz Hugh, and in some sense Fitz Hugh continues to exist, but that is about all that is currently true of Fitz Hugh. He is not alive. He is not a writer. He does not take up space (although perhaps his remains do). He is not much more than a bare particular. As Williamson said, a past table is not a table. Similarly, a former writer is not a writer.

How does any of this help? Williamson's story is attractive, in that it affords us something to link our temporal anaphors to, but it does not do so in a way that traditional B-theoretic accounts do. On a standard B-theoretic approach if I refer to Fitz Hugh Ludlow I am referring to an individual that is (tenselessly) bearded,

---

[26] Thanks to Josh Brown for discussion here.

is glassy-eyed, is a writer, etc. On Williamson's approach that simply isn't the case. We have no reason to say that Fitz Hugh is (detensed-is) bearded or a writer or anything else.

The view is presentism *strictly speaking*, but only because everything that did exist still exists and everything that will exist exists now. But that is about all that they do. Fitz Hugh Ludlow exists but he is bereft of life. He rests in peace. He is an ex-person. The only problem is that he exists. But that problem is a feature; because the bare particular that remains is the thing we can refer to with our temporal anaphors.

Let's suppose that this is close enough to presentism so that a presentist can let it slide; let's call it *weak presentism*. There remains a problem. We were compelled to adopt this position so that we could supply referents for our temporal anaphors and for past and future objects, but is it enough that these objects simply exist? Does reference (anaphoric, or cross-temporal, or any other kind of reference) not require more? To put it another way, can anaphoric reference (or any notion of reference) come this cheaply?

For Gareth Evans (1982), reference did not come easily at all. There had to be an information-theoretic chain linking us and the object to which we refer. But there are plenty of cases in which we have no information-theoretic access to the targets of our anaphors. To take one of Evans' most famous cases (discussed earlier), we may lose a ball bearing in a bucket of nearly identical ball bearings, but most of us would be willing to say that it can still be the target of anaphoric reference. Even for an account of reference like Kripke's, which involves a causal relation with the reference target, it is not clear how *future* targeted anaphors would work.

There is a broad range of opinion on the nature of connection necessary to secure the reference relation. Russell (1910–11), for example, thought that we would have to be directly acquainted with something to refer to it, and thus the only suitable targets of the reference relation were "egocentric particulars" like the referent of 'I'. On the other end, there is recent work by Hawthorne and Manley (2012), which holds that the reference relation is easily secured—perhaps by anything in our forward or backwards-looking light cones—by treating it as existential quantification with a singular restriction.

I don't propose to solve the problem of the reference relation here, because there is another point to be made: The problem of reference is also a problem for the detenser. For example, someone who is a detensing four-dimensionalist about time will want to hold that all future and past events exist (and indeed are just as real as present events) but may not be able to explain how we refer to such things—something necessary for them to be the targets of referential anaphors.

For example, if we deploy the type of temporal anaphora envisioned by Partee, or the event anaphora of the type anticipated by Reichenbach, but have an account of reference like that of Evans or Kripke, we simply won't be in the relevant causal relation or information-theoretic relation to support the needed temporal anaphora. That is, we won't have the right relation to refer to many past events (perhaps *most* past events), and the prospects of referring to future events (crucial in the analysis of some complex tenses) will be dim to nonexistent. In effect, even B-theorists need some alternative to reference in providing an account of temporal anaphora.

If one goes down the Hawthorne and Manley route and liberalizes reference to the point where it is simply existential quantification with a singular restriction, it is far from clear that a presentist can't also help herself to this notion of "reference," and hook it to the kinds of objects proposed by Williamson.

The upshot of this is that while running temporal anaphora off Williamson-style eternal objects raises interesting questions about how it is done, the same how-is-it-done questions are raised by traditional detensed four-dimensionalist theories. Whatever is anchoring the needed reference relation, it is an equal opportunity mystery.

Bibliography

Abusch, D., 1997. "The Sequence of Tense and Temporal *De Re.*" *Linguistics and Philosophy* 20, 1–50.

Anscombe, G.E.M., 1975. "The First Person." In S. Gutenplan (ed.), *Mind and Language: Wolfson College Lectures 1974.* Oxford: Clarendon Press, 45–64.

Arpaly, N., 2003. *Unprincipled Virtue: An Inquiry into Moral Agency.* Cambridge: Cambridge University Press.

Atkins, P.W., 1986. "Time and Dispersal: The Second Law." In R. Flood and M. Lockwood (eds.), *The Nature of Time.* Oxford: Basil Blackwell, 80–98.

Bigelow, J., 1988. *The Reality of Numbers.* Oxford: Oxford University Press.

Bohr, N., 1934. *Atomic Theory and the Description of Nature.* Cambridge: Cambridge University Press.

Bohr, N., 1961. *Atomic Physics and Human Knowledge.* New York: Science Editions, Inc.

Boltzmann, L., 1964. *Lectures on Gas Theory* 1896–1898 (trans. S. Brush). Berkeley: University of California Press, 446–7.

Bourne, C., 2006. *A Future for Presentism.* Oxford: Oxford University Press.

Branquinho, J., 2006. "On the Persistence of Indexical Belief." Paper given to the APA Eastern Division Meeting, December 2005, revised 2006. http://www. joaomiguelbranquinho.com/uploads/9/5/3/8/9538249/persistence.pdf (last accessed September 15, 2016).

Bratman, M., 1987. *Intention, Plans, and Practical Reason.* Cambridge: Harvard University Press.

Brennan, S.E., and Clark, H.H., 1996. "Conceptual Pacts and Lexical Choice in Conversation." *Journal of Experimental Psychology: Learning, Memory, and Cognition* 22, 1482–93.

Brennan, S.E., and Schober, M., 1999. "Uhs and Interrupted Words: The Information Available to Listeners." In *Proceedings of the 14th International Congress of Phonetic Sciences, Satellite Meeting on Disfluency in Spontaneous Speech* (19–22). Berkeley, CA.

Broad, C.D., 1923. *Scientific Thought.* New York: Harcourt, Brace, and Company.

Brogaard, B., 2007. "Span Operators." *Analysis* 67, 72–9.

Brogaard, B., 2008. "In Defense of a Perspectival Semantics for 'Know'." *Australasian Journal of Philosophy* 86, 439–59.

Brogaard, B., 2012. *Transient Truths: An Essay in the Metaphysics of Propositions.* Oxford: Oxford University Press.

Burge, T., 1979. "Individualism and the Mental." In French, Euhling, and Wettstein (eds.), *Studies in Epistemology.* Vol. 4, *Midwest Studies in Philosophy.* Minneapolis: University of Minnesota Press, 73–122.

Burge, T., 1986. "Individualism and Psychology." *The Philosophical Review* 95, 3–45.

Burgess, J., 1984. "Basic Tense Logic." In D. Gabbay and F. Guenthner (eds.), *Handbook of Philosophical Logic*, vol. 2. Dordrecht: D. Reidel, 89–133.

Burton, S.C., 1997. "Past Tense on Nouns as Death, Destruction, and Loss." In K. Kusimoto (ed.), *Proceedings of NELS 27*, University of Massachusetts, Amherst: Graduate Linguistics Student Association, 65–77.

Byrne, A., 2005. "Perception and Conceptual Content." In E. Sosa and M. Steup (eds.), *Contemporary Debates in Epistemology.* Oxford: Blackwell, 231–50.

Cappelen, H., and Dever, J., 2013. *The Inessential Indexical.* Oxford: Oxford University Press.

Casati, R., and Varzi, A., 1995. *Holes and Other Superficialities.* Cambridge: MIT Press.

Castañeda, H.-N., 1967. "Indicators and Quasi-Indicators." *American Philosophical Quarterly* 4, 85–100.

Castannñeda, H.-N., 1989. *Thinking, Language, and Experience.* Minneapolis: The University of Minnesota Press.

Chierchia, G., 1984. *Topics in the Syntax and Semantics of Infinitives and Gerunds.* PhD thesis, Dept. of Linguistics, University of Massachusetts, Amherst.

Chomsky, N., 1959. "Review of B.F. Skinner, *Verbal Behavior.*" *Language* 35, 26–57.

Chomsky, N., 1970. "Remarks on Nominalization." In R. Jacobs and P. Rosenbaum (eds.), *English Transformational Grammar.* Waltham: Ginn, 184–221.

Chomsky, N., 2000. *New Horizons in the Study of Language and Mind.* Cambridge: Cambridge University Press.

Clark, H., 1992. *Arenas of Language Use.* Chicago: CSLI Publications and The University of Chicago Press.

Collins, J., 2007. "Meta-scientific Eliminativism: A Reconsideration of Chomsky's Review of Skinner." *British Journal for the Philosophy of Science* 58, 625–58.

Craig, W.L., 1996. "Tense and the New B-Theory of Language." *Philosophy* 71, 5–26.

Crisp, T., 2004a. "On Presentism and Triviality." In D. Zimmerman (ed.), *Oxford Studies in Metaphysics 1.* Oxford: Oxford University Press, 15–20.

Crisp, T., 2004b. "Reply to Ludlow." In D. Zimmerman (ed.), *Oxford Studies in Metaphysics 1.* Oxford: Oxford University Press, 37–46.

Crisp, T., 2007. "Presentism and the Grounding Objection." *Noûs* 41, 90–109.

Davidson, D., 1967a. "Truth and Meaning." *Synthese* 17, 304–23.

Davidson, D., 1967b. "The Logical Form of Action Sentences." In N. Rescher (ed.), *The Logic of Decision and Action.* Pittsburgh: University of Pittsburgh Press, 81–120.

Davidson, D., 1986. "A Nice Derangement of Epitaphs." In E. LePore (ed.), *Truth and Interpretation: Perspectives on the Philosophy of Donald Davidson.* Oxford & New York: Blackwell, 433–46.

Dennet, D., 1987. *The Intentional Stance.* Cambridge: MIT Press.

Dever, J., 2007. "Low-grade Two-dimensionalism." *Philosophical Books* 48, 1–16.

Dowty, D., 1982. "Tenses, Time Adverbs, and Compositional Semantic Theory." *Linguistics and Philosophy* 5, 23–55.

Dummett, M., 1964. "Bringing about the Past." *Philosophical Review* 73, 338–59.

Enç, M., 1986. "Towards a Referential Analysis of Temporal Expressions." *Linguistics and Philosophy* 9, 405–26.

Enç, M., 1987. "Anchoring Conditions for Tense." *Linguistic Inquiry* 18, 633–57.

Evans, G., 1982. *The Varieties of Reference.* Oxford: Oxford University Press.

Evans, G., 1996. "Understanding Demonstratives." In *Collected Papers.* Oxford: Oxford University Press, 291–321.

Everett, H., 1957. "Relative State Formulation of Quantum Mechanics." *Reviews of Modern Physics* 29, 454–62.

Fine, K., 2005. "Tense and Reality." In *Modality and Tense: Philosophical Papers.* Oxford: Oxford University Press, 261–320.

Fodor, J., 1975. *The Language of Thought.* Cambridge: Harvard University Press.

Forbes, G., 2011. "The Problem of Factives for Sense Theories." *Analysis* 71, 654–62.

Frege, G., 1892. "Über Begriff und Gegenstand," in *Vierteljahresschrift für wissenschaftliche Philosophie* 16, 192–205. Translated as "Concept and Object" by P. Geach in *Translations from the Philosophical Writings of Gottlob Frege,* P. Geach and M. Black (eds. and trans.), Oxford: Blackwell, third edition, 1980, 182–94.

Frege, G., 1956. "The Thought" (trans. by A.M. and M. Quinton). *Mind* 65, 289–311.

Galistel, C.R., and King, A., 2009. *Memory and the Computational Brain: Why Cognitive Science Will Transform Neuroscience.* Chichester: Wiley-Blackwell.

Gerstein, M. et al., 2007. "What Is a Gene, Post-ENCODE? History and Updated Definition." *Genome Research* 17, 669–81.

Giorgi, A., and Pianesi, F., 1997. *Tense and Aspect.* Oxford: Oxford University Press.

Glanzberg, M., 2007. "Context and Unrestricted Quantification." In A. Rayo and G. Uzquiano (eds.), *Absolute Generality.* Oxford: Oxford University Press, 45–74.

Grünbaum, A., 1963. *Philosophical Problems of Space and Time*. New York: Knopf.

Hanson, N.R., 1958. *Patterns of Discovery*. Cambridge: Cambridge University Press.

Hawthorne, J., 2015. "Comments on *Transient Truths: An Essay in the Metaphysics of Propositions* (Berit Brogaard)." *Inquiry* 58, 619–26.

Hawthorne, J., and Manley, D. 2012. *The Reference Book*. Oxford: Oxford University Press.

Heck, R., 2002. "Do Demonstratives Have Senses?" *Philosophers' Imprint* 2, #2, http://www.philosophersimprint.org/002002 (last accessed February 5, 2018).

Heisenberg, W., 1930. *The Physical Principles of Quantum Theory*. Chicago: University of Chicago Press.

Higginbotham, J., 1995. "Tensed Thoughts." *Mind and Language* 10, 226–49.

Higginbotham, J., 2009. *Tense, Aspect, and Indexicality*. Oxford: Oxford University Press.

Hinrichs, E., 1981. *Temporale Anaphora im Englishen*. Unpublished Staatsexamen thesis. University of Tubingen, Tubingen, Germany.

Hinrichs, E., 1986. "Temporal Anaphora in Discourses of English." *Linguistics and Philosophy* 9, 63–82.

Hornstein, N., 1990. *As Time Goes By*. Cambridge, MA: MIT Press.

Hornstein, N., 1999. "Movement and Control." *Linguistic Inquiry* 30, 69–96.

Horwich, P., 1987. *Asymmetries in Time: Problems in the Philosophy of Science*. Cambridge: MIT Press.

Horwich, P., 1990. *Truth*. Oxford: Basil Blackwell.

Kaplan, D., 1977. "Demonstratives." Manuscript UCLA. Reprinted in J. Almog et al. (eds.), *Themes from Kaplan*. Ithaca: Cornell University Press, 1989, 481–563.

Kaplan, D., 1979. "On the Logic of Demonstratives." *The Journal of Philosophical Logic* 8, 81–98.

Kaplan, D., 1990. "Thoughts on Demonstratives." In P. Yourgrau (ed.), Demonstratives. Oxford: Oxford University Press, 34–49.

Kapranov, P., Drenkow, J., Cheng, J., Long, J., Helt, G., Dike, S., and Gingeras, T., 2005. "Examples of the Complex Architecture of the Human Transcriptome Revealed by RACE and High-density Tiling Arrays." *Genome Research* 15, 987–97.

Kripke, S., 1979. "A Puzzle about Belief." In A. Margalit (ed.), *Meaning and Use*. Dordrecht: D. Reidel, 239–83.

Kripke, S., 1980. *Naming and Necessity*. Cambridge: Harvard University Press.

Kripke, S., 1982. *Wittgenstein on Rules and Private Language*. Cambridge: Harvard University Press.

Ladusaw, W., 1977. "Some Problems with Tense in PTQ." *Texas Linguistics Forum* 6, 89–102.

Laplace, P.S., 1798. *Traité de mécanique céleste*. Paris: Duprat.

Larson, R., 1998. "Events and Modification in Nominals." In D. Strolovitch and A. Lawson (eds.), *Proceedings from Semantics and Linguistic Theory (SALT) VIII*. Ithaca, NY: Cornell University Press, 145–68.

Larson, R., and Ludlow, P., 1993. "Interpreted Logical Forms." *Synthese* 95, 305–56.

Larson, R., and Segal, G., 1995. *Knowledge of Meaning*. Cambridge: MIT Press.

Lechalas, G., 1896. *Étude sur L'espace et le Temps*. Paris: Félix Alcan.

Lewis, D., 1972. "General Semantics." In D. Davidson and G. Harman (eds.), *Semantics of Natural Language*. Dordrecht: D. Reidel, 169–218.

Lewis, D., 1979. "Attitudes *De Dicto* and *De Se*." *Philosophical Review* 88, 513–43.

Lewis, D., 1986. *Philosophical Papers*, vol. 2. Oxford: Oxford University Press.

Lewis, D., 1992. "Review of D.M. Armstrong, A Combinatorial Theory of Possibility." *Australasian Journal of Philosophy* 70, 211–24.

Lewis, D., 1999. "Zimmerman and the Spinning Sphere." *Australasian Journal of Philosophy* 77, 209–12.

Lewis, D., 2004. "Tensed Quantifiers." In Dean Zimmerman (ed.), *Oxford Studies in Metaphysics*, vol. 1. Oxford: Oxford University Press.

Lewis, D., and Lewis, S., 1970. "Holes." *Australasian Journal of Philosophy* 48, 206–12.

Ludlow, P., 1982. "Substitutional Quantification and the Problem of Expression Types." *Logique et Analyse* 100, 415–24.

Ludlow, P., 1994. "Conditionals, Events, and Unbound Pronouns." *Lingua e Stile* 29, 3–20.

Ludlow, P., 1999. *Semantics, Tense, and Time: An Essay in the Metaphysics of Natural Language*. Cambridge: MIT Press.

Ludlow, P., 2000. "Interpreted Logical Forms, Belief Attribution, and the Dynamic Lexicon." In K.M. Jaszczolt (ed.), *Pragmatics of Propositional Attitude Reports*. Oxford: Elsevier Science, Ltd.

Ludlow, P., 2004. "Presentism, Triviality, and the Varieties of Tensism." In D. Zimmerman (ed.), *Oxford Studies in Metaphysics*, vol. 1. Oxford: Oxford University Press, 21–36.

Ludlow, P., 2011. *The Philosophy of Generative Linguistics*. Oxford: Oxford University Press.

Ludlow, P., 2012. "Tense and the Philosophy of Language." In R. Binnick (ed.), *Oxford Handbook on Tense and Aspect*. Oxford: Oxford University Press.

Ludlow, P., 2014. *Living Words: Meaning Underdetermination and the Dynamic Lexicon*. Oxford: Oxford University Press.

Ludlow, P., 2015. "Tense, the Dynamic Lexicon, and the Flow of Time." *Topoi* 34, 137–42.

Ludlow, P., 2016. "Tense, Perspectival Properties, and Special Relativity." *Manuscrito* 39, 49–74.

Ludlow, P., and Martin, N. (eds.), 1998. *Externalism and Self-Knowledge*. Stanford: CSLI Publications. Distributed by Cambridge University Press.

MacDonald, H., 2016. "Your Brain and the Second Law of Thermodynamics." *PsychologyToday.com*, posted April 17, 2016. https://www.psychologytoday.com/blog/time-travelling-apollo/201604/your-brain-and-the-second-law-ther modynamics (last accessed December 11, 2017).

Mach, E., 1959. *The Analysis of Sensations*. New York: Dover.

Markosian, N., 2004. "A Defense of Presentism." In D. Zimmerman (ed.), *Oxford Studies in Metaphysics*, vol. 1. Oxford: Oxford University Press.

Martin, C., 1996. "How It Is: Entities, Absences and Voids." *Australasian Journal of Philosophy* 74, 57–65.

Maudlin, T., 2007. *The Metaphysics Within Physics*. Oxford: Oxford University Press.

McDowell, J., 1980. "On the Sense and Reference of a Proper Name." In M. Platts (ed.), *Truth Reality and Reference*. London: Routledge and Kegan Paul, 111–30.

McDowell, J., 1996. *Mind and World*. Cambridge: Harvard University Press.

McGinn, C., 1983. *The Subjective View: Secondary Qualities and Indexical Thought*. Oxford: Clarendon Press.

McTaggart, J., 1908. "The Unreality of Time." *Mind* 68, 457–74.

McTaggart, J., 1927. *The Nature of Existence*, vol. 2. Cambridge: Cambridge University Press.

Mehlberg, H., 1935. "Essai sur la théorie causale du temps." *Studia Philosophica* 1, 119–260.

Mehlberg, H., 1962. "Theoretical and Empirical Aspects of Science." In E. Nagel, P. Suppes, and A. Tarski (eds.), *Logic, Methodology and Philosophy of Science*. Stanford: Stanford University Press.

Mellor, D.H., 1981. *Real Time*. Cambridge: MIT Press.

Mellor, D.H., 1998. *Real Time*, 2nd ed. Cambridge: MIT Press.

Minkowski, H., 1915. "Das Relativitätsprinzip." *Annalen der Physik* 352, 927–38.

Mulligan, K., Simons, P., and Smith, B., 1984. "Truth-Makers." *Philosophy and Phenomenological Research* 44, 287–321.

Noë, A. 2012. *Varieties of Presence*. Cambridge: Harvard University Press.

Oaklander, N.L., 2010. "McTaggart's Paradox and Crisp's Presentism." *Philosophia* 38, 229–41.

Oaklander, N.L., and Smith, Q. (eds.), 1994. *The New Theory of Time*. New Haven: Yale University Press.

Parsons, C., 1984. *Mathematics in Philosophy*. Ithaca: Cornell University Press.

Parsons, C., 2007. "The Problem of Absolute Universality." In A. Rayo and G. Uzquiano (eds.), *Absolute Generality*. Oxford: Oxford University Press, 203–19.

Partee, B., 1973. "Some Structural Analogies between Tenses and Pronouns in English." *The Journal of Philosophy* 70, 601–9.

Partee, B., 1984. "Nominal and Temporal Anaphora." *Linguistics and Philosophy* 7, 243–86.

Perry, J., 1977. "Frege on Demonstratives." *Philosophical Review* 86, 474–97.

Perry, J., 1979. "The Problem of the Essential Indexical." *Noûs* 13, 3–21.

Perry, J., 2001. *Reference and Reflexivity*. Stanford: CSLI Publications.

Price, H., 1996. *Time's Arrow and Archimedes' Point: New Directions for the Physics of Time*. New York: Oxford University Press.

Prior, A.N., 1959. "Thank Goodness That's Over." *Philosophy* 34, 12–17.

Prior, A.N., 1967. *Past, Present and Future*. Oxford: Oxford University Press.

Prior, A.N., 1968. *Papers on Time and Tense*. Oxford: Oxford University Press.

Pryor, J., 1999. "Immunity to Error through Misidentification." *Philosophical Topics* 26, 271–304.

Putnam, H., 1975a. "The Meaning of 'Meaning'." In Gunderson (ed.), *Language, Mind and Knowledge*. vol. 7, *Minnesota Studies in the Philosophy of Science*. Minneapolis: University of Minnesota Press, 131–93.

Putnam, H., 1975b. "Philosophy and Our Mental Life." In *Mind, Language, and Reality: Philosophical Papers*, vol. 2. Cambridge: Cambridge University Press, 291–303.

Putnam, H., 1988. *Representation and Reality*. Cambridge: MIT Press.

Quine, W.V.O., 1960. *Word and Object*. Cambridge: MIT Press.

Railton, P., 2006. "Normative Guidance." In R. Schaefer-Landau (ed.), *Oxford Studies in Metaethics*, vol. 1. Oxford: Oxford University Press, 3–34.

Rayo, A., and Uzquiano, G., 2007. *Absolute Generality*. Oxford: Oxford University Press.

Recanati, F., 2004. "Indexicality and Context-Shift." Workshop on Indexicals, Speech Acts and Logophors, Nov. 2004, Harvard University. https://jeannicod.ccsd.cnrs.fr/ijn_00000552/document (last accessed December 20, 2017).

Recanati, R., 2007. *Perspectival Thought: A Plea for (Moderate) Relativism*. Oxford: Oxford University Press.

Reichenbach, H., 1947. *Elements of Symbolic Logic*. New York: Macmillan.

Reichenbach, H., 1956. *The Direction of Time*. Los Angeles: University of California Press.

Reichenbach, H., 1958. *The Philosophy of Space and Time*. New York: Dover.

Reinhart, T., 1976. *The Syntactic Domain of Anaphora*. PhD dissertation, Department of Linguistics, MIT.

Rey, G., 2003. "Intentional Content and a Chomskyan Linguistics." In A. Barber (ed.), *Epistemology of Language*. Oxford: Oxford University Press, 140–86.

Rödl, S., 2007. *Self-Consciousness*. Cambridge: Harvard University Press.

Ross, J., 1967. *Constraints on Variables in Syntax*. PhD dissertation, Department of Linguistics, MIT.

Rovelli, C., 1996. "Relational Quantum Mechanics." *International Journal of Theoretical Physics* 35, 1637–78.

Russell, B., 1905. "On Denoting." *Mind* 14, 479–93.

Russell, B., 1910–11. "Knowledge by Acquaintance and Knowledge by Description." *Proceedings of the Aristotelean Society*. Reprinted in *Mysticism and Logic*, London: George Allen and Unwin, 1917, and New York: Doubleday, 1957.

Schein, B., 2017. *And: Conjunction Reduction Redux*. Cambridge: MIT Press.

Searle, J., 1980. "Minds, Brains, and Programs." *Behavioral and Brain Sciences* 3, 417–57.

Searle, J., 1990. "Is the Brain's Mind a Computer Program?" *Scientific American* 262, 26–31.

Searle, J., 1995. *The Rediscovery of the Mind*. Cambridge: MIT Press.

Segal, G., 1989. "A Preference for Sense and Reference." *The Journal of Philosophy* 86, 73–89.

Shannon, C., 1948. "A Mathematical Theory of Communication." *The Bell System Technical Journal* 27, 623–56.

Shannon, C., and Weaver, W., 1949. *The Mathematical Theory of Communication*. Urbana, IL: University of Illinois Press.

Shimony, A., 1993. *Search for the Naturalistic World-View*, vol. 2. Cambridge: Cambridge University Press.

Shoemaker, S., 1968. "Self-Reference and Self-Awareness." *The Journal of Philosophy* 65, 555–67.

Sider, T., 2001. *Four-Dimensionalism*. Oxford: Oxford University Press.

Siegel, S., 2016. "The Contents of Perception." *The Stanford Encyclopedia of Philosophy* (Spring 2016 Edition), Edward N. Zalta (ed.). http://plato.stanford.edu/archives/spr2016/entries/perception-contents (last accessed September 10, 2016).

Smith, C., 1975. "The Analysis of Tense in English." *Texas Linguistic Forum* 1, 71–89.

Smith, C., 1978. "The Syntax and Semantics of Temporal Expressions in English." *Linguistics and Philosophy* 2, 43–99.

Smith, Q., 1993. *Language and Time*. Oxford: Oxford University Press.

Soames, S., 1997. "Skepticism about Meaning: Indeterminacy, Normativity, and the Rule-Following Paradox." In A. Kazmi (ed.), *Meaning and Reference. The Canadian Journal of Philosophy, Supplementary Volume* 23, 211–49.

Soames, S., 2005. *Reference and Description: The Case Against Two-Dimensionalism*. Princeton: Princeton University Press.

Sorabji, R., 1983. *Time, Creation, and the Continuum*. Ithaca: Cornell University Press.

Spilianakis, C., Lalioti, M., Town, T., Lee, G., and Flavel, R., 2005. "Interchromosomal Associations between Alternatively Expressed Loci." *Nature* 435 (7042), 637–45.

Stowell, T., 1995a. "The Phrase Structure of Tense." In J. Rooryck and L. Zaring (eds.), *Phrase Structure and the Lexicon*. Dordrecht: Kluwer Publications, 277–91.

Stowell, T., 1995b. "What Is the Meaning of the Present and Past Tenses?" In P.-M. Bertinetto, V. Bianchi, and M. Squartini (eds.), *Temporal Reference: Aspect and Actionality*. Vol. 1, *Semantic and Syntactic Perspectives*. Torino: Rosenberg & Sellier, 381–96.

Tolman, R.C., 1917. *The Theory of Relativity of Motion*. Berkeley: University of California Press.

Turing, A., 1936. "On Computable Numbers, with an Application to the Entscheidungs-Problem." *Proceedings of the London Mathematical Society* 42, 230–65.

Uzquiano, G., 2007. "Unrestricted Unrestricted Quantification: The Cardinal Problem of Absolute Certainty." In A. Rayo and G. Uzquiano (eds.), *Absolute Generality*. Oxford: Oxford University Press, 305–32.

van Fraassen, B., 1970. *An Introduction to the Philosophy of Time and Space*. New York: Random House.

van Fraassen, B., 1980. *The Scientific Image*. Oxford: Clarendon Press.

Velleman, J.D., 2006. "The Voice of Conscience." In D. Velleman, *Self to Self*. Cambridge: Cambridge University Press, 110–28.

von Neumann, J., 1955. *Mathematical Foundations of Quantum Mechanics*. Princeton, NJ: Princeton University Press. [First published in German in 1932: *Mathematische Grundlagen der Quantenmechank*, Berlin: Springer.]

Weatherson, B., 2016. "David Lewis." The Stanford Encyclopedia of Philosophy. https://plato.stanford.edu/archives/win2016/entries/david-lewis (last accessed January 19, 2018).

Webber, B. 1988. "Tense as Discourse Anaphor." *Computational Linguistics* 14, 61–73.

Wettstein, H., 1986. "Has Semantics Rested on a Mistake?" *Journal of Philosophy* 83, 185–209.

Williams, D.C., 1951. "The Myth of Passage." *The Journal of Philosophy* 48, 457–72.

Williamson, T., 1999. "Existence and Contingency." *Proceedings of the Aristotelian Society*, Suppl. Vol. 73, 181–203.

Wittgenstein, L., 1961. *Tractatus Logico-Philosophicus*. London: Routledge and Kegan Paul.

Wittgenstein, L., 1991. *Philosophical Investigations*. New York: Wiley.

Zimmerman, D., 1998a. "Temporary Intrinsics and Presentism." In P. van Inwagen and D. Zimmerman (eds.), *Metaphysics: The Big Questions*. Oxford: Basil Blackwell, 206–19.

Zimmerman, D., 1998b. "Temporal Parts and Supervenient Causation: The Incompatibility of Two Humean Doctrines." *Australasian Journal of Philosophy* 76, 265–88.

Zimmerman, D., 2005. "The A-Theory of Time, the B-Theory of Time and 'Taking Tense Seriously'." *Dialectica* 59, 401–57.

Index